How to grow
Perennial
Vegetables

How to grow
Perennial
Vegetables

Martin Crawford

green books

First published in 2012 by

Green Books,
Dartington Space, Dartington Hall,
Totnes, Devon TQ9 6EN

Reprinted 2012

Design by Jayne Jones
Illustrations by Marion Smylie-Wild (www.marionsmylie.co.uk)

For photograph credits see page 218

ISBN 978 1 900322 84 3

Printed on Arctic Matt paper
by Latimer Trend, Plymouth, UK

3 1357 00149 3920

Disclaimer: Many things we eat as a matter of course – potatoes, beans, rhubarb,
sorrel (to name but a few) – are all toxic to some degree if not eaten in the right
way, at the right time and with the right preparation. At the time of going to press,
the advice and information in this book are believed to be true and accurate, and
if plants are eaten according to the guidance given here, they are safe. However,
someone, somewhere, is allergic to almost anything, so if you are trying
completely new plants to eat, try them in moderation to begin with. The author
and publishers accept no liability for actions inspired by this book.

Page 2 image: sea kale

Contents

"Martin is a true pioneer and his work deserves respect and celebration."
Permaculture magazine

"Martin Crawford has spent 15 years creating what is almost certainly the best forest garden in the temperate world. He's also a remarkable researcher of information on plants and their ecology, and the breadth of his knowledge matches the depth of his experience."
Patrick Whitefield, author of *Permaculture in a Nutshell*

"Martin Crawford is a frontiersman, a pioneering teacher and an inspiration. Both his work and his garden are national treasures."
Chris Nichols, Director of the Ashridge MSc in Sustainability and Responsibility

"There can be nothing, absolutely nothing, more important to the future of humankind and of our fellow creatures than agroforestry: raising trees, crops and livestock in productive and sustainable harmony. People worldwide have known this for millennia, but we in the West, as is our way, have put agriculture in one camp, forestry in another, and wildlife conservation in a third – and engineered a turf war between the three. Martin Crawford is among the few brave souls who have stood out against the Western trend."
Colin Tudge, author of *The Secret Life of Trees* and *Consider the Birds*

To Rosie and Tom, with love.

Acknowledgements

It seems appropriate to thank a few people who, over the years, have guided and nudged me in various ways and without whom I may have ended up doing something quite different. So thanks to John Dalby, Ben Foley and Pam and Nick Rodway.

Thanks to Marion for her great drawings and calm enthusiasm.

Thanks to the folks at Green Books for turning my text into a magnificent-looking book.

My greatest thanks, as ever, are due to Sandra, for her constant encouragement and sense of humour.

Foreword

Even the most enthusiastic of us vegetable growers tend to be a bit set in our ways – hidebound by tradition and convention; drawing on decades of well-hoed wisdom. We might be converts to raised beds and no-dig systems, but rarely do we question or seek to expand the range of proven veg crops that has served so many generations for so long. For some, even growing things like bulb fennel or rocket seems a bit racy!

This lovely book makes it clear that we are not just missing a trick, we are missing a feast. As one who loves to forage, and not just for berries and nuts but also for shoots, stems and leaves, I find the case argued here particularly compelling. Almost by definition, wild plants that yield edible crops are perennials – including irresistible seasonal favourites like nettles, sorrel, alexanders and elderflowers.

To me, growing perennial vegetables is the perfect fusion of foraging and gardening – because you are growing low-maintenance plants that more or less take care of themselves, and offer up their edible harvest year after year. You are basically planting plants that you can then 'forage' for just a few steps from your own back door.

If that makes sense to you in principle, then Martin's expert advice in the pages that follow will help you turn a great idea into a growing reality. And you will reap the rewards for many years to come.

Hugh Fearnley-Whittingstall
River Cottage, East Devon, April 2012

Introduction

We in Europe or North America are not very used to growing or eating many perennial vegetables. There are a few that most people know – globe artichoke and rhubarb probably being the most familiar – and some, like potatoes, are grown as replant perennials (see page 21). However, the way agriculture has developed, into an almost entirely short-lived-plant-based and mechanised method of growing vegetables and grains, means that perennials have been somewhat left behind.

Why should this be? Perhaps it is partly because the soil is easily tilled between annual crops to keep it weed-free. With perennials, once they are established then mechanical or chemical weeding is not usually quite so easy.

Another factor is yield. Most short-lived vegetables are either killed when they are first harvested or are exhausted at the end of the growing season by regular harvesting. They have short lives and have to grow fast.

Poke root – a North American wild edible that is easy to grow. The cooked shoots are delicious.

Perennials, on the other hand, are usually harvested in a sustainable manner, allowing the plant to continue its growth, so yields can often be less per unit area than those of annual crops.

But things are changing. More and more people are starting to understand that measuring the success of a growing system only in yield or output gives only part of the story. What about carbon emissions? You'll find that tilling the soil annually is one of the worst offenders in agriculture. What about inputs of chemicals? Increasingly, people are unhappy with food grown using chemicals. What about human health? We are what we eat, and you'll find that foods from perennial plants almost always contain far more nutrients than those from short-lived plants (see pages 16-17). What about ecosystem health? The growing systems used for perennial plants disturb the environment much less than annual tillage.

What's more, you don't always have to go far to discover perennial vegetables. Lots of those mentioned in this book grow wild in forests and hedgerows. But why delineate between the wild and the cultivated? You can grow perennial vegetable plants in your own garden in a number of ways and turn harvesting times into an enjoyable forage!

Key to plant descriptions

Under each plant in Part 2 of this book is a symbol indicating which part(s) of the plant are edible (see box). Also given is the hardiness zone.

Edible parts symbols

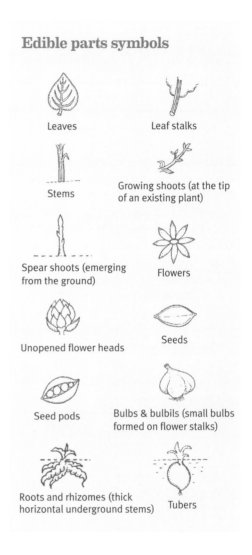

Leaves

Leaf stalks

Stems

Growing shoots (at the tip of an existing plant)

Spear shoots (emerging from the ground)

Flowers

Unopened flower heads

Seeds

Seed pods

Bulbs & bulbils (small bulbs formed on flower stalks)

Roots and rhizomes (thick horizontal underground stems)

Tubers

Hardiness zones

This American system of numbering climate zones has been applied to Europe and other parts of the world with varying success. The zone number given for a plant is an indication of the minimum average winter temperatures that a plant can tolerate – hence a plant hardy to zone 7 (say) can tolerate a minimum temperature of -18°C (0°F).

In the UK the system does not work quite so well, because here the cooler summers must also be taken into account – sometimes after a poor summer, new growth is either insufficient or does not harden off, which can also affect plant survival over winter. A new system of hardiness rating is being created by the Royal Horticultural Society (RHS), which should be better for the British climate, but meanwhile the zone system is still of use.

Most of the UK is classed as zone 8, with upland areas zone 7 and areas adjacent to coasts, especially in the south, as zone 9. But the microclimate you create in your garden can move your hardiness zone rating one higher – so if in theory you are in a zone 8 area, in a well-sheltered garden you may be able to grow zone 9 species. Another complication is that the hardiness of a species may vary according to its origins, with provenances further north leading to hardier plants.

Remember that minimum air temperatures are not the same as minimum soil temperatures – so a zone 8 plant, for example, is likely to tolerate soil temperatures down to only about -5°C (23°F).

Hardiness zone maps for Europe and North America can be found at: http://en. wikipedia.org/wiki/Hardiness_zone.

The zone system of plant hardiness		
Zone number	Average min temp (°C)	Average min temp (°F)
1	Below -46	Below -50
2	-46 to -40	-50 to -40
3	-40 to -34	-40 to -30
4	-34 to -29	-30 to -20
5	-29 to -23	-20 to -10
6	-23 to -18	-10 to 0
7	-18 to -12	0 to 10
8	-12 to -7	10 to 20
9	-7 to -1	20 to 30

Metric and imperial values

Values throughout this book are given in metric, with imperial conversions for lengths, weights and temperature. Other metric-to-imperial conversions are as follows

$1m^2$ = 1.2 sq yards
1 hectare = 2.5 acres
1 litre = 1.75 pints (UK); 2.1 pints (USA)
100 litres = 22 gallons (UK); 26 gallons (USA)

Saltbush – a Mediterranean shrub with superb salty leaves.

Part 1

An introduction to perennial vegetables

Chapter 1

Why grow perennial vegetables?

Most gardeners who want to grow some of their own food have a combination of annual vegetables and fruit bushes and/or trees, but few have perennial vegetables (apart from, perhaps, rhubarb). This seems such a shame, because there are some fantastic food plants out there with delicious flavours that are often very easy to grow.

Oca is a crop widely grown in the Andes, with delicious lemon-flavoured tubers.

What is a perennial vegetable?

For the purposes of this book, a perennial vegetable is defined as a plant that lives for at least three years, and is raised for some edible part of it – such as the leaves, shoots, leaf stems, roots or flowers. The edible part might be used raw or cooked. The plant must also be capable of being harvested without killing the plant itself. You'll also find some well-known fruiting plants included here as a vegetable – strawberries, for example. These are included only if a part other than the fruit can also be eaten.

There is a distinction, rather blurry, between a vegetable and a herb. A herb (in the culinary sense) is a plant with a strong, distinctive taste, used as a flavouring in relatively small amounts. So I have not included, say, lovage as a perennial vegetable, even though it is perennial, and is edible. However, I do include some plants that we often think of as herbs if they can be used in bulk amounts in salads or cooked dishes – so you will find entries for some of the mints, and for sweet cicely.

In the context of this book, I am talking about plants being perennials in the climatic conditions found in the temperate and continental climates of Europe and North America. Some annuals of course become perennials if the climate is warm enough, and these are not usually included unless, like runner beans, they can be grown as a replant perennial (i.e. a plant that is perennial in a warm climate but in a cold climate can still be grown by lifting plant parts in autumn, storing them over winter and replanting in spring).

Also in this book are some replant perennials such as potatoes and mashua, where it is common practice to save some of the tubers in the autumn for replanting next year.

The case for growing perennials

There are lots of reasons why growing perennial vegetables makes sense.

Less work

You don't have to cultivate the soil every year. Turning the soil over takes a lot of energy, whether it is tractor energy in ploughing or human energy in digging. Because perennials are planted only once (or once every few years), you do not have to disturb the soil so often.

If you stop turning the soil, and keep on top of the flush of weeds you'll get from the initial soil preparation, then the weed seed bank in the top layer of the soil will not get replenished with deeper dormant seeds. You'll find that the weeding required decreases over time, especially if you mulch around your perennials.

Because most perennials do not need digging up every year, it is more important to weed out pestiferous perennial weeds when small. (When growing annual crops, the weeds can always be dug out in winter.) Nevertheless, even in the first year after planting, the weeding demanded should not be any greater than that for an annual crop.

Fewer carbon emissions

A few years ago, nobody considered what carbon emissions were resulting from agriculture and horticulture, but that is changing rapidly. Growing food and other materials creates a lot of carbon in the atmosphere, not least because almost all crops are short-lived, requiring the energy-intensive cultivating of soil every year. Cultivating the soil exposes soil organic matter (humus) to air both on the soil surface and in the soil itself, leading to release of carbon in the form of carbon dioxide.

Once you stop digging soil, carbon emissions are vastly reduced, and quite possibly reversed – you may start to actually store more carbon in the soil. This is because certain fungi (mycorrhizal fungi – see page 42) are critical in storing carbon in soils, and soil cultivation kills them.

Better for the soil

When you stop digging the soil and grow perennial crops that cover and protect the soil, the soil structure is maintained, which in turn helps everything growing in it. Soil humus levels build up, nutrients don't wash out so easily, and water is retained in drought, yet drains in very wet weather.

If you think about it, annual plants are not very widespread in the natural world. They appear whenever soil is disturbed by animals, plants falling over, and so on. But they persist for only a year or two before they are succeeded by perennial plants. In nature, most plants are perennial, and in basing our whole civilisation on short-lived plants we may have been down a productive but nevertheless destructive cul-de-sac.

Healthier food

Most perennial plants contain higher levels of mineral nutrients than the common short-lived plants grown as vegetables, which is not surprising really, considering that they have larger and permanent root systems, able to exploit soil space more effectively and thus take up more nutrients.

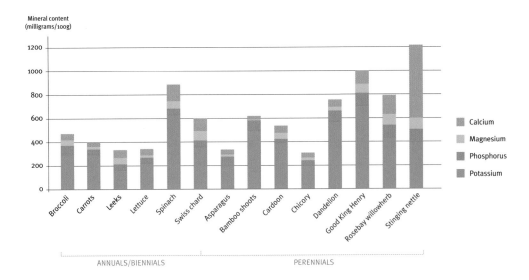

Mineral content of some common annual/biennial and perennial vegetables.

Data for the charts on these two pages comes from the USDA National Nutrient Database for Standard Reference at http://www.ars.usda.gov/ba/bhnrc/ndl and from *Cooking Weeds* by V. Weise.

Vitamin levels in perennial vegetables are more variable, but can certainly be as high or higher than those in short-lived vegetables, even those known for high vitamin levels.

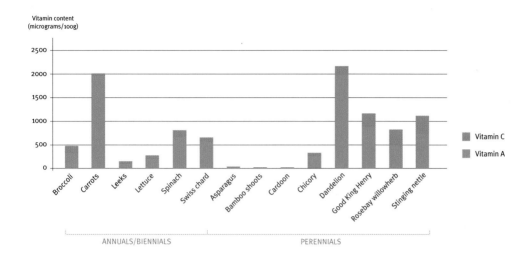

Vitamin content of some common annual/biennial and perennial vegetables.

Protein levels in green vegetables can be high, and the protein content of perennial vegetables is frequently higher than that of annuals and biennials.

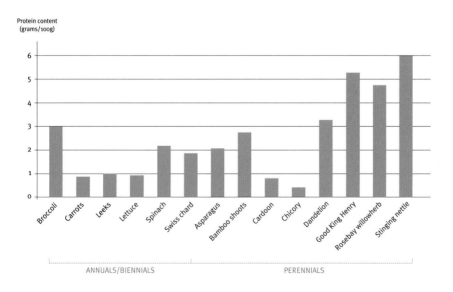

Protein content of some common annual/biennial and perennial vegetables.

Extension of the harvesting season

Short-lived crops are distinctly seasonal. How seasonal depends on your climate, mainly on how cold the winter is. But there is nearly always a gap in annual production – the 'hungry gap' between April and June, when overwintering annuals have been harvested but newly sown crops are not yet ready.

Cropping of perennial vegetables is more evenly distributed over the year. Perhaps the most useful time for perennial vegetables is spring, as there are plenty of perennials in which the edible crop is the young shoots that emerge in April, May or even June – for example, Solomon's seals – from a perennial rootstock. There are also various perennial leaf vegetables that leaf out in the same period – for example, lime trees – which can begin to be harvested.

Other good reasons

You may well already have beds of perennials growing in your garden for ornament, for attracting bees or for fragrance. Why not have perennial beds with the same functions, but where the plants also have edible virtues? Some of the plants featured in this book, such as Solomon's seals and hostas, may already feature in your ornamental beds.

Perennial vegetables tend to be of more value to bees, other pollinating insects and beneficial insects in general; most are allowed to flower, whereas most annual vegetables are not. If you grow annual vegetables as well, you might well find that you get fewer pest problems on these because of the perennials nearby – you can even deliberately interplant annuals and perennials in various ways (see Chapter 2, page 26, for more on planting mixtures).

Chapter 2

Growing perennial vegetables

In normal gardening lingo, 'perennial' is usually used to describe a low-growing herbaceous or evergreen non-woody perennial plant. However, this book takes a much wider perspective. For example, trees and shrubs are also perennials, and in fact there are many nice edible leaves from them – lime leaves, saltbush leaves and mulberry leaves, to name but three.

Aquatic perennial plants are also included here, as are some bulbs, and one fern.

Good King Henry – a hardy perennial spinach-type plant.

Types of perennial plant

This book describes plants of the following types.

Trees

A number of trees have edible parts that may be used as a vegetable, one example being the snowbell tree. A tree like this, which is grown for the young fruits, is not usually coppiced (see below) as this would cut off the fruiting wood.

Shrubs

Likewise, a number of shrubs provide vegetables. One is the American elder, whose flowers can be fried as a fine vegetable. I include bamboos – one of the finest of the spring vegetables – in shrubs, even though they are strictly speaking perennial grasses.

Coppiced trees

Trees that provide a leaf vegetable are often coppiced – cut off low down so they will produce vigorous new shoots the next year – to maintain them as more of a compact bush and so make leaf harvesting easier and more practical. The branchwood from coppicing may also be of use for firewood or for growing mushrooms on. The coppice cycle can be anything from one to five or more years, depending on the vigour of the tree and the desired size. I coppice large-leaved lime annually, and small-leaved lime every three to five years, and use the young leaves widely as a salad vegetable.

Herbaceous and evergreen perennials

Most of the plants described in these pages fall into this category, which gardeners often call simply 'perennials'. Herbaceous perennials – for example, asparagus – die down to underground roots, rhizomes or tubers in the winter. Evergreen perennials – for example, globe artichoke – retain some or all of their leaves over winter. Some perennials do not fit so neatly into these categories: for example, many mallows retain a rosette of green leaves over the winter in milder areas but may not do so in colder areas. From here on, herbaceous and evergreen perennials will be referred to as 'non-woody perennials'.

Perennial bulbs

The alliums are good examples of perennial bulbs, and there are several described here. The top growth of bulbous plants usually dies back for a part of the year – though not necessarily winter. So, for example, Babington's leek dies back to a bulb from late July to early September, whereas ramsons dies back from late June to February. The bulbs that die back for part of the summer usually prefer well-drained sunny sites and can be particularly useful for a supply of leaves in winter.

Perennial ferns

Well, 'fern', actually – there is only one mentioned in this book, ostrich fern, whose young 'fiddleheads' are a well-known wild edible in North America and Scandinavia. Other ferns – for example, bracken – have been eaten in the past but are no longer considered safe to eat.

Climbers

There are both climbing herbaceous perennials (e.g. hops) and climbing shrubs (e.g. grape vines) that can be used as vegetables. These plants can be grown in many ways, from bushy plants kept small by harvesting to climbers covering walls, fences, trees and so on.

Aquatic perennials

These are plants growing in water, usually dying back to bulbs or rhizomes for the winter. An example is American arrowhead or duck potato, which forms tubers that can be cooked in various ways.

Replant perennials

This term refers to plants that are perennial in warm climates and sometimes mild temperate climates, usually producing tubers or rhizomes, but are not hardy enough to survive winters in colder temperate climates. I have included some of these, even though they are not truly perennial in colder regions, because plants such as mashua and cinnamon vine, or Chinese yam, can be grown in milder temperate regions such as the south of England, and in warmer microclimates. Potato is a replant perennial (though the ones that evade harvesting often survive the winter and regrow), and runner beans can also be grown in this way.

Perennial root and tuber crops

It is common for folk to say to me, "It's all very well having all these leafy vegetables, but where are the substantial bulb and root vegetables to take the place of onions, carrots and parsnips?" Well, several of the above categories of vegetable have roots or tubers as the main crop. These are listed in the table, right.

Tuber, bulb and root perennials	
Vegetable	**Crop type**
Arrowheads	Tubers (underwater)
Babington's leek	Bulbs
Chinese artichoke	Tubers
Egyptian onion	Bulbs
Elephant garlic	Bulbs
Garlic	Bulbs
Groundnut	Tubers
Jerusalem artichoke	Tubers
Marsh mallow	Roots
Mashua	Tubers
Multiplier onions	Bulbs
Oca	Tubers
Potato	Tubers
Rocambole	Bulbs
Scorzonera	Roots
Sea kale	Roots
Silverweed	Roots
Skirret	Roots
Sweet cicely	Roots
Sweet potato	Tubers
Ulluco	Tubers
Water caltrop	Tubers (underwater)
Water chestnut	Bulbs (underwater)
Water lotus	Rhizomes (underwater)
Yacon	Tubers
Yams	Tubers
Yellow asphodel	Roots

Soils

You can grow edible perennials in any type of soil. Most soils can be improved, if necessary, by adding organic matter of whatever kind you can source. Loose mulches can help a lot too. A mulch is a material laid over the ground, either to clear weeds or to keep a planted area weed-free with minimal effort.

Perennial beds

Beds can be pretty much whatever shape or size you like, and the planting design can be anything from a formal geometric arrangement to a much more random and semi-natural layout. Bear in mind the shade tolerance of the perennials you are growing (most prefer sun), and in general plant taller perennials towards the north side and/or shadier side, with shorter plants towards the south/lighter side.

It is really worth trying to make sure that the bed is free of perennial weeds before you plant out. In a smallish garden this may mean digging over the area, or alternatively you can use a sheet mulch (see opposite). Some of the perennial vegetables described in this book can be grown as a good

Perennial vegetables suited to specific soils		
Dry soil	**Wet soil**	**Poor soil**
Asparagus	Arrowheads	Bellflowers (alpine)
Babington's leek	Day lilies	Chicory
Bellflowers (alpine)	Giant butterbur	Dandelion
Cardoon	Golden saxifrage	Day lilies
Chives	Groundnut	Groundnut
Daffodil garlic	Ostrich fern	Mashua
Day lilies	Ramps	Perennial sweet peas
Fennel	Skirret	Perennial wall-rocket
French scorzonera	Tiger nut	Poke root
Globe artichoke	Watercress	Red valerian
Ground plum		Rock samphire
Iceplant and orpine		Saltbush
Nopale cacti		Sweet potato
Perennial wall-rocket		Ulluco
Red valerian		
Rock samphire		
Saltbush		
Sheep's sorrel		

ground-cover layer – so in effect they self-mulch – sometimes even under trees. See the table on page 31 for some examples of these.

Sheet mulches

A sheet mulch is a flat material (as opposed to, for example, compost or bark chippings) used over a whole area of soil, either to clear it for planting or to maintain a weed-free area when nothing else is growing there (for example, over winter). Sheet mulches are fairly quick and easy to lay but are not always aesthetically pleasing.

Various materials can be used for sheet mulching, including thick card, newspaper, carpet, black plastic, permeable woven plastic and biodegradeable mulch matting rolls made of flax, hemp, jute, etc. The plastic mulches are also available in rolls, which makes them quick and easy to lay. If using a roll of mulch when there are plants already in the ground to retain, you'll need to cut slits or holes in the mulch for them.

Using plastic mulches in the garden is a compromise in 'eco' terms, but they are very efficient and some can be reused again and again for many years. In a storm, large areas of sheet mulch can blow away if they start flapping wildly. To prevent this they should usually be weighed down with branches or prunings, or pinned down with pegs or 'staples' made of wire. If you don't like the look of plastic sheet mulches, you can cover them with a few centimetres' depth of loose chipped bark or similar organic material, though you will need to move the loose material once the sheet mulch has done its work in to lift the mulch material back up.

Most grasses, apart from couch grass, are killed after 3-4 months without light in the growing season, while 12 months is really needed to kill off dandelions, docks, couch grass and other pernicious weeds. Bindweed, horsetail and other nightmare weeds can take years to kill by mulching.

If your soil is not very fertile, you can put down fertility-building materials such as compost and animal manures beneath the sheet mulch.

There is often strong weed growth at the edge of the mulch where it meets existing grass. Plants in this situation exploit the fine soil conditions under the edges of the mulch to grow faster than normal, and you might find this growth needs cutting or strimming more often than other grass areas.

Planting time

In mild temperate climates, as in most of the UK, planting of perennials is ideally done in autumn or winter, though spring planting is also possible. In recent years the climate in the UK seems to have been tending towards warm and very dry springs, and planting in autumn or winter means that you should not have to water plants during dry spring weather.

In colder climates, where the ground freezes for the whole of winter or is covered with snow for long periods, spring planting is more common, but if spring weather is hot and dry, extra watering is likely to be required.

Loose mulches

After planting out, you can mulch the new plants with a loose mulch if you want. Many different loose organic materials can be used for this. The advantages are less weeding while the plants establish, and better soil conditions, especially in a dry first spring or summer; a loose mulch also provides a good habitat for beetles and other beneficial insects.

Disadvantages are the extra work involved, good conditions for slugs/snails and perhaps more expense. Whether it is worth it or not may depend on how quickly the plants will establish and whether they will form a weed-suppressing canopy of leaves.

If you decide to mulch newly planted perennials, plant first and put the mulch around the plants afterwards. Some materials – for example, leafmould (rotted leaves), garden compost or rotted farmyard manure – are likely to have weed seeds in, while others – for example, chipped bark, grass mowings (applied thinly) and fallen autumn leaves – may be weed-seed-free.

Planting patterns

When you plant out, the density of planting and planting pattern will affect how the plants grow – close planting may lead to more competition and to plants growing taller but narrower. It will also affect the maintenance required, as closer planting means that more of the soil surface is covered so there is less chance for weeds to become established (see Diagram 1).

Another advantage of closer spacing is that when plants are harvested, more of the ground cover is left intact (for example, if leaves or shoots are harvested from a number of plants in the patch). Keeping the ground covered with plant growth as far as possible is a priority for any kind of ecological agriculture, because this keeps the soil in best condition, which benefits everything that grows in it.

If you are growing patches of several species, keep in mind most of all the sun requirements, and position taller plants where they won't cast too much shade on smaller ones. Diagrams 2 to 4 show examples of planting patterns that take into account the sun requirements of the different species.

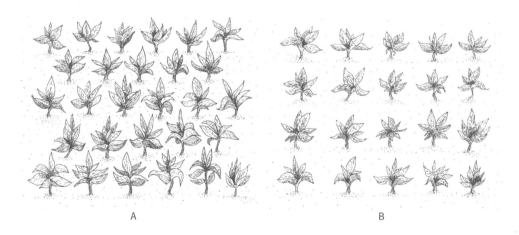

A   B

Diagram 1. Staggered planting (A) covers the soil much better than square planting (B).

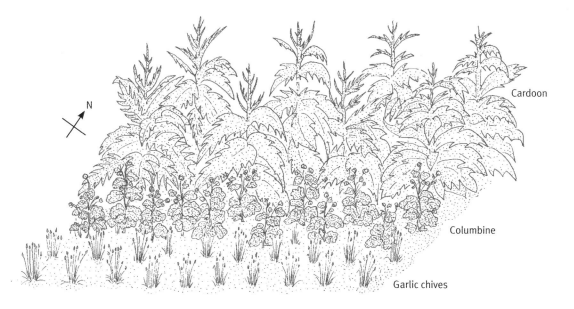

Cardoon

Columbine

Garlic chives

Diagram 2. An open bed showing graduation of species height, getting higher towards the north.

Columbine

Siberian purslane

Hostas

Daffodil garlic

Diagram 3. Perennial bed beneath fruit trees. Hostas, columbine and Siberian purslane are all shade-tolerant. The daffodil garlic on the southern side gets enough light, even though the tree canopies are partly above it.

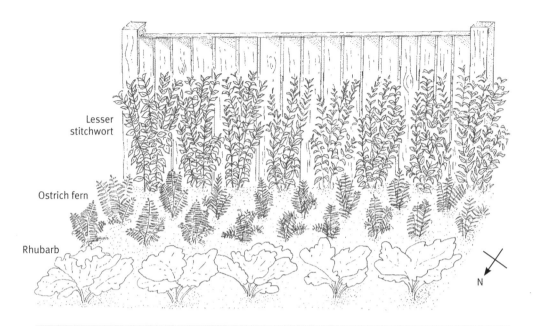

Lesser
stitchwort

Ostrich fern

Rhubarb

N

Diagram 4. A bed against a north-facing fence. All the species used are shade-tolerant, and again are graduated in height.

Perennial polycultures

Polycultures of plants are mixtures deliberately grown together, using species that do not quickly outcompete each other. You don't have to mix plants together like this in your planting schemes, but it does lead to gardens with a more natural feel to them and which tend to be more resilient to pests, diseases and extreme weather conditions. A disadvantage of mixing plants together can be that harvesting becomes more complicated – other species may get in the way of the one you are harvesting.

Choosing plants for perennial polycultures

When mixing plants together in a single area, try to choose plants of different heights so that they are not both competing for light in the same aerial space. Plants of the same type (e.g. non-woody perennials or trees) should be of similar vigour. Also, think about seasonal differences in growth and choose plants to complement each other (e.g. an early spring herbaceous perennial beneath a late-leafing shrub.)

Examples of perennial polycultures

In the simplest type of polyculture, two clump-forming species are growing together. In most cases it is best to arrange the planting so there are 'islands' of several plants of one species – usually the taller – in a 'sea' of the other (see Diagram 5), which tends to stop one species outcompeting the other too much. The lower species needs to be able to tolerate a little more shade than the taller one. Either species can be evergreen, but this will of course change the dynamics of the species interactions.

Diagram 5. Two clump-forming species: 'islands' of giant butterbur in a 'sea' of day lilies.

In a different type of mixture (see Diagram 6), a larger, clump-forming plant is underplanted with a small, spreading or running plant. The larger plant does not necessarily need to be planted in groups; rather, individuals can be scattered over an area. The lower plants spread and fill in any gaps after planting. The lower plant must be somewhat shade-tolerant if it is to cover the ground well beneath the taller plants.

Spreading plants are sometimes seen as a nuisance – and indeed they may at times need controlling – but they are valuable since they rapidly fill gaps where plants die, and often fewer plants are needed when planting out.

Diagram 6. A large clump-forming plant (perennial kale), underplanted with a small running plant (strawberries).

A more complex polyculture involves coppiced trees (see page 20) for leaf crops underplanted with a mixture of shade-tolerant crops (see Diagram 7).

Diagram 7. Coppiced lime and mulberry trees underplanted with shade-tolerant violets, which are themselves also interplanted with patches of tall cardoons and shorter orpine – the latter on the south side of the coppiced trees so they get more light to thrive.

In a different complex arrangement, shrubs, including bamboo, are underplanted with a mixture of herbaceous perennials, and climbing plants are trained into the shrub canopy. In the example shown in Diagram 8, bamboo and American elder are underplanted with ramsons. The bamboo shoots come up after most of the ramsons harvest. Dwarf varieties of hops are trained into the elder canopy after their initial shoots are cut as a vegetable. Elsewhere, poke root also interplants well with ramsons, as its shoots come up in late spring when ramsons is almost finished flowering. After the ramsons dies back to bulbs at the end of June, the ground cover beneath the larger plants will be very thin – in these situations you may need to add a mulch to reduce weed growth for the period until the winter.

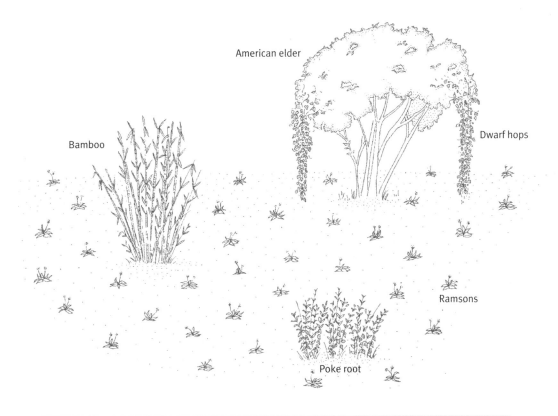

American elder

Bamboo

Dwarf hops

Ramsons

Poke root

Diagram 8. Bamboo and American elder underplanted with ramsons and poke root. Dwarf hops are trained into the elder canopy.

Perennial grains

The onward march of mechanised agriculture has made us believe that it is not worth growing your own grains on a small scale. The excellent *Small-scale Grain Raising* by Gene Logsdon makes it clear this is not the case. A grain plot 3m x 30m (10' x 100') can grow about 18kg (40lb) of rye or 25kg (55lb) of wheat, an amount of grain that goes a long way in cooking.

There is some interesting ongoing research in the US on perennial grains – particularly perennial rye and relatives of wheat – that have great potential. I know that grains aren't really counted as a vegetable, but I have included perennial rye and wheat in this book. Cultivation of land to grow annual grains – on which a large proportion of the human population depends – is one of the factors that make agriculture a large emitter of carbon dioxide, the main greenhouse gas. As was noted in Chapter 1, moving towards perennial crops – grains as well as vegetables – is desirable because not only do they save time and effort but they also reduce carbon emissions.

Grains are grasses and, unfortunately, cast very little shade and are thus rather prone to weed competition. Perennial grain plants are usually spaced much more widely than annual grain plants and are allowed or encouraged to tiller (branch) in order to increase the number of flowers. An intercrop of something like clover might work well and reduce weed problems.

Perennial tuber and root crops

The cultivation of these types of crop, which include groundnut, Chinese artichoke, Jerusulem artichoke, mashua, oca and yams, differs from that of most of the other perennial vegetables in that (obviously) the crop must be dug up and thus the soil disturbed each year.

On occasion, or even every year if preferred, these crops can be treated as replant perennials – i.e. the entire crop is dug up in autumn or winter and selected tubers are replanted in spring.

If you are going to grow some tuber or root crops as replant perennials, it is probably best to rotate the species grown through different areas – perhaps integrating the perennials with annual vegetables. Rotations prevent the build-up of species-specific pests and diseases that can seriously affect many annual vegetables, though it must be said that most perennial vegetables are far more resilient than annuals.

Interplanting non-woody perennials with perennial tuber or root crops is tricky because often the interplants will also be dug up along with the roots or tubers. If the interplant is a spreading plant, such as strawberry or mint, then it is much more likely to survive the digging and regrow successfully. Alternatively you may want to grow a single-species tuber/root patch to maximise yield – any interplant is likely to reduce tuber yields a little.

With some perennial roots and tubers it is difficult or virtually impossible to dig all the roots/tubers out – hence Jerusulem artichoke's reputation for being a truly permanent crop! Regrowth from those left in the ground is usually sufficient to ensure a crop the following year.

Perennial vegetables and ground-cover plants

Some perennial vegetables make a good ground cover by themselves (see table opposite), which usually makes them lower-maintenance and potentially useful for planting under trees, shrubs or other, larger, perennial vegetables.

There are numerous opportunities for interplanting perennial vegetable plants

Perennial vegetables forming a good ground cover	
Vegetable	Light conditions tolerated*
Apple mint	Sun to partial shade
Bellflowers (alpine)	Sun
Cardoon	Sun
Chinese artichoke	Sun to light shade
Columbine	Sun to partial shade
Day lilies	Sun to light shade
False strawberry	Sun to full shade
Giant butterbur	Full shade – needs shade
Globe artichoke	Sun
Golden saxifrage	Partial shade – needs shade
Hostas	Partial shade to full shade
Lemon balm	Sun to part shade
Lesser stitchwort	Partial shade – needs shade
Lucerne	Sun
Ostrich fern	Full shade – needs shade
Poke root	Partial to full shade
Ramps	Full shade – needs shade
Ramsons	Full shade – needs shade
Redwood sorrel	Full shade – needs shade
Sorrel (French & sheep's)	Sun to light shade
Siberian purslane	Sun to full shade
Silverweed	Sun to light shade
Solomon's seals	Sun to full shade
Sweet potato	Sun
Turkish rocket	Sun to partial shade
Violets	Light shade to full shade
Wild strawberry	Sun to partial shade
Wood sorrel	Full shade – needs shade

* *'Light shade' means just a few hours of shade per day, whereas 'partial shade' means perhaps half the day in shade, and 'full shade' means barely any full sunlight at all.*

with low-growing ground-covering plants to form a 'base' layer beneath and around them. There are advantages in this even if the lower plants are not cropped themselves, as they give a number of other benefits.

- Keeping the soil covered with plant growth helps maintain the soil in maximum health. It is protected from drying sun and beating rain and keeps its texture better, thus benefiting all soil life and ultimately everything that grows in it.

- In addition, the lower plants may have 'system' functions which aid garden health – for example, they may be bee plants, beneficial insect plants, nitrogen fixers or mineral accumulators (plants that can 'mine' nutrients and bring them up to the topsoil layers) – see page 43.

The following two tables give an indication of the root structure of a number of base-layer plants; bear this in mind when planting perennial vegetables amongst them, and try to mix shallow- and deep-rooted plants where possible. Some of the plants in these tables are perennial vegetables themselves.

Recommended very low base-layer plants		
Plant*	Root structure	Extra functions
Alum root	Moderately deep	Bee plant
Asarabacca	Shallow	None
Barren strawberry (*Waldsteinia ternata*)	Shallow	Bee plant
Barren strawberry (*Waldsteinia fragarioides*)	Shallow	Bee plant
Bird's foot trefoil	Moderately deep	Bee plant, nitrogen fixer
Bloodroot	Deep	Bee plant
Bugle	Shallow	Bee plant
Creeping dogwood	Shallow	Edible fruit
Creeping jenny	Shallow	Bee plant
Dwarf comfrey	Deep	Bee plant, mineral accumulator
False strawberry	Shallow	Edible leaves, fruit
Foam flower	Shallow	Beneficial insect plant
Golden saxifrage	Shallow	Edible leaves
Ground elder	Shallow	Edible leaves
Ground ivy	Shallow	Edible leaves for teas
Groundcover raspberry (*Rubus pentalobus*)	Shallow	Edible fruit, bee plant
Lady's mantle	Shallow	Medicinal

(Cont.)

Plant*	Root structure	Extra functions
Lesser periwinkle	Shallow	Bee plant
Lungwort	Very deep, taprooted	Bee plant, mineral accumulator
Nepalese raspberry	Shallow	Edible fruit, bee plant
Partridge berry	Shallow	Bee plant
Ramps	Shallow, bulbs	Edible (all)
Ramsons	Shallow, bulbs	Edible (all)
Redwood sorrel	Moderately deep	Edible leaves
Siberian purslane	Shallow, tuberous	Edible (all)
Silverweed	Deep, taprooted	Edible roots, bee plant
Strawberries	Shallow	Edible leaves, fruit
Sweet woodruff	Shallow	Edible leaves for flavouring
Violets	Shallow	Edible leaves & flowers
Wand flower	Moderately deep	Mineral accumulator
Wild ginger	Shallow	None
Wintergreen	Shallow	Medicinal
Wood sorrel	Deep	Edible leaves

* Those in bold are perennial vegetables in their own right and appear in the species listing in Part 2.

Recommended low base-layer plants		
Plant	**Root structure**	**Extra functions**
Rock cranesbill	Moderately deep	Bee plant
Horse mint	Shallow	Beneficial insect plant
Apple mint*	Shallow	Edible leaves & stems, beneficial insect plant
Groundcover raspberry (*Rubus* 'Betty Ashburner')	Shallow	Edible fruit
Chinese bramble	Shallow	Edible fruit
Soapwort	Moderately deep	Soap plant, bee plant
Comfrey	Very deep	Bee plant, mineral accumulator, medicinal
Russian comfrey	Very deep	Bee plant, mineral accumulator, medicinal
Periwinkles	Shallow	Bee plant

* This is a perennial vegetable in its own right and appears in the species listing in Part 2.

Forest gardens

A forest garden is a garden modelled on the structure of young natural woodland, using plants of direct and indirect benefit to people – most often edible ones. The trees, shrubs and non-woody perennials are planted in a way that aims to minimise competition and make use of beneficial interactions between them. Forest gardens are self-fertilising, through plants that fix nitrogen from the air (e.g. clovers) and others that raise minerals from deep in the soil up into the topsoil. Plants are chosen to include those that attract predators of insect pests and to help reduce disease problems. A diverse system is important to give long-term resilience.

The term 'forest garden' is perhaps not the right term for these gardens in temperate climates, where the word 'forest' implies a large number of high trees with canopies touching and deep shade beneath. Forest gardens can be as small as an urban back garden, but in the UK climate they must allow light beneath trees to enable lower crops to grow. They are not often neat, tidy gardens – but then nature is rarely neat and tidy.

The plants in a forest garden are mainly perennial. In terms of growing perennial vegetables, this kind of growing system is perhaps the most ecological in that the aim is to provide as near to natural conditions for the plants as possible. Sun-loving

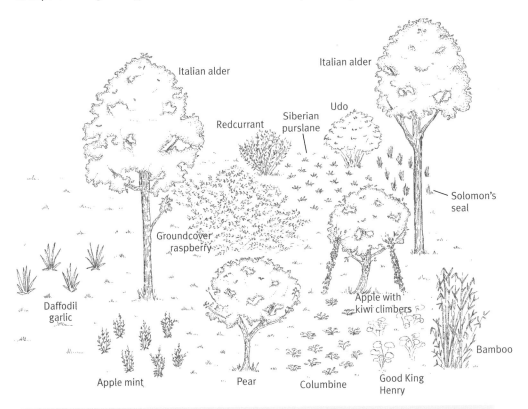

Diagram 9. A forest garden. This example illustrates the multiple layers, with large and small trees, shrubs of various sizes, climbers and non-woody perennials growing together. The positioning of lower plants in relation to larger ones is critical so that they receive enough light to perform well.

perennials will need open spaces left for them, though shade-tolerant ones can often be located beneath and between trees.

A forest garden almost always includes plants other than perennial vegetables. Many of the plants used are multi-purpose; they may have a main function or crop but very often have a number of other uses too.

For in-depth information about all aspects of forest gardens and how to set one up, see my book *Creating a Forest Garden*.

The amount of shade in forest gardens varies, but there will certainly be shadier parts. The following table lists some of the perennial vegetables that can be grown in such areas. (Note that the table shows tolerance to partial shade but not the total range of light conditions a plant can tolerate. Hence, partial shade could be at the sun end of one plant's range and at the shade end of another's range.)

Perennial vegetables tolerating partial shade*
American elder
Apple mint
Babington's leek
Bamboos
Beech
Bellflowers (hardy) – not alpines
Bladder campion
Bowles's mint
Caucasian spinach
Columbine
Dandelion
European elders
False strawberry
Giant butterbur
Golden saxifrage
Good King Henry
Grape vine (for leaves)
Horseradish
Hostas
Lemon balm
Lesser stitchwort
Limes
Mallows
Marsh mallow
Mitsuba
Ostrich fern
Plantains
Poke root
Ramps
Ramsons
Redwood sorrel
Rhubarbs
Siberian purslane
Solomon's seals
Strawberries
Stinging nettle
Sweet cicely
Turkish rocket
Udo
Violets
White deadnettle
Wood sorrel

* *'Partial shade' here means around 50 per cent of the day spent in shade.*

Growing perennial vegetables under existing trees

In some gardens you may be starting with a woodland situation – high trees casting quite a lot of shade beneath. A number of shade-tolerant perennial vegetables can be introduced into the lower layers beneath the trees, including those in the following table. (Again, this table shows plants with tolerance to substantial shade, but does not indicate the total range of light conditions that each plant can tolerate.)

Perennial vegetables tolerating substantial shade
Apple mint
Babington's leek, perennial leek
Bamboos
Beech
Bellflowers
Bowles's mint
Columbine
Daffodil garlic
Dandelion
False strawberry
Giant butterbur
Hostas
Lesser stitchwort
Limes
Mallows
Ostrich fern
Poke root
Ramps
Ramsons
Redwood sorrel
Siberian purslane
Solomon's seals
Sorrels
Strawberries
Stringing nettle
Udo
Violets
Wood sorrel

If you are starting with a fairly wild site, you are likely to have a mixture of brambles, nettles, seedling trees and other plants beneath the trees. You'll need to clear areas of these before planting out perennial vegetables, and using sheet mulches is the obvious way to do it – you won't be able to dig over the soil easily because of the root systems of the trees.

Once areas have been cleared, planting out small plants is the best way to proceed – larger ones will need bigger holes dug for them, and you'll find that the tree root systems in the soil are often in the way. Smaller plants can often be slipped into tiny holes alongside or between existing roots.

You could also try broadcasting seed for some species. For example, wood mallow and Siberian purslane usually germinate quickly after sowing. Other plants, though, require their seeds to go through a winter (i.e. undergo stratification – see page 54) before they will germinate – so the seed will be vulnerable to predation over a long period. Also for some, seed is not often available.

If the high trees on your site are native, you might well find that each year you need to weed out tree seedlings that germinate in

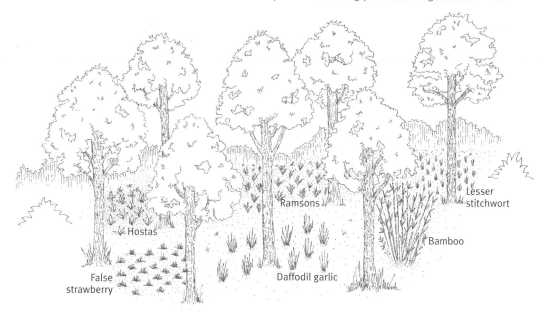

Diagram 10. Growing perennial vegetables under trees.

your perennial beds. Brambles too are likely to need watching out for.

Growing aquatic perennial vegetables

Growing perennial vegetables that need aquatic conditions introduces a new set of challenges. How to grow in a pond or an artificial container? How, for example, do you harvest the produce? A pond system is more aesthetically pleasing, and integrates easily with other plants nearby. On the other hand, harvesting is often more difficult from a pond than from a container and, where the pond becomes deep, is potentially dangerous. However, some plants require a depth of water that is practical only with a pond system.

Aquatic perennial vegetables	
Vegetable	**Depth required**
Arrowheads	Marginal plants – 0-45cm (0-18") deep, planted in mud or pots
Water caltrop / water chestnut	Floating plant – in water 10-30cm (4-12") deep, with a little soil beneath
Water chestnut / Chinese water chestnut	Marginal plant – 10-30cm deep (4-12"), planted in mud or pots
Water lotus	Semi-marginal plant – 30-45cm (12-18") deep, planted in mud or deep pots
Watercress	Can be grown in constantly damp soil or in shallow water up to 15cm (6") deep

How to create an aquatic perennial vegetable garden

If using a plastic pool, be sure to place it on a smooth surface free of stones or other sharp objects. You can put some old carpet, thick card, plastic sheet, etc. beneath to protect it.

1. Fill the container with normal garden soil to a depth of 15-20cm (6-8") – if filling a plastic pool, take special care not to puncture the plastic with stones or spades. Try not to include too much plant matter with the soil, as it may ferment and make the container smelly. Water caltrop does not require soil to root into, but a thin layer is useful for supplying nutrients for it.

2. Level the soil and plant tubers, bulbs or rhizomes, choosing the best-looking ones, in mid- or late spring. Bury the tubers just beneath the soil (by hand if in a plastic pool). Water chestnut bulbs should have started into growth, and arrowhead tubers should have a pointed shoot. Space the tubers/bulbs 10-15cm (4-6") apart for arrowhead; 30-40cm (12-16") apart for water chestnut. Watercress is grown from seed, usually in smaller containers and then transplanted.

3. Fill the container with water (preferably rainwater) so that the soil surface is covered with a minimum of 10cm (4") of water. Water caltrop tubers can just be floated on to the water surface.

4. Keep the container topped up with water over the summer. Usually, very little weeding is required.

5. When the foliage starts to die down in autumn, the tubers will have matured. Allow the container to dry out, then when the soil is not saturated (but still moist), sift through it to harvest tubers. Arrowhead tubers are hardy and can be left stored in the soil (which should be kept moist) until required.

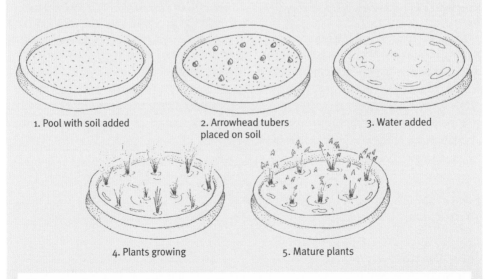

1. Pool with soil added

2. Arrowhead tubers placed on soil

3. Water added

4. Plants growing

5. Mature plants

Diagram 11. Growing water plants in a pool.

The advantage of growing in artificial containers is that the water level can usually be reduced easily – often aiding the formation of tubers – and can be reduced completely at harvest, making the crop much easier to get at. However, water levels may need topping up more regularly.

Many types of container can be used, for example:
- Old baths or sinks
- Plastic paddling pools
- Purpose-built pools dug in the ground and lined.

Of these, plastic paddling pools are the easiest to use: they are cheap to buy, an ideal size (about 1.2m/4' in diameter) and can be stored over the winter if not required. It is also easy to place them inside a greenhouse or polytunnel, which in a climate like the UK is required for water chestnuts to crop well.

If you are not near grazing livestock – i.e. there are no cattle or (especially) sheep in adjacent fields – then water plants should be safe to eat raw after washing, or of course cooked. If there are grazing animals nearby, then any water plants (notably watercress, which is sometimes used raw) should be washed and well cooked before eating, because of the risk of transmission of liver fluke. The risk is increased if there is a population of dwarf pond snails, since these are an intermediate host for the parasite.

Native and non-native plants

During the 1990s and the first decade of the twenty-first century, there was an increasing tendency to question the origin of plants introduced into gardens and agricultural systems, with the assumption that natives are always better and that non-natives might suddenly take over and wreck ecosystems. Now, nobody can argue that there haven't been instances of introduced plants causing problems – for example, Japanese knotweed in the UK – but the full story is much more complex. Japanese knotweed is a good example, as it is also a nice perennial vegetable (the young shoots are eaten as a vegetable in Japan); however, I have not included it in this book as not only is it unwise to plant it in your garden, it is also illegal to do so in the UK. This plant has covered several hundred acres of land here. But wait a minute – compare that with the most troublesome invasive plant in the UK, bracken, which is covering 40,000+ hectares and is entirely native.

The fact is that in the UK we have a poor native flora compared with mainland Europe, and we could not possibly feed 60 million people on available edible native plants – we have no choice but to eat non-natives, which currently include wheat, barley, onions, garlic, potatoes, sweetcorn, squash, carrots, parsnips and most brassicas. To rail against non-natives while eating a loaf of wheat bread is muddled thinking!

As a general rule, I welcome plants from elsewhere that increase self-reliance and the efficiency of growing systems. Where any of the plants mentioned in this book could potentially expand a little too much for comfort, I have mentioned it. But bear in mind that a plant in one climate or context may be a vigorous spreader – for example, water caltrop in parts of North America – while in a different climate it may often be completely well-behaved, as water caltrop is in the UK.

Chapter 3
Maintenance of perennial vegetables

Keeping your vegetables and garden healthy is about much more than simply being on the lookout for pests or diseases and then treating the damage. A truly sustainable garden incorporates techniques that mean pests and diseases hardly get a chance to even appear. You can include plants that attract lots of predators, so potential pests get eaten; use lots of aromatic herbs to reduce disease levels; and, by utilising the beneficial soil fungi that thrive in uncultivated soil, you can make your garden resilient against drought and soil-borne diseases.

Perennial wild cabbage. Wild cabbage grows on the cliffs around much of Europe's coastline.

To have a sustainable, perennial-based garden we must let go of the attitude that 'every inch of soil must produce a crop for us', and dedicate some proportion of our plots to plants that have 'system' functions, such as mineral accumulators or nitrogen-fixing plants (see page 43).

Feeding

Most perennial vegetables require much less feeding than annual vegetables. The common annual vegetables have been selected and bred over many years to respond to large amounts of nutrients and grow to large sizes accordingly. This level of fertility is rarely found in nature, and with the resulting excessive growth come associated problems of pests and diseases. Few growers are going to stop growing all annual vegetables, but bear in mind that the fertility they require has unwelcome consequences in terms of both maintenance and ecological costs.

Most perennial vegetables require a lower nutrient input from us because:

- Their root systems are more efficient at finding their own nutrients. Obviously the root systems of perennials are fairly permanent and are nearly always more extensive than those of annual plants, so they can exploit a much larger soil volume to find food.

- In a perennial-based system, a mat of beneficial fungi (called mycorrhizal fungi) grows through the topsoil layer. These fungi have a huge role in sustaining natural ecosystems as well as perennial-based horticulture. Amongst other things, they help feed plants in a symbiotic relationship: the fungal hyphae (their equivalent of roots) are much finer than plant roots and can exploit soil much more efficiently than plants. They supply plants with hard-to-get nutrients in return for some sugars from the plant. These fungi are described in more detail overleaf.

- Most perennial vegetables have been less highly selected and bred than annual vegetables. This means that some have lower crop yields over a single season than an equivalent annual vegetable, though of course over its lifetime the perennial will usually yield many times the yield of the annual. However, a comparison of yields is meaningless unless it is related to the inputs into the growing system and a wider view of the system (see below).

If you make your own garden compost, then the first plants you should think of mulching are the tuber, root and bulb crops (see table on page 21), as a bit of extra fertility will increase the size of the crop, which makes life easier in the kitchen when the vegetables are being prepared. Leafy perennial crops are much less nutrient-demanding and are easy to provide for with occasional mulches of leafy material, leafmould or cut leaves (e.g. of comfrey). Or, if you are growing trees within your system, the leaf litter from them is often enough and you'll not need to deliberately feed at all.

Utilising plants for feeding the perennial system

I prefer to garden in a way whereby most or all of the nutrients required are obtained via plants grown on site – a closed-loop system. This, in combination with the return of some human urine, has got to be the basis of any sustainable growing system. In standard

Mycorrhizal fungi

Mycorrhizae are structures which develop where certain fungi colonise the tissues of fine roots of plants. The fungi help source minerals for the plant in return for carbohydrates and other substances. This mutually beneficial relationship is called a symbiosis.

As well as providing plant nutrition, these fungi provide other benefits too. They protect plant roots from pests and diseases, they can move nutrients large distances through the soil, and they are critical in the sequestering of carbon in soils. Recently it has been discovered* that plants can even send 'messages' to each other via the fungi,

warning, for example, of a pest outbreak and enabling other plants to start producing defensive chemicals before they even encounter the pest!

In a perennial-based system, mycrorrhizal fungi will appear in time by themselves if you do nothing, but they make take years to arrive. Their spores circulate in the air, and they can spread underground from nearby established sites (e.g. from established trees or hedges). You can buy inoculant which contains the spores of 15-20 species, intended for use when planting trees, though many of the same fungi will associate with non-woody perennials.

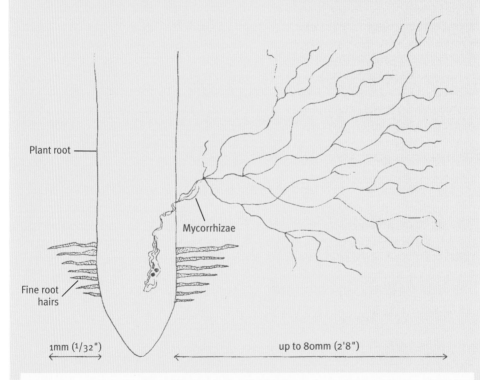

Plant root

Mycorrhizae

Fine root hairs

1mm (1/32")

up to 80mm (2'8")

Diagram 12. A mycorrhizal root. The fungus usually develops after the root, and grows around it and actually inside it.

*See Ferris Jabr, 'Heard it on the grapevine: The secret society of plants', *New Scientist*, 29 March 2011.

cultivation of annuals, the on-site provision of nutrients is largely achieved by using short-lived green manures, although you do need to devote 30-50 per cent of the land to green manures at any one time to maintain the fertility that annuals require.

Because most perennial vegetables are much less demanding than annuals, the amount of land you need to devote to plants that feed the system is also much less – around 10-15 per cent should be sufficient unless you are growing a lot of one of the demanding tuber crops. This 10-15 per cent of the growing area should be devoted to a mixture of nitrogen-fixing and mineral accumulator plants, all or most of which can be perennials themselves.

Nitrogen-fixing plants, unsurprisingly, supply nitrogen into the system. This is especially needed to sustain growth and productivity.

Mineral accumulator plants help provide other nutrients, including potassium, phosphorus and trace elements. These plants have particularly deep roots that are very efficient at extracting minerals from the soil deep down and accumulating them in the upper parts of the plant. When the leaves die down in autumn, some of the nutrients go back into the topsoil layers; some plants, such as comfrey, can also be cut to increase the nutrient flow upwards – the leaves can be used as a mulch where needed, or the cut parts can be used to make compost or as a compost activator.

Where to grow nitrogen fixers and mineral accumulators

The nutrients which these plants are able to supply to other plants in your growing system first get into the soil from litterfall, root turnover (the death of fine annual roots, which is a natural cycle in most plants), dieback of herbaceous parts and leaching from roots. Much of this initial transfer takes place in the vicinity of the nitrogen fixer or accumulator plant itself.

However, what then happens in a growing system comprised of perennial plants, where the soil is for the most part not physically disturbed, is what also happens in natural ecosystems: the nutrients are moved to where they are needed by mycorrhizal fungi. These fungi can move nutrients at least 30-40m (around 100-130'), perhaps more, which means that you don't have to have your nitrogen fixers and accumulator plants right next to other perennial crops; certainly not for the less demanding perennials. So you may be able to utilise some of the larger plant sources of nutrients (for example, nitrogen-fixing trees) some way away so that they will not overshade your perennials.

For the more demanding perennial crops (e.g. tuber crops), though, it would be wise to have nutrient sources relatively close – say, within 10m (33') or so – just so the fungi have less work to do; the fungi get their energy from plants, so the more they need to do, the more plants have to feed them. Although this is not necessarily detrimental to the plants, it is still astonishing to think that 20 per cent of all the energy a tree produces in the form of sugars via photosynthesis may be devoted to feeding mycorrhizal fungi.

Probably the most important factor about placement of plants that are helping to feed other plants, then, is not proximity but issues of shading. If your perennial crops prefer sun or only light shade, then larger nitrogen-fixing or mineral accumulator plants should be sited so as not to shade them – i.e. to the north, for example.

Nitrogen fixation in plants

Although the air we breathe is 78 per cent nitrogen gas (N_2), plants can usually use none of this and rely on nitrogen in solution in the soil. The exceptions are nitrogen-fixing plants, which live in symbiosis with particular bacteria; the bacteria take nitrogen out of the air within the soil, and pass it in soluble form to plants in exchange for sugars.

This process leads to nitrogen-fixing plants being high in nitrogen in their leaves and stems. Farmers tend to grow annual or short-lived perennial legumes and plough them in to gain the nitrogen from them; however, in perennial growing systems we can still benefit from nitrogen-fixing plants without necessarily killing them. Leaf litter and dieback of herbaceous growth in autumn, along with leaching from roots and root turnover (the death of fine annual roots), returns a huge amount of nitrogen to the soil.

Once in the soil, the nitrogen can then get moved to where it is needed by mycorrhizal fungi – but only if you have a system where the soil is predominantly not disturbed.

There are two families of nitrogen-fixing plants: the legumes (which includes clovers, lupins and vetches) and actinorhizal plants (which include alders and *Elaeagnus* species). Farmers have long used legumes to maintain soil fertility, and increasing numbers of gardeners are turning to nitrogen-fixing plants to provide some of the fertility their garden requires.

Recommended nitrogen-fixing plants

In general, the legumes tend to need better drainage than the actinorhizal plants. In the trees and shrubs tables below and opposite, the actinorhizal plants are the alders, *Elaeagnus* spp. (including autumn olive, goumi, oleaster and silverberry), *Myrica* spp. (bog myrtle, northern bayberry and wax myrtle) and sea buckthorn.

There is a limited number of useful large nitrogen-fixing trees, which can be helpful for a more forest-like structure to the garden.

Tall nitrogen-fixing trees	
Tree	Comments
Black locust, false acacia	Conical, fast-growing; thorny and can sucker. Thin canopy which allows lots of light through.
Himalayan sea buckthorn	Thorny and can sucker.
Italian alder	More tolerant of dry summer conditions than most alders; conical form.
Japanese pagoda tree	Often used ornamentally.
Red alder	Very fast-growing.

For sunny or lightly shaded sites, there is a good number of nitrogen-fixing shrubs and small trees. Most are legumes and need good light conditions.

Shrubs and small nitrogen-fixing trees	
Plant	**Comments**
Autumn olive	Fast, bushy. Produces masses of excellent edible fruits.
Bladder senna	Open shrub.
Bog myrtle	Spice shrub to grow in boggy and wet conditions.
Brooms	Fast, short-lived (10-15 years).
Bush clover	Ornamental shrub with flowers loved by bees.
Ceanothus	Ornamental shrubs used in sunny areas.
Dyer's greenweed	Small, scruffy shrub.
Elaeagnus x *ebbingei*	Evergreen, shade-tolerant. Bears early-ripening fruits in spring.
Gorse	Very prickly!
Goumi	Bears cherry-sized edible fruits in summer.
Green alder	Can be pruned or coppiced regularly.
Indigofera spp.	Used ornamentally in milder areas.
Laburnums	Used ornamentally for their yellow flowers.
Amur maackia	Slow-growing, tolerates dry soils and chalk.
Northern bayberry	A smaller version of wax myrtle.
Oleaster	Fast-growing.
Redbuds	Small trees used ornamentally.
Sea buckthorn	Thorny and suckering, so can sometimes become troublesome. Nutritious acid fruits.
Siberian pea tree*	Slow-growing, edible small pods and seeds.
Silverberry	A fast-growing bushy shrub bearing edible fruits.
Sitka alder	Can be pruned or coppiced regularly.
Sweet fern	Has spicy leaves and fruits, good in acid poor soils.
Tree lupin	Evergreen shrub. Needs a well-drained soil.
Wax myrtle, bayberry	Evergreen spice shrub.
Wisterias	Climbing shrubs used ornamentally.

* This is a perennial vegetable in its own right and appears in the species listing in Part 2.

Most non-woody nitrogen fixers (and all those in the table below) are legumes and need good sun and reasonable drainage. A few are shade-tolerant.

Non-woody nitrogen-fixing plants	
Plant*	Comments
Bird's foot trefoil	Great bee plant.
Clovers	Many species used.
Crown vetch	A good soil stabiliser on slopes.
Earthnut pea	Tendril climber with edible starchy tubers.
Everlasting pea	Tendril climber.
Greater bird's foot trefoil	Great bee and wildlife plant.
Gunnera	Likes moist soil; not so hardy. Shade-tolerant.
Groundnut	Twining climber with starchy edible tubers.
Ground plum	Grown for its edible young pods.
Kidney vetch	Pasture plant on alkaline soils.
Liquorice	Roots used for food, medicine and more!
Lucerne	Major agricultural fodder and green manure crop.
Lupins	Used ornamentally and in horticulture.
Milk vetch	Shade-tolerant.
Perennial sweet peas (wood pea and everlasting pea)	Tendril climbers. Wood pea is shade-tolerant.
Runner bean	Replant perennial grown for its edible pods and seeds.
Vetches	Used for green manure.

* Those in bold are perennial vegetables in their own right and appear in the species listing in Part 2.

Most nitrogen-fixing plants are pioneer species, which are sun-demanding; they often disappear when shaded. Whereas the preceding tables list the best all-round nitrogen-fixing species, the following table (opposite) gives a number of the most useful shade-tolerant species.

Nitrogen-fixing plants tolerating partial shade		
Trees	**Shrubs**	**Non-woody perennials**
Common alder	Autumn olive	Bird's foot trefoil
Red alder	Northern bayberry	Chilean rhubarb
	Californian bayberry (evergreen)	Earthnut pea
	Elaeagnus x *ebbingei* (evergreen)	Everlasting pea
	Elaeagnus glabra (evergreen)	Greater bird's foot trefoil
	Elaeagnus pungens (evergreen)	**Groundnut***
	Goumi	Gunnera
	Green alder	Hog peanut
	Oleaster	Liquorice
	Silverberry	Russian liquorice
	Sitka alder	White clover
	Sweet fern	Wood pea
	Wax myrtle (evergreen)	Wood vetch

* This is a perennial vegetable in its own right and appears in the species listing in Part 2.

Recommended mineral accumulator plants

All trees tend to accumulate minerals to a degree, through their fairly deep-rooted nature. Many perennial plants do the same by being deep-rooted and/or particularly efficient at mineral extraction (probably in combination with fungi). The perennial plants listed in the table overleaf are known to be particularly good, but it is likely that nearly all deep-rooted perennials are beneficial in this respect.

Mineral accumulator plants	
Plant*	**Comments**
Asparagus	Well-known spring vegetable.
Bracken	A well-known weed that you won't want to introduce, but can be useful as a cut mulch if you have it already.
Burnets	Edible young leaves.
Chicory	Often grown as an annual but many forms are perennial.
Chives	Well-known herb.
Cleavers, goosegrass	A well-known hedgerow and forest weed.
Clovers	Many species are used in agriculture and gardening; nitrogen fixers as well.
Coltsfoot	Sometimes regarded as a weed; a good early bee plant; medicinal.
Comfrey	One of the best accumulators. Comfrey and Russian comfrey are tallest and good for mulching, while dwarf comfrey makes a good ground cover in part shade. Great bee plants; also medicinal. Some may self-seed.
Daisy	Has edible young leaves and flowers.
Dandelion	Well-known weed.
Docks	Well-known weeds that you may not wish to deliberately encourage! Same family as sorrels.
Fennel	Well-known herb (not Florence fennel).
Garlic	Well known in two main forms.
Horseradish	Well-known herb.
Horsetail	Another noxious weed but high in nutrients.
Lemon balm	Well-known aromatic herb.
Liquorices	Deep-rooted perennials with edible roots.
Lucerne	Well known as a green manure.
Lungworts	Great early bee plants; shade-tolerant.
Lupins	Many species used ornamentally; also nitrogen fixers.
Marsh mallow	The plant is less well known than the confectionary!
Milk vetches	Also nitrogen-fixing.
Mulleins	For well-drained sites; many bee plants.
Plantains	Well known as weeds.
Poke root	North American foragers know this well.
Restharrow	A nitrogen fixer; edible young shoots.

(Cont.)

Plant*	Comments
Rhubarbs	Well known as a spring edible.
Salad burnet	Formerly much eaten.
Sanicle	A shade-loving ground-cover plant. Medicinal.
Scorzonera	Known for its roots but other parts are edible too.
Silverweed	Well known as a weed.
Skirret	Formerly much cultivated but long forgotten.
Sorrels	The same family as docks, only the leaves are much nicer!
Spurges	Often used ornamentally.
Stinging nettle	Well known as a weed.
Sweet cicely	A much overlooked herb.
Tansy	A well-known herb.
Toadflax	An excellent bee and butterfly plant.
Turkish rocket	A fine perennial brassica.
Udo / Japanese asparagus	Well known in Japan as a vegetable.
Valerian	Tall, good insect plant, medicinal uses. Likely to self-seed.
Vetches	All good bee plants and also nitrogen fixers.
Watercress	Well known but not so often cultivated.
Yarrow	Well-known grassland herb.

* Those in bold are perennial vegetables in their own right and appear in the species listing in Part 2.

Soil pH

Soil pH measures the acidity or alkalinity of a soil and is determined by the availability of calcium. The scale runs from 0 (most acidic) to 14 (most alkaline), with 7 being neutral.

Most plants are happy in soil with a pH of 5.5-7.0. The ideal is usually 6.0-6.5. Legumes prefer neutral (pH 7.0). If your soil is more acidic than pH 5.5, you should consider liming with ground limestone or dolomite, which are rock minerals.

If you do need to lime, the quantity of calcium (lime) needed to amend the soil pH will depend on the type of soil – sandy soils need most, clay soils need least to increase the pH by a given amount. A decent pH testing kit will give you recommendations for liming based on your soil type.

To apply lime, broadcast the liming material over the soil surface. Worms will take it down and it will become available to plants over the following couple of years.

Disease management

As a grower of perennial vegetables you will have an immediate advantage over your annual-growing friends and neighbours, because most perennial crops suffer from few very damaging diseases. The high-fertility diet that annual vegetables need makes the plants very susceptible to insect problems, and you'll find that most perennials grow with no disease problems whatsoever.

You can further promote the health of your plants by ensuring that you have lots of diversity. This will give your system overall resilience, and if one crop should suffer from disease problems, it is likely that nothing else will share quite the same susceptibility. Try mixing plants in various ways in your planting design (see Chapter 2, pages 26-9) – this will make it more difficult for a disease to move from plant to plant.

Recently it has been discovered (see footnote on page 42) that plants can send warning messages to each other (at least to others of the same species) via the mycorrhizal fungi that will establish in a perennial system. Thus, if one plant is attacked by a disease or pest, it will warn others, which can then start producing chemical defences even before the problem affects them. This must contribute to the healthiness of most natural ecosystems, where diseases rarely sweep through a whole area. There are probably many more unseen happenings in the (physically uncultivated) soil that we know nothing about, which aid plants grown in no-dig conditions.

Perennial plants do not, of course, live for ever. If a particular plant dies out, then consider replanting it in a different location rather than back in the same place. This will reduce the chance of any disease becoming established.

Pest management

The same principles apply to pest problems as to diseases. There are far fewer insect pests that can become problematic on perennial vegetables than on annuals, and, since many perennial vegetables do not belong to the same plant families as those of the common annual vegetables, pests of annuals are not often a problem on the perennials.

There are a few larger pests which might need attending to. One is pigeons – all vegetable growers will know the damage they can do to brassicas, and this extends to the perennial brassicas (broccoli, collards, kale, wild cabbage, sea kale). The usual protective measures (e.g. netting) may be needed if pigeons are a problem.

The other pests are browsers – rabbits and deer – who will delight in eating some of your choicest perennial vegetables if they get the chance. Rabbits should be fenced out: use wire mesh bent horizontal on the ground facing outwards from the protected area (see Diagram 13). If deer are a problem – for example, if you are adjacent to woodland – then fencing may also be the answer, though it is much more expensive. Roe deer need a fence 1.8m (6') high, while red deer need 2.1m+ (7+') high. Repellents have some effect against deer: human urine, human hair (e.g. from hairdressers) and lion dung (from zoos) have all been suggested as partially effective. Of course you could also harvest the offending rabbits and deer.

Diversity is very important in pest prevention, because most insect pests smell their way

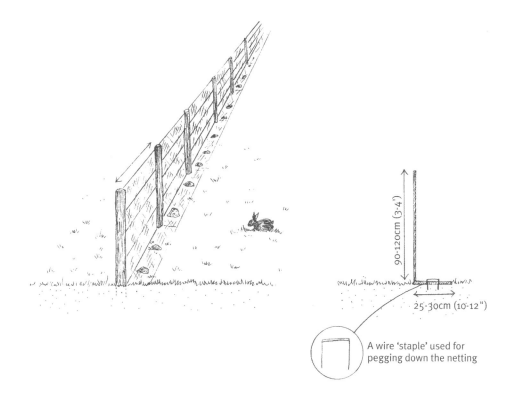

90-120cm (3-4')

25-30cm (10-12")

A wire 'staple' used for pegging down the netting

Diagram 13. Rabbit fencing. Rather than dig a trench in the traditional way, the wire mesh can be laid on the ground and either weighted down with stones or pegged down.

to the plant they want to eat. If there are lots of mixed-up plants, they just get confused and are unable to find their way to a host.

A good quantity of aromatic plants is especially useful in confusing insect pests, as the essential oils liberated are excellent at masking the smell of the plant they want to attack. You might have aromatic herbs as some of your perennial vegetables (for example, lemon balm and apple mint), but if you have space it is well worth considering planting out areas of aromatic herbs – mints are especially good, and I use a lot of oregano as well – as pest confusers, even if

you don't require them in a culinary sense. It is not a waste of space to devote areas to plants that will reduce pest problems.

There are also many plants that are excellent at attracting beneficial predatory insects, including all members of the Compositae (which attract hoverflies) and Umbelliferae (which attract hoverflies and parasitic wasps). Again, some of these plants are perennial vegetables themselves and you may be growing them already, but if you don't have many then you should consider including some of the species listed in the table overleaf.

Beneficial insect attractant plants*
Alexanders
Angelicas
Anise hyssops
Artemesias
Asters
Beans
Bee balms
Betony
Bindweeds
Borage
Breadroot
Brooms
Burdocks
Burnets
Burnet saxifrage
Butterburs
Cabbages
Catsfoot
Chamomile
Chickweed
Chicory
Clovers
Comfreys
Coneflowers
Cow parsnips
Daisy
Dandelion
False lupins
Fennel
Feverfew
Giant fennels
Golden marguerite

Goldenrods
Groundnut
Hemp agrimony
Hollyhock
Knapweeds
Lemon balm
Liquorices
Lovage
Lucerne
Lupins
Meadow parsnips
Milk vetches
Mints
Mitsuba
Mountain mint
Musk mallow
Oregano
Pig nut
Pignut
Pilotweed
Rosemary
Sages
Savorys
Scorzonera
Sea hollies
Skirret
Stinging nettle
Sunflowers
Sweet cicely
Sweet peas
Sweet roots
Sweet vetches
Tansy

| Thymes |
| Tickseeds |
| Vetches |
| Wild indigos |
| Wild strawberry |
| Yarrows |

* Those in bold are perennial vegetables in their own right and appear (or particular species of that 'family' appear) in the species listing in Part 2.

Harvesting and yields

Harvesting of perennial plants is often approached differently from harvesting of annuals, because you want the crop plants to continue growing: harvesting is not usually destructive.

Where young shoots – 'spear shoots' – coming through the ground are the crop (e.g. asparagus, bamboo shoots and Solomon's seal), the shoots are harvested for only a short period, usually by cutting off at or just below soil level, then they are allowed to grow so that the plant can make enough energy to continue its life.

Where the harvest is a crop of leaves (e.g. Good King Henry), leaf stalks (e.g. rhubarb), stems (e.g. apple mint) or growing shoots – the growing tips of an existing plant (e.g. Caucasian spinach) – it is wise not to take too much from any one plant. In this way, plants are not set back too much and the leaf coverage over the ground stays more intact, which means that weeds are much less likely to become a problem. So it is best to grow patches of these plants and to harvest just a little from each plant.

Flowers (e.g. from day lilies) and flower heads (e.g. from Turkish rocket) are best harvested

intensely from each plant – in other words, you should usually try to pick all the flowers or flower heads available; this will encourage the plants to produce more. Similarly, seed pods (e.g. from runner beans) should be harvested intensely if you want the plant to continue producing more pods.

Seeds (e.g. from Siberian pea tree or runner beans) are harvested when they are fully ripe. You can harvest whole pods of seeds and dry them further before shaking them in a sack to loosen the seeds.

Bulbils (small bulbs formed on flower stalks, e.g. from Babington's leek) can be harvested young before the outer layer dries and becomes papery – in which case they can be used whole – or when ripe, in which case the papery layer has to be removed, as with garlic.

Bulbs (e.g. garlic) are usually harvested once the aerial parts of the plant have died down in summer or autumn. Most of those described in this book are hardy and will overwinter in the ground if they are not harvested in a particular year.

With tubers, roots and rhizomes, in a temperate climate where the ground does not freeze much in winter and does not get waterlogged, the best place to store them is usually in the ground. Dig as required throughout the winter. Where winter temperatures do get colder and where you are growing replant perennials, dig up the underground parts in autumn and store in slightly moist sand or compost, in a cool place or in a root cellar. Replant these parts in spring to grow the next season's crop, either by planting directly in the ground or by starting them off in small containers first.

As I've mentioned in the Introduction, yields in a single season of a perennial vegetable might be lower than those of an annual equivalent. But of course over the plant's lifetime the yield will be many times that of a single season. Yield figures are simply unavailable for most perennial vegetables because they are fairly unknown in Western countries, even though most have been grown for ages in other parts of the world.

Propagation

Most folk growing perennial vegetables will want to propagate their plants, just as annual vegetable growers do. But, while annual vegetables are mostly seed-grown, perennial vegetables are propagated by a wider variety of methods.

Seed sowing

Unlike annual vegetables, which have been selected for fast-germinating seeds, most perennials are not only slower to germinate but many also require some form of pre-treatment before they will germinate. This is usually either cold stratification or scarification.

- **Cold stratification** is a period of moist, cold conditions, with temperatures of about 5°C (41°F). Typically, many species need 3 months of these conditions. If you have reliably cold winters, then you can sow seeds in autumn in seed trays, using a well-drained seed compost, and allow them to experience winter temperatures (make sure you cover the seed trays to stop the seeds being eaten by rodents). Otherwise, mix the seeds with moist (not wet) sand, put the mix in a plastic bag (labelled) and place in a fridge for the required time; then take out and sow.

- **Scarification** is the softening of the seed coat to allow moisture into the embryo to start germination. Sometimes physical scratching, cutting or sanding is used; sometimes a hot-water treatment. Long-domesticated legumes, such as peas and beans, have been selected for good germination and no longer need stratification; however, most less common legumes need this treatment because they have very hard seed coats. Pour water just under boiling hot (90-95°C / 194-203°F) over the seeds, and allow them to soak in it as it cools for 24 hours before sowing. Legumes are adapted for fire – you won't be harming the seeds!

When sowing perennials, it is usually wise to sow in seed trays rather than soil beds, simply because most perennials are slow germinators and in the meantime you are likely to get a lot of weed seeds growing in soil. Seeds in seed trays should be covered (I use a second seed tray upside down) to exclude both light (to stop algae growth of the seed surface) and rodents. Check frequently for germination, when the covering should be removed. Those few species with tiny seeds (e.g. mints, ice plant, orpine) should be sown on the surface of pre-moistened seed compost, but most should be buried to about a seed's depth.

Pot up seedlings soon after they emerge and grow on in a compost with reasonable nutrient content. Many species can be sown in spring and will be large enough to plant out by summer, should conditions permit, though I almost always grow my perennials for a whole season before planting them out in late autumn or winter, which vastly reduces the chance of having to water plants in a dry summer following planting.

Summer cuttings

Cuttings can be taken of soft growth in late spring (softwood cuttings) or summer (semi-ripe cuttings).

Cuttings should be taken from non-flowering shoots; straight cuttings without a heel are fine for the majority of plants. Early morning is the best time for taking softwood cuttings because the shoots are fully turgid and the air temperatures cooler – if taken later in the day, make sure you keep the cuttings cool and moist.

Cuttings should average 10-12cm (4-5") long with several nodes. The lower cut is made just beneath a leaf node; the higher one just above and sloping to shed water. The cuttings should be processed as soon as possible, though they may keep in a fridge for a day or two. The leaves are removed from the lower half of the cutting by carefully snipping with a sharp knife; all flower buds are removed. If the remaining leaves are large, it may be necessary to trim these by half to reduce water loss while the cutting puts out new roots – but note that this makes cuttings more susceptible to fungal infections.

With a few species (mints and watercress), cuttings can just be placed in water and they will soon produce roots. After 2 weeks or so they can be potted up.

Soft summer cuttings respond well to hormones, and even easy-to-root species root more uniformly and profusely when treated. A standard hormone rooting powder or liquid is fine; these often contain a fungicide which reduces cutting mortality. Alternatively, or in addition to bought-in hormones, a willow rooting substance (WRS) can easily be home-made and can significantly improve the rooting of some

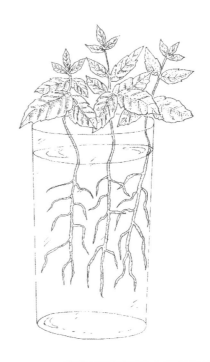

Diagram 14. Summer cuttings rooting in water.

plants. To make WRS, cut willow stems from the current year's growth into small pieces, pack into a container, cover with water for 24 hours, then drain off the water and store it. Cuttings should be placed upright in the WRS for 24 hours and then potted. (See Diagram 15 overleaf.)

Use a cuttings compost that is well drained with plenty of air in it – for example, two parts perlite or vermiculite to one part potting compost or composted bark. Unless the cuttings are to be left to root for a long time in the compost, there is no benefit in incorporating extra plant food. The rooting container should be at least 9-10cm (3½-4") deep to allow for reasonable drainage.

Once the cuttings are placed into the compost and watered, place a few small sticks or canes in the pot and cover the whole thing with a large clear plastic bag, tying it around the pot. This ensures a moist atmosphere, which is essential.

The vast majority of plants do not require bottom heat for cuttings to root. Ideal temperatures for rooting are 18-24°C (64-75°F); if a particularly cool spell occurs after taking the cuttings, then some heat – e.g. via a heated bench or propagator – may be desirable. Some shading may also be necessary in summer.

As the cuttings root and start to produce new growth, a hole can be made in the plastic bag, and gradually made larger, to slowly reduce the moist atmosphere and acclimatise the cuttings.

Most perennials root from cuttings quite quickly and can be potted up in late summer and grown on. Once roots start appearing through the holes at the bottom of the pot, they are generally safe to pot up. Slower ones should not be potted up until the following spring.

Diagram 15. (a) The freshly taken cutting, and after removal of leaves.

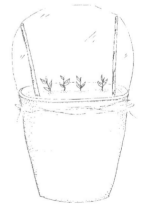

(b) Dipping the cutting into a hormone rooting powder or liquid.

(c) The cuttings placed into a pot of suitable compost, then covered with a polythene bag.

Hardwood cuttings

These are cuttings made of mature, firm, dormant wood from trees or shrubs after the leaves have fallen. They are prepared during the dormant season – late autumn, winter or early spring. Cuttings can be taken from the time when the leaves can be removed without tearing the bark, though waiting until the leaves have fallen saves work.

Cuttings are usually taken from wood of the previous season's growth. Tip portions of a shoot are discarded; the top cut (sloping to shed water) is made just above a node, and the bottom cut just beneath a node, so cuttings are about 20-30cm (8-12") long and 6-12mm (1/4-1/2") in diameter (see Diagram 16). They need a minimum of two buds.

Use a similar rooting compost as with summer cuttings (see page 55) and containers at least 10-15cm (4-6") deep, or place cuttings direct into the ground in well-drained beds. Grow on for at least one season (until the following autumn) before transplanting.

- **Autumn planting:** In regions with mild winters (e.g. most of the UK) or reliable snow cover, cuttings can be made in the autumn and planted immediately in

Diagram 16. (a) Cutting taken from current year's growth.

(b) Cutting trimmed to suitable length with angled top cut.

(c) Cuttings placed in a pot.

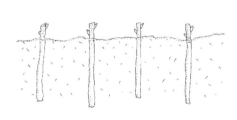

(d) Cuttings placed into soil.

nursery beds. Rooting may take place during the dormant season, or the formation of roots and shoots may occur simultaneously the following spring. The low and declining soil temperatures mean that rooting takes some time.

- **Spring planting:** With easy-to-root species, the cuttings can be gathered during the dormant season and wrapped in newspaper or slightly damp peat in a polythene bag, and stored at 0-4.5°C (32-40°F) – in a fridge, for example – until spring. The cuttings must not be allowed to dry out or become too wet during storage; if buds start to grow, the cuttings must be planted immediately. In spring, cuttings are planted directly into nursery beds. Rising soil temperatures may make rooting quick.

Basal cuttings

Basal cuttings are those taken from the base of a plant. These can be taken in spring: find shoots 10cm (4") long, growing from the plant's base, dig away the earth a little and cut them off close to the crown with a knife. Pot up in a well-drained compost and provide bottom heat. In a few weeks the cuttings should root and can be grown on before planting out.

Root cuttings

Root cuttings can be used to propagate some species. Dig up some or all of the roots of a mother plant: you generally want roots 7-12mm (1/4-1/2") diameter. Chop these into sections 2.5-10cm (1-4") long and insert into a pot. (If the root was horizontal in the ground then it can go horizontal in the pot; if more vertical in the ground then insert vertically in the pot.) Grow on for several months before planting out.

Division

Division is mainly applied to non-woody perennials and is the easiest method of vegetative propagation; also, no special conditions are needed to look after the young plants. Extra plants are produced as smaller, younger pieces of the clump are generated, and, where many are needed, plants can be split into small sections or single-bud divisions.

Plants are usually divided when they are dormant or just starting into growth – autumn or spring are best, with spring preferable if the soil is heavy, cold or wet, or if plants are somewhat tender. Spring- and early-summer-flowering perennials are best divided immediately after flowering.

All divisions should have plenty of roots (always aim to have more root than shoot for good results) and if there are few roots, the leaves should be trimmed to reduce water loss during establishment. Evergreen grasses and bamboos benefit from leaf reduction, and the latter should have canes cut down to 30cm (12").

The new plants should be planted in their new positions to the same depth as before.

Tight-clump-forming perennials

These should be lifted carefully with a fork and split into portions 5-8cm (2-3 1/4") across with a sharp spade or knife; larger pieces, with more shoots and roots, will flower sooner than small ones. Always discard the centre portions of clumps and retain the young outer parts (see Diagram 17).

Clump-forming species suitable for division include most bamboos, bellflowers, day lilies, hostas, lemon balm, rhubarbs, sea kale, sorrels and sweet cicely.

Diagram 17. Division of tight clumps.

Loose mats and clumps

Many perennials form loose mats and clumps, which are easy to divide. Lift them with a fork and pull apart with your hands or two garden forks if congested. Bamboos should be divided in mid-spring, when growth has just started. Species that are suitable for division this way include bamboos, hostas, ice plant, mints, orpine, strawberries and violets.

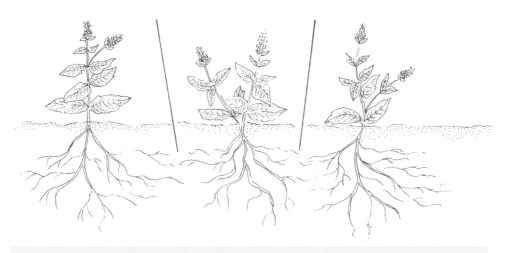

Diagram 18. Division of loose clumps.

Single-bud division

In addition to clump-forming plants, some single plants can be divided. Plants that can be divided are those that produce a mass of closely knit shoots or buds forming a crown of growth which can be split off, each portion possessing at least one shoot or bud together with an adequate root system for establishment. Because these portions are usually small, they often benefit from growing on in a nursery bed or pots before planting out.

Herbaceous perennials with fibrous crowns, such as day lilies, are easy to divide; the best time is after the flowers have died down and new shoots and roots have started to form – for late-summer- and autumn-flowering plants, this will be in spring. The crowns are lifted and prepared by trimming off dead and dying growth, removing surplus soil and washing the crowns as clean as possible. Portions of the crown may then be pulled off or cut off into manageable portions.

Young crowns are generally easier to manage than older ones, and the most suitable pieces for growing on are found on the periphery of the crown – the woody central material is difficult to split and lacks vigour. Large, tough crowns may need to be levered apart with two garden forks. Divisions can be planted immediately back into the soil or potted up to grow on.

Some non-woody perennials, e.g. hostas, have tough, compacted crowns with pronounced fleshy buds and roots, which are difficult to pull apart. These should be lifted in late winter or early spring, when the crown buds will be starting growth. After washing, the crowns are cut with a knife, ensuring that each part possesses at least one shoot or bud with adequate roots. These divisions are prone to fungal rots and hygiene is important – many growers use fungicides (alternatively, sulphur dust may be acceptable to organic growers).

Bulb division

The simplest ways to propagate bulbs are by bulblets (i.e. dividing excess bulbs formed in the bulb clump) and bulbils (small bulbs formed on flower stalks) – many alliums are vegetatively propagated this way, as is quamash.

Layering

Spreading perennials that naturally layer – for example, strawberries and false strawberry – are easily deliberately layered to produce new plants (see Diagram 19).

As these plants produce runners, they will root at the stem nodes (where leaves start to emerge) if the nodes are in contact with the ground. You can peg down or weight these down with soil so they root into the soil around the mother plant (to be dug up later), or you can do the same into pots.

Runners are produced from July onwards, and runners that are pegged down by mid-August are usually rooted enough to transplant in autumn.

Layering also works with many woody plants, but rooting takes much longer – a year or more. Shoots are pegged down to the ground and covered with soil.

Diagram 19. Layering plants that produce runners.

Maintenance

Once your perennial vegetables are established, minimal care is required for most species. However, there is *some* maintenance needed – growing perennials is not 'do-nothing gardening'!

Trees and shrubs

Woody plants grown as a leaf crop and tolerant of cutting (e.g. limes, mulberries, goji berry) are usually best treated as a coppice crop to maintain a plentiful supply of new shoots with tender leaves. They

should be grown for several years (4-6) to get well established before the first cut. They can then be either coppiced (cut off low down near the soil) or pollarded (cut off at chest height), removing all branches and leaving a series of branch stubs. These will then grow vigorous new shoots the following year.

The best time to coppice or pollard is in winter, though there is flexibility – if you wait until late winter then the new shoots will be delayed a month or more in late spring, which can sometimes be useful. You can continue coppicing every 1-4 years, depending on how large you want to let the plant grow. Grape vines can be treated similarly if they are used only as a leaf crop, though if you want fruits then it is better to pick the leaves of plants trained and pruned in the normal ways for fruit production.

Beech and saltbush do not respond well to coppicing. Beech is better trimmed as a low mound or hedge, while saltbush probably needs no extra pruning after shoots have been cut for harvesting.

Other perennial tree vegetables (e.g. elders, Siberian pea tree, snowbell tree) generally need no pruning at all. The only exceptions are the European elders, which can be trimmed back to 1.5m (5') high every few years to maintain the trees so that the flowers are still easily harvested.

Herbaceous perennials

Most of the perennials described in this book are herbaceous, usually with tops dying down in winter and persisting as roots or tubers over winter. Much of this section also applies to evergreen non-woody perennials.

Weeding

It is important to keep on top of weeds among your herbaceous perennials. Whereas with annual vegetables you would usually dig the soil every year and have the opportunity to remove pernicious weeds before they become too established, with most perennial vegetables you do not, and weeds such as docks, couch grass or bindweed may well enjoy the conditions.

Before planting, ensure that the ground is weed-free. Either dig it over, use a sheet mulch (see Chapter 2, page 23) or use some other means of removing all pernicious weeds.

Initial mulches of a suitable loose mulch material (see page 23), used when you plant out young plants, will both reduce the weeding needed and also help the plants to establish.

With many species – for example, Good King Henry – you can plant at a density such that the plants will form a fairly impervious ground cover with no detrimental effects, and this makes complete sense, resulting in very little weeding needed in the future. In the case of a few species, however – potatoes are an example – growing them very densely may cause them to become susceptible to fungal diseases because of a lack of air flow, so these plants need to be spaced out more.

Some species – such as most of the onion family – create very little shade and will not make a weed-suppressing cover. For these, the best options are either to use a loose mulch, topping it up every so often, or to interplant with some lower creeping plants – see Chapter 2, pages 26-9, for more information.

Hand weeding will still be necessary from time to time – I weed my perennial beds about once a month between spring (April) and summer (July). I am not worried by low weeds that compete little (for example, ground ivy), as they often have benefits in terms of being good bee plants or beneficial insect attractants. Larger weeds usually get chopped (I weed with garden shears) and left to decompose where they fall. They may regrow again to be chopped again later, but eventually most weeds die with this treatment. Many weeds are good mineral accumulators, so by growing and being cut down they are still contributing to the system as a whole.

Pruning

Dead stems of perennials should be left intact over winter rather than being cut in autumn, as is traditional. Lots of beneficial insects overwinter both inside dead stems and beneath the stem mulch often formed from fallen dead stems, and you should encourage them rather than joining in the over-zealous attempts to keep gardens 'tidy'. Every bit of garden tidiness not only increases the work required but also reduces the sustainability of your garden.

Thinning and dividing

Traditionally, beds of garden perennials that spread are thinned by dividing and removing excessive plants every few years, mainly because crowded plants may put up far fewer flowers. However, perennial vegetables are mostly grown for their leaves, shoots or roots, and for these thinning is not nearly such a requirement. If productivity for the crop you want declines a lot, then dividing plants and thinning the bed may be sensible. You can replant some of the thinnings elsewhere too if you wish. See pages 58-60 for more about dividing different types of plants.

In summary

Looking after perennial plants is mostly very easy, as once they are planted they tend to look after themselves. But which plants to choose? The A–Z that follows in Part 2 lists more than 100 perennial vegetables, but even this is a small proportion of those that are eaten throughout the world.

I have tried to choose plants that are generally easy to grow anywhere, and that are accessible in terms of obtaining seed or planting stock. Few people will grow all these plants, but you might find that once you get started on the perennial vegetable path, you will want more!

Orpine has wonderfully succulent edible leaves.

Part 2

Perennial vegetables A–Z

Air potatoes
See Yams (*Dioscorea* spp.)

Alfalfa
See Lucerne (*Medicago sativa*)

American elder
(*Sambucus canadensis*)

American elder is quite different from the European elders (see page 101) in character, being a lower suckering deciduous shrub rather than a tree, reaching 2-2.5m (6.6-8') high and wide. Each stem lives for 4-6 years before dying down to the ground, being replaced by new shoots. It does not spread vigorously, no more than 15-20cm (6-8") horizontally each year. The creamy-white flowers are large – up to 20cm 8" in diameter.

As its name suggests, it is native to North America, where in the far north of its range it becomes a herbaceous perennial, dying down to the ground each year.

This is a wonderful flowering shrub, and if elder flowers are a crop you value, then you should consider growing this. The big advantage that American elder has over European elders is that it flowers later than them and over a long period – from July to November (or even December sometimes here in Devon), so you can have a constant supply of fresh flowers over that period.

If the flowers are pollinated, then the fruits are similar to those of European elder (*S. nigra*).

Hardiness zone: 3

Cultivation

It tolerates most soils and considerable shade (though flowering will reduce in shade). A soil that stays moist in summer is preferred. It is happy in hedges.

Allow most new suckering shoots to emerge, as these are needed to replace old shoots dying off.

American elder is not self-fertile, so if you have only one bush (or one variety) then fruits will not set – this encourages extra flowering (which is a good thing if flowers are your crop). It does not cross-pollinate with European elder, as their flowering times do not overlap.

Varieties: If you have two different varieties, then fruits will form after flowering. These are similar in size and flavour to the fruits of the European elderberry. Two varieties are commonly in cultivation, 'Johns' and 'York'. Of these, 'York' has larger flowers and a slightly longer flowering season.

Harvest: Wait till flowers are fully open on dry days when pollen is falling freely (lightly tap the flower to check), as this is when the flavour is at a maximum. When harvesting flowers, try to minimise the amount of green stalk you pick. Use or process flowers within a few hours.

Propagation: By hardwood cuttings in autumn.

Culinary uses

The flowers can be used in the same ways as those of European elders, but they have a stronger vanilla fragrance. They can be eaten as a vegetable – especially nice dipped in batter and fried. They are also often used as a flavouring in parts of Europe – in tarts and fritters, and in batters.

I also like making soft drinks from them – just soak in water overnight (6-10 heads with 5 litres of water) and use within a day or two. If you also add 2-4 chopped lemons and sugar you'll end up with a cordial, which stores for longer. Very nice still and bubbly elderflower wines are easy to make. They can also be used to make an eau de vie spirit.

Maintenance and potential problems

Maintenance just involves cutting out old dead stems – and even this is optional if you don't mind the bush looking scrappy.

There are no pests or diseases of note. This species does not seem to suffer from aphid problems in the way that European elder can do.

Apple mint
(Mentha suaveolens)

Whereas a pungent mint like peppermint would not count for me as a vegetable – it is rather a strong flavouring – apple mint is a mild mint that we use in bulk.

Apple mint is a vigorous, spreading aromatic plant, herbaceous in most areas but evergreen where winters are mild. Plants can reach 60-90cm (2-3') high and make a thick, spreading, weed-surpressing clump. Plants are not deep-rooted and spread via shallow rhizomes. The leaves have a woolly feel to them, and the flowers are mauve.

Hardiness zone: 6

Cultivation

Grow in any moist soil that does not dry out too much in summer. Apple mint grows in sun or in substantial shade.

Varieties: The two common popular varieties are 'Grapefruit' and 'Pineapple'.

Harvest: Harvest leaves and young stems throughout the growing season.

Propagation: Sow seed, which is very fine, on the top of seed compost in spring and keep moist – germination is quite quick. Also propagate by root cuttings.

Culinary uses

Apple mint can be used as a bulk ingredient chopped in salads – it's particularly good in grain-based salads. It is also used chopped or as whole leaves for flavouring.

Maintenance and potential problems

It may need containing in places – bordering it with a cut or mown path is a good way to contain it. I prefer to leave the dead stems in place over winter, to aid overwintering insects, but try to cut them roughly in spring to maximise the light available to young growth.

Arrowheads
(*Sagittaria* spp.)

This is a family of aquatic herbaceous perennials, including the American

arrowhead, or duck potato or wapato (*S. latifolia*), the European grassy arrowhead (*S. graminea*) and the Asian swamp potato (*S. sagittifolia*) – the latter pictured below left. They are found in shallow, still or slowly flowing water, and are highly recognisable by their arrow-shaped leaves, which are held above the surface of the water on long stalks. These species can reach 0.3-1m (1-3') high or so and bear pretty white flowers. They spread via rhizomes to form colonies.

The plants produce clusters of round tubers, 1.5-3cm (5/8-1 1/8") in diameter, at the end of long slender roots around the bases of the plants. The tubers are an important food crop in Japan and some other parts of Asia.

Hardiness zone: 7

Cultivation

It is easiest to grow plants from tubers, though these are not always easily available to purchase. Grassy arrowhead tubers can sometimes be bought from Asian food stores. If your aquatic growing area has earth spread over the base, tubers can be pushed into the soil underwater. Otherwise you'll need to plant them in a pond planter pot.

You can also grow from seed (which needs to be fairly fresh), sowing in a pot which is kept in 5cm (2") of water. Seeds can take 2-6 weeks to germinate. Once seedlings have been potted up, the water depth can be gradually increased until the roots are fully submerged. Plant out into mud/earth below water or into planters – which are best shallow and wide.

Harvesting is easiest if plants are grown in a container with 15-20cm (6-8") of soil covered with at least 10cm (4") of water (see Chapter 2, page 38). Plants can also be grown in wet, boggy soils, but there is likely to be more weed competition. Plant tubers with pointed shoots in spring, 10-15cm (4-6") apart. Arrowheads need a position in full sun.

Once the tubers are fully formed, plants rapidly die down. Tubers are usually harvested in autumn and winter, but those of grassy arrowhead can be harvested all year round. The tubers of this species should not be allowed to freeze.

In Asia, arrowheads are grown in paddy culture like rice – sprouted tubers are planted in fields which are then flooded.

Varieties: There are no varieties.

Harvest: To harvest the tubers from earth beds, you'll need to dig down into the mud with your hands and ferret them out! It's no good trying to pull the plants up, because the tops will just break off. Of course, if you have grown plants in planters, these can be lifted out and the earth dissected rather more easily to locate the tubers. And if you have grown them in a pond planter, you may be able to drain it and let it dry out to make harvest easier. The tubers of American arrowhead and swamp potato are cold-hardy and can be left *in situ* to harvest over winter if you wish. Those of all species can be stored in plastic bags in a little water in a fridge.

Propagation: To maintain a supply of plants, make sure you replace some tubers if you have harvested all the previous autumn.

Arrowhead tubers.

Culinary uses

The tubers are starchy and are used as a cooked vegetable, boiled for 5-10 minutes or roasted. They have a good, slightly sweet, nutty, potato-like flavour. The skins and sprout can be somewhat bitter after boiling, so these are best rubbed off after cooking. They make a good accompaniment to meat and fish.

Tubers can also be ground and dried, then used as a flour in baking and as a thickener.

Maintenance and potential problems

As the name 'duck potato' implies, ducks like to eat the plants. In a small pond or growing system this should not be a problem, but in a larger pond which ducks visit you might need to scare them off (e.g. by using model herons) or use nets to deter them.

The water lily aphid can sometimes cause damage, so ideally make sure to grow a good diversity of plants nearby to attract hoverflies and other aphid predators.

In North America, muskrats can be a serious pest.

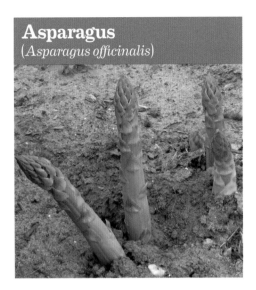

Asparagus
(Asparagus officinalis)

One of the best-known perennial vegetables, asparagus is a slowly expanding tuberous and herbaceous perennial, growing 1-1.5m (3-5') high with feathery foliage. The new shoots in spring are cut and used as a vegetable.

Asparagus originates from the eastern Mediterranean and occurs wild in maritime areas throughout Europe. It likes a fertile, well-drained soil, ideally with near-neutral pH (7.0).

Hardiness zone: 4

Cultivation

Normally asparagus is planted as crowns of named varieties. This is worthwhile, because it can suffer from many pests and diseases, and newer varieties have been bred with resistance. Shoots can be harvested 2 years after planting crowns.

Asparagus can also be grown from seed, but you may need to thin out weak female plants of low vigour. Plants also take longer to establish by seed and you'll need to wait 3 years before harvesting shoots.

Before planting, the soil should be carefully prepared. If your soil is not very well drained, you'll need to make a raised bed for asparagus to be happy. Potential perennial weeds must be removed, because asparagus is prone to weed competition at the best of times. Fertility materials – manures, composts, etc. – should be incorporated into the soil beforehand. Crowns should be planted 10-15cm (4-6") deep, in rows 60-80cm (2'-2'8") apart, with plants 40-60cm (1'4"-2') apart in the rows. It is worth making trenches, and making a ridge of soil at the bottom of the trench, on top of which the crown is placed, with roots trailing down either side.

Asparagus beds should be kept with a permanent organic mulch on the soil surface, or otherwise be interplanted with an undemanding low-growing intercrop (e.g. milk vetch, which trails over the soil surface but does not root from trailing stems). The alternative is endless weeding, because the feathery foliage casts little shade. Irrigation may be required in dry summers, especially on sandy soils.

After the harvesting season, stems grow tall and these are worth supporting – they can snap in winds and the swaying can make holes in the soil, which fill with water and cause roots to rot. Place canes or sticks along the sides of the bed and connect with twine to support the mass of stems. In autumn, cut down the stems to 5cm (2") above ground when the foliage turns yellow.

Varieties: Recommended varieties include the following. They are all mid-season unless indicated otherwise.

Open-pollinated varieties (will include male and female plants):
These older varieties will produce male and female plants when grown from seed – shoots from either are delicious, but male plants give a bigger yield. Female plants can also self-seed and lead to overcrowded beds, so collect and remove seeds before they fall. Shoot diameter will be more variable from these varieties, but many folk believe the flavour is superior to that of the newer F1 varieties.

'Argenteuil' – good on heavier soils.
'Connover's Colossal' – good on sandy soils, heavy cropping for an open-pollinated variety.
'Giant Mammoth' – good on heavier soils.
'Mary Washington' – has long, thick spikes, resistant to asparagus rust.
'Pacific Purple' – produces heavy yields of purple spears.

F1 hybrid male varieties:
'Backlim' – produces good yields of thick spears, mid- to late season, resistant to rust, compact foliage.
'Cito' – very high-yielding, much used commercially.
'Eros' – produces large, purple-tipped spears, good on sandy and clay soils.
'Franklim' – produces heavy yields, quickly builds up production.
'Gijnlim' – produces heavy crops on both sandy and clay soils, has high rust resistance. Early season.
'Grolim' – produces good yields of thick spears, needs sandy soils.
'Guelph Millennium' ('Millennium') – very cold-tolerant, good in northern locations and even in poor soils. Late season.
'Jersey Giant' – produces thick spears of good flavour. Early season.
'Jersey Knight' – produces thick, tasty spears, mid- to late season.
'Lucullus' – late-season variety with medium-sized spears.
'Marte' – good yields.
'Mondeo' – high yielding, disease-resistant variety with a long harvesting season and good flavour.
'Purple Passion' – produces high yields of purple spears.
'Thielim' – good yields, resistant to grey mould (*Botrytis*), upright foliage – recommended for organic cultivation.

Harvest: Once plants are established, harvesting can take place over 4-6 weeks in spring. Cut or snap the spear-shaped shoots when about 25cm (10") long, at or just below soil level.

Propagation: Sow seed in spring. Many varieties are propagated by dividing crowns. Bought or divided crowns are planted in spring.

Culinary uses

Try to cut your asparagus at the last minute before you cook it, to maximise the flavour.

Just steam or boil for a few minutes and serve with butter or a sauce.

Maintenance and potential problems

In the autumn, cut foliage down to near soil level and mulch the bed. In spring you may need to mulch with more fertility materials to maintain production.

The main pests are the adults and larvae of the asparagus beetle, which damage shoots and foliage. Easily identified, with black-and-white striped backs and red rims, they can be picked off by hand and disposed of.

The main disease is asparagus rust, which can be severe in wet summers and reduce the following year's crop substantially. Diseased tops should be cut and removed in autumn and burnt or buried.

Babington's leek
(*Allium ampeloprasum* var. *babingtonii*)

Also known as perennial leek

This interesting perennial is native to the seashore around the British Isles, and has edible parts at all stages of its life cycle. In early autumn, the underground bulb starts into growth, the growth appearing just like that of an annual leek. If the plant is very young, the stem will be quite small, but it gets thicker with age and by 3 years or so it can be 2cm (3/4") diameter. This stem grows over the winter, getting to maximum size by early spring, typically 45cm (1'6") high.

As spring progresses, the plant puts up a flowering stem, which is tough (like that of annual leek) and up to 1.5m (5') high, topped with a cluster of small, pale pinkish-purple flowers that attract bees. The flowers do not set seed, but instead the plant forms a head of bulbils (like small cloves of garlic), which remain in a green state for 4-6 weeks before ripening. A head of bulbils is quite heavy, and the plant often naturally bends over and the head touches the ground – this is the main way in which new plants spread in nature. If the head does touch the ground, then the bulbils in contact with the ground will soon root once they are ripe.

As the bulbils ripen, the plant dies back to the underground bulb. This bulb is the size and shape of a large bulb of garlic, but is not subdivided into cloves. The bulbs remains dormant for about a month and then start back into growth again.

Hardiness zone: 6

Cultivation

Babington's leek is easy to grow. It needs sun or partial shade, and is undemanding as to soil as long as there is reasonable drainage. The first-year growth is 25-30cm (10-12"); by the third year plants are large enough to harvest and will start to flower.

Varieties: There are no named varieties, but as well as the species there is apparently a rare form with red bulbs and bulbils.

Harvest: The 'leeks' can be harvested in two ways between late autumn and spring:

- They can be dug up whole – in which case you get a longer leek stem, but you have removed the plant completely and there is a bulb to use as well.
- they can be cut off at soil level – in which case you get less leek but the plant should recover and regrow.

Bulbils are harvested green in July and August, or ripe in late August or early September. If harvesting them ripe, you can dig the bulb at the same time if you want to harvest it. That is the end of the perennial plant of course, but you have the bulbils to start off new plants.

Bulbs and bulbils, once properly dry, store for a long time – over a year – while retaining vitality.

Propagation: Start with bulbils, which can be bought commercially. These can be sown in rows or broadcast in autumn or spring, even where there are existing plants, as long as the plant growth is not too dense nor higher than about 15cm (6"). Aim for a spacing of about 10cm (4") between bulbils.

Established plants can also produce offsets – daughter bulbs next to the mother bulb – from which new plants can be raised. Simply dig out and divide the daughters, then they can be transplanted at any time.

Babington's leeks growing beneath deciduous trees.

Culinary uses

The leeks can be used in exactly the same ways as annual leek: the only differences are that the outer leaves can be a bit tougher – you may want to discard them – and the flavour is stronger and more garlicky.

The bulbils can also be eaten. The ripe ones have papery skins like cloves of garlic, which are a bit fiddly to remove (the easiest way is to half-crush the bulbils on a flat surface with the flat edge of a knife, then the papery skin comes cleanly away). It is easier to use the green bulbils, as they don't need peeling and can be put whole into soups or stews.

The bulbs too can be eaten, as a kind of easy-grow garlic. Again, the plants need to be a few years old before the bulbs are big enough. The bulb has a strong garlic-leek flavour, and can be used in the same ways as either.

Maintenance and potential problems

Like many alliums, Babington's leek does not suppress weeds very well, though my experience is that it grows well mixed in with other plants. It is important in plant mixtures that the new shoots in autumn get plenty of light, i.e. are not too overshaded.

Baker's garlic
See Rakkyo (*Allium chinense*)

Balm, lemon
See Lemon balm (*Melissa officinalis*)

Bamboos
(*Phyllostachys* spp., *Pleioblastus* spp., *Pseudosasa japonica*, *Arundinaria gigantea*, *Semiarundinaria* spp. and *Yushania* spp.)

There are many bamboo species, ranging from dwarf shrubs to giant tree-sized species. Although all have edible shoots, it is only those of the larger ones that are thick enough to be worth harvesting. My favourites are the *Phyllostachys* species, which are medium-to-large shrub-sized grasses growing 3-8 metres (10-26') high, with shoots and canes 2-8cm (3/4-3¹/4") in diameter.

Bamboo shoots are a great nutritious vegetable, in season through the spring when many annual vegetables are in short supply.

Bamboos sometimes have a reputation for being uncontrollable and invasive, and certainly some types (and many of the *Phyllostachys* species) try to expand, but harvesting is the management – cut the shoots coming up where they are not wanted (preferably when small enough to eat too), and those shoots will not regrow. Alternatively, you can put in rhizome barriers to stop the spread (see page 76).

New shoots emerge from the ground mainly from April to July and are the same diameter as the cane would be when fully grown. To be worth harvesting, shoots need to be at least 1.2cm (1/2") across.

Hardiness zone: 6

Cultivation
Bamboos tolerate most soils but prefer moist soil in summer. Sun or light shade is ideal. Most bamboos do not like positions exposed to strong winds.

Varieties: The following table gives information by species, on shoot quality and the start of shoot emergence, for bamboos that are productive and large enough to make good eating.

Bamboos for edible shoots			
Common name	Latin name	Emergence*	Comments
Anceps bamboo	*Yushania anceps*	Summer–early autumn	Free of bitterness – good
Arrow bamboo	*Pseudosasa japonica*	Summer–early autumn	Free of bitterness – good
Big node bamboo	*Phyllostachys nidularia*	Early spring	Slight bitterness
Black bamboo	*Phyllostachys nigra*	Summer	Bitter when raw
Cane reed	*Arundinaria gigantea*	Spring	Some bitterness
Chinese weeping bamboo	*Phyllostachys flexuosa*	Late spring	Very bitter raw
Fishpole bamboo	*Phyllostachys aurea*	Early autumn	Free of bitterness – good
Giant timber bamboo	*Phyllostachys bambusoides*	Summer	Bitter when raw
Green sulphur bamboo	*Phyllostachys sulphurea* f. *viridis*	Late spring	Slight bitterness – fair
Greenwax golden bamboo	*Phyllostachys viridiglaucescens*	Early summer	Free of bitterness – good
Maculata bamboo	*Yushania maculata*	Summer–early autumn	Free of bitterness – good
Moso bamboo	*Phyllostachys edulis*	Late spring	Prized, major Japanese edible shoot
Narihira bamboo	*Semiarundinaria fastuosa*	Early autumn	Slightly bitter
Nuda bamboo	*Phyllostachys nuda*	Spring	Very slight bitterness – good
Pitt White bamboo	*Yushania anceps* 'Pitt White'	Midsummer	Free of bitterness – good
Red margin bamboo	*Phyllostachys rubromarginata*	Summer	Good quality
Simon bamboo	*Pleioblastus simonii*	Summer–early autumn	Fair quality
Smooth-sheathed bamboo	*Phyllostachys vivax*	Early autumn	Slightly bitter
Stone bamboo	*Phyllostachys angusta*	Late spring	Free of bitterness
Sweetshoot bamboo	*Phyllostachys dulcis*	Early spring	Prized, major Chinese edible shoot
Violet bamboo	*Phyllostachys violascens*	Late spring	Slight bitterness
Yellow grove bamboo	*Phyllostachys aureosulcata*	Late spring	Free of bitterness
Yunzhu bamboo	*Phyllostachys glauca*	Late spring	Slight bitterness

*Early spring = April/May, late spring = late May/June, summer = late June/July/early August; early autumn = late August/September. NB these dates are for southern England – add on a week for central UK and two weeks for the north.

Harvest: The new shoots can be cut from when they begin to show through the soil until they are about 1m (3') high, but only the top 30cm (1') is edible. It is easiest to cut the new shoot at soil level, but you can also dig the soil away and cut it where it joins the rhizome, for a longer shoot.

All bamboos also have edible seeds, which are like a sweet nutty rice. However, most flower very irregularly, so the seeds cannot be considered a reliable crop. The ripe seeds can be beaten from the canes into a basket. After flowering, bamboo plants often die off; in nature there is strong regeneration from seed.

Propagation: This is usually by division of clumps, which can involve saws and axes – not just spades – because the rhizomes can be as tough as the canes. Plants can also be grown quite easily from seed, but seed is rarely produced and not often available commercially.

Culinary uses

Bamboo shoots are prepared by halving lengthwise, then removing the outer tough leafy sheaths in layers to expose the white and pale green flesh.

The flesh of a few species is free of bitterness and can be eaten raw in salads. Most, however, are bitter when raw and require steaming for 5-10 minutes, which completely removes the bitterness. Cooked shoots have a mild, courgette-like flavour with hints of celery and peas. They are great as a mild vegetable on their own, or added into stews or stir-fries, for example.

With bamboo seeds, like most grass seeds, the papery husk must be removed before

eating. The seeds are then usually cooked like rice, or they can be dried and ground into a flour.

Maintenance and potential problems

Regularly harvested bamboos will require plentiful nitrogen, otherwise the shoot size will decrease.

If you want to be extra sure that the bamboo cannot expand past a certain point, you can enclose the area with a rhizome barrier. These are usually made of thick, flexible plastic and must be dug in at least 45cm (1'6") deep.

Basswood
See Limes (*Tilia* spp.)

Beech
(*Fagus sylvatica*)

A well-known European large tree, beech has been planted in many parts of the UK, though it is thought to be native only to parts of the south. It is only moderately fast-growing, 60-80cm (2'-2'8") per year once established, and reaching up to 30m (100') high. It is often used in trimmed hedges because young and trimmed trees retain old leaves over the winter and thus give fairly good winter shelter.

Hardiness zone: 5

Cultivation

Beech is easy to grow. It has exceptional climatic tolerance, happy both in the continental eastern USA and in cool oceanic Scotland. It does require good rainfall (at least 70cm/2'4" per year), and is happy in any pH of soil as long as it is well drained but moist. It tolerates exposure except for coastal exposure. Young trees are especially shade-tolerant; older trees need sun or partial sun.

Varieties: Copper beech, or purple beech (*F. sylvatica* Atropurpurea Group), is widely grown and has the same uses as the species.

Harvest: Beech is mainly listed here as a leaf crop. It comes into leaf relatively late (May in the UK), and the young leaves make good eating for about 3 weeks, after which they become tough. If you are growing beech as a leaf crop, it makes absolute sense to keep your tree(s) trimmed – you could have a dual-purpose edible hedge or dedicated trimmed beech bushes in the garden, as I do.

The kernels of the seeds (beech nuts) make a very nice nibble, but they are small and fiddly. In the past they have been crushed to produce an edible oil, even on a commercial scale in France. The seeds are harvested in September and October.

Beech trees do not usually start producing seed until about 50 years of age, so if you want beech seed as a crop, you'll probably need to find someone else's trees you can crop!

Propagation: Beech trees are usually grown from seed: the seeds require 3-4 months of stratification and can either be sown in the autumn or stratified and then spring-sown. Seedlings do not produce a strong taproot.

Culinary uses

The leaves have a lovely lemony zing to them and are great in salads and soups. Some chefs recommend eating them (raw) with asparagus dishes.

The seed kernels can be eaten raw or added to cakes, biscuits, crumbles and other desserts.

Maintenance and potential problems

The main maintenance needed is trimming, in the case of hedges or trimmed bushes. Hedges are usually trimmed in summer (June–July) instead of winter, so that the old leaves can remain over the winter and aid in sheltering. But trimmed bushes can be trimmed in winter – or indeed at any time of the year.

Beech has few problems unless trees get drought-stressed on well-drained soils, when beech bark disease, caused by coral spot fungus, can be a serious problem. To avoid this, make sure trees are mulched before dry spells and irrigate if really necessary.

Bellflowers – alpine
(*Campanula* spp.)

Also known as harebells

Alpine species of bellflower include fairy thimbles (*C. cochlearifolia*), Adria bellflower (*C. portenschlagiana*) and trailing bellflower (*C. poscharskyana* – pictured above). These evergreen species are most commonly seen in the UK growing in and on walls, where they thrive. They are all garden escapees, native to Eastern Europe, all producing pretty funnel-shaped bluish-purple, pink or white flowers that are very attractive to bees. They grow to 30cm (1') high and often no wider, though trailing bellflower can cover walls more effectively.

Hardiness zones: 3-5

Cultivation
Alpine bellflowers require very well-drained soils, and need full sun or light shade. They are tolerant of nutrient-poor soils. The easiest way of introducing them is to plant small plants into cracks of walls, or even to mix the seed with sand and sprinkle it along and into walls.

Varieties: Several ornamental varieties exist, all of which can be used for food.

Harvest: Harvest young leaves, stems and flowers (as well as roots) at any time during the growing season.

Propagation: Propagate by seed or basal cuttings in spring. The seed is very fine, like dust, and needs careful handling – it should be sprinkled on to the surface of a fine seed compost and not buried. Plants often self-seed in the right conditions.

Culinary uses
The flowers, leaves, stems and roots of all bellflower species are edible in salads or cooked. The flowers in spring and summer are sweet and make a nice nibble or addition to salads. The leaves are a little tough and hairy, but they can be eaten raw, and are improved by using an oily or thick dressing. The leaves and the stems can also be cooked as greens, or added to other cooked dishes, such as soups or stews.

The roots of these species, while sweet and edible, are not particularly large and are also usually difficult to harvest because the plants are growing in walls.

Maintenance and potential problems
Little maintenance required and no problems!

Bellflowers – hardy
(*Campanula* spp.)

Also known as harebells

Hardy perennial bellflowers include clustered bellflower (*C. glomerata*), milky bellflower (*C. lactiflora* – pictured above), giant bellflower (*C. latifolia*), peach-leaved bellflower (*C. persicifolia*), creeping bellflower (*C. rapunculoides*) and nettle-leaved bellflower (*C. trachelium*). Most are herbaceous perennials, but a few (e.g. peach-leaved bellflower) are evergreen. They are native to various parts of Europe, some to the UK, and all bear pretty funnel-shaped flowers (white to bluish and purple), which are much loved by bees.

These species are larger than the alpine bellflowers, with flower spikes growing to 1m or 1.5m (3' or 5') high, though the plants themselves are still quite narrow, about 20-30cm (8-12") wide.

Hardiness zones: 2-8

Cultivation
Hardy bellflowers tolerate most ordinary soils. They all prefer sun but tolerate more shade than the alpine species.

Varieties: Several ornamental varieties exist, all of which can be used for food.

Harvest: Harvest young leaves, stems and flowers (as well as roots) at any time during the growing season.

Propagation: Propagate by seed or basal cuttings in spring. As with alpine bellflowers (see opposite), the seed is very fine and needs careful handling. Plants often self-seed in the right conditions.

Culinary uses
The flowers, leaves, stems and roots of all bellflower species are edible in salads or cooked. For flowers, leaves and stems, treat as for alpine bellflowers – see opposite.

The roots of all species are sweet and edible, with a delicate, earthy flavour – use boiled, in soups, or finely sliced raw or cooked in salads. Many species bear only small roots, but creeping bellflower bears larger and fleshier roots and is the most worthwhile.

Maintenance and potential problems
Little maintenance required and no problems.

Bladder campion
(*Silene vulgaris*)

This is a European herbaceous perennial growing up to 90cm (3') high. It has smooth waxy grey leaves, white flowers and a distinctive bladder-shaped seed pod. It is found widely in hedge banks, open woodland and fields on reasonably well-drained soils. Flowers are pollinated by bees and moths.

There is a long history of using the leaves in European cuisine.

The closely related sea campion (*Silene uniflora*) requires a well-drained soil or sand/gravel to grow in, and is hardy to zone 3.

Hardiness zone: 6

Cultivation

Grow bladder campion in any reasonably well-drained soil that is not too acid; grow sea campion on a well-drained soil. Full sun or partial shade is required.

Varieties: there are no varieties.

Harvest: The best leaves to harvest are the basal leaves (the leaves around the base of the plant) – there are more of these and it is easier to harvest a good quantity, and they are sweeter than later leaves. Older leaves can be somewhat bitter.

Propagation: By seed (easy) or division.

Culinary uses

The young basal leaves have a sweet honey-and-pea flavour and make excellent eating – use in salads, or cook these and older leaves by steaming or stir-frying. Use fried with scrambled eggs.

Maintenance and potential problems

No maintenance required and no problems.

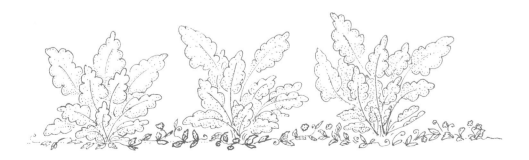

Bowles's mint
(*Mentha* Bowles's mint)

This is the other mint (apart from apple mint) that I think is worth using as a bulk ingredient and so counts for me as a vegetable.

Bowles's mint is an aromatic herbaceous plant that spreads irregularly, not forming a ground cover but good interplanted with something low. Plants grow 60-120cm (2-4') high, with a few stems appearing here and there, each with a small spread of 20-30cm (8-12"). The plants are not deep-rooted and spread via shallow rhizomes.

The leaves have a slightly woolly feel to them and a flavour between that of apple mint and spearmint.

Hardiness zone: 5

Cultivation

Bowles's mint grows in any moist soil that does not dry out too much in summer. It is happy in sun or in deep shade.
Varieties: Bowles's Mint is a variety itself.

Harvest: Harvest leaves and young stems throughout the growing season.

Propagation: By root cuttings in winter or division in spring.

Culinary uses

It can be used as a bulk ingredient chopped in salads – particularly good chopped in grain-based salads. It's also used chopped or as whole leaves for flavouring.

Maintenance and potential problems

This mint may need containing in places to stop it from spreading too far, though it does not suppress all competition like apple mint does. Bordering it with a cut or mown path is a good way to contain it.

I prefer to leave the dead stems in place over winter – they aid overwintering insects – but try to cut them roughly in spring to maximise the light available to young growth.

Brassicas, perennial
See Perennial brassicas (*Brassica* spp.)

Broccoli, Chinese
See Chinese broccoli (*Brassica oleracea* Alboglabra Group)

Broccoli, perennial
See Perennial broccoli (*Brassica oleracea* Botrytis Group)

Buffalo pea
See Ground plum (*Astragalus crassicarpus*)

Bunching onion
See Welsh onion, scallion & bunching onion (*Allium fistulosum*)

Burnet saxifrage
(*Pimpinella saxifraga*)

This is a European herbaceous perennial found at woodland edges, in meadows and in pastures. Related to aniseed (*Pimpinella anisum*), it bears basal leaves (at the base of the plant) very similar to salad burnet leaves, while leaves on the stems are fleshier and smaller. White flowers are borne in summer on solid hairy stems, up to 1m (3') high. Greater burnet saxifrage (*Pimpinella major* – pictured left) is used similarly.

Hardiness zone: 4

Cultivation
This plant likes a fairly sunny site and a well-drained soil with a neutral to alkaline pH. It persists well in grasses.

Varieties: There are no varieties.

Harvest: The young basal leaves are harvested before the emergence of the flower stem.

Propagation: Sow seed in spring.

Culinary uses
The leaves have a cucumber-parsley flavour, and can be used in salads and as a flavouring, e.g. in sauces, cheeses or salsa verde. They are good with meat or fish. The seeds are unpleasantly pungent and not recommended.

Maintenance and potential problems
None of either.

Bush kale
See Perennial kale (*Brassica oleracea* Ramosa Group)

Camass
See Quamash (*Camassia quamash*)

Cardoon
(*Cynara cardunculus*)

This large, grey-leaved Mediterranean evergreen perennial thistle has big leaves and tall flowering stems. The leafy plants reach about 80cm (2'8") high and a similar or slightly larger width, and the flowering stems reach 1.5-2.1m (5-7') high. At the top of the flowering stems, large flower buds form, which open into intensely blue-purple flowers much loved by bees.

Cardoon is closely related to globe artichoke, and they are sometimes difficult to tell apart. The flower buds on cardoon do not get as large as those of globe artichoke – the latter has been selected for large buds.

Hardiness zone: 7

Cultivation
Cardoon likes well-drained to moderately well-drained fertile soils. Winter cold may knock back the larger leaves but the below-ground parts are hardier than those of globe artichoke and survive winter weather better in the UK.

Full sun or only light shade is required, and protection from cold winds.

Varieties: There are few cardoon varieties available commercially. Notably there are seedless varieties, which come more or less true from seed; otherwise good forms can be propagated by division in November or March. Most named varieties are less spiny than the species.

'Bianco Gigante Inerme a Foglia Intera' – Italian productive variety.
'Blanco de Peralta' – Spanish variety, heavy yielding with over 30 per cent leaf stem of very high quality.
'Blanco de Valencia' – Spanish variety, heavy yielding with over 30 per cent leaf stem of very high quality.
'Gigante de Romagna' – very vigorous.
'Gobbo di Nizza' – Italian variety with thick ribs, almost spineless.
'Lleno de España' – Spanish variety.
'Lumbier' – Spanish variety.
'Plein Blanc Inerme' – French variety, vigorous.
'Porto Spineless' – leaves and stems bear fewer spines, also used for cut flower use.
'Rojo de Agreda' – Spanish variety, low yielding.
'Rojo de Corella' – Spanish variety.
'Tafalla' – Spanish variety, moderately productive.
'Verde de Calahorra' – Spanish variety, very productive.

'Verde de Peralta' – the major variety grown in Navarre, Spain; a compact plant, leaf stalks have low fibre content and are very tender. Very productive.

Harvest: Leaf ribs and stalks can be harvested from mature leaves. The ribs have some bitterness to them and can sometimes be tough. However, the leaf stalks can be blanched, and if this is done then the leaf ribs will also be more tender.

To blanch leaf stalks, in late summer they should be bundled together (tied near the top) and wrapped with sacking, card or black plastic to cover 45-60cm (1'6"-2") of stalk to exclude light for up to 6 weeks. The blanched stalks are then harvested in autumn; the unblanched leafy tops cut and discarded. You can do this every second year – the plant will need a year without being harvested to recover reserves.

Unopened flower heads (buds) are usually picked from cardoons only when immature.

Propagation: Sow seeds in early spring, making sure you pot up seedlings regularly so they do not become pot bound. Plant out in late spring into moist soil of good fertility, about 80cm (2'8") apart.

Culinary uses

The leaf ribs and stalks are usually boiled or steamed, then peeled before eating. They have a celery-type flavour which in the leaf ribs can be slightly bitter, though less so if blanched. If tender, the leaf ribs can be peeled and eaten raw in salads or dipped in olive oil and eaten. Cardoon stalks go particularly well with eggs and cheese.

Cardoon flower head.

Immature flower heads (buds) can be boiled and eaten whole, when they are similar to globe artichokes, though the flavour is not as fine.

Cardoon roots are also edible, though by digging them up you'll kill the plant of course. They are cooked like parsnips and taste like sweet celery.

Cardoon seeds yield an oil similar in composition, quality and uses to sunflower oil. The plants contain an enzyme that is

Cardoon in flower.

extracted and used as a vegetable rennet in the making of many regional cheeses in Portugal.

Maintenance and potential problems

In the UK the main problem is excessively wet winter weather, which can kill plants unless they are in well-drained soils. In early spring, when the leaf canopy will be thinnest, there is potential for weed competition.

Caucasian spinach
(Hablitzia tamnoides)

A plant that has come to light only in the last couple of years, this perennial climber/ scrambler has a puzzling recent history, having been grown as a perennial vegetable for some time in Scandinavia, though it originates from the Caucasus (Georgia, etc.). It is a somewhat untidy sprawling plant of the Chenopodium family, with leaves that look quite similar to those of Good King Henry (*Chenopodium bonus-henricus*). It will scramble over the ground and if there is anything to clamber up, it will reach a few metres (10 feet or so).

Hardiness zone: 4

Cultivation

Caucasian spinach seems happy in most soils as long as they are well drained, and should be quite drought-tolerant as it has deep taproots. It prefers light shade.

Varieties: There are no varieties.

Harvest: New shoots appear early in spring and harvesting of shoots and leaves can begin as soon as there is enough growth.

Propagation: By division of established plants in winter or by layering (see Chapter 3, page 60). Plants do not seem to produce much seed, but if you can source seed – it is sometimes available on seed exchange websites – then it should germinate readily in spring after a period of cold stratification (see Chapter 2, page 54).

Culinary uses

Treat the shoots like spinach and just steam for a few minutes.

Maintenance and potential problems

None of either.

Chard
See Perpetual spinach & chard
(Beta vulgaris subsp. cicla)

Chicory
(Cichorium intybus)

Also known as radicchio

Chicory is a small, deep-rooted dandelion-like European plant with many biennial and perennial forms – only the latter are discussed here. It is about 30cm (1') wide, but with a flower spike up to 1.2m (4') high, topped with pretty blue flowers. It is a good mineral accumulator and grows wild in fields and meadows and roadsides. Note that Witloof chicory, used to force chicons, is a biennial.

Radicchio is a variety of chicory that resembles a small red cabbage. It forms a compact head of dark red leaves, veined in white. The size ranges from that of a large radish to that of a large grapefruit.

Hardiness zone: 3

Cultivation

Chicory grows in any reasonably drained soil; most lushly in fertile soils. It prefers full sun but will tolerate light shade.

Varieties: Most varieties bred for leaf production are perennial, and include the following.

'Cerolio' – has tight dark rosettes.
'Da Taglio Foglia Larga' – pale green leaves, very productive.
'Dentarella' ('Italian Dandelion') – green-leaved, resembles a large dandelion.
'Grumolo Bionda' – pale green leaves in open rosettes.
'Grumolo Verde' – small plant with green leaves, very cold-tolerant.
'Italo Rossico' ('Red Rib Dandelion') – green-leaved with deep red mid-ribs.
'Puntarella' – has thick, succulent, contorted stems.
'Rossa di Treviso' – bears long leaves, turning dark purple-red in autumn. (Pictured left.)
'Rossa di Verona' – bears medium-sized leaves that turn dark purple-red in autumn.
'Spadona' – has long rounded leaves.
'Zuccherino of Trieste' – small green leaves, very productive.

Harvest: Leaves are harvested throughout the growing season but become more bitter on flowering plants – flower stalks can be cut back to lengthen the harvest. Roots can be harvested in autumn and winter and roasted to make a coffee-like beverage. They can be stored in sand or a similar moist medium.

Plants can be blanched in spring to improve the flavour of the leaves (much like rhubarb – exclude light with a large upturned pot or other rigid cover).

Propagation: Chicory is usually grown from seed, which germinates quickly.

Culinary uses

The slightly bitter leaves are widely used in salads and added to cooked dishes (they only need a few minutes' cooking). If wilted over a flame for a few seconds, they lose most of the bitterness. Don't hold over a flame for long or you'll have crispy chicory.

The roots are cleaned and roasted before being ground for use as a coffee substitute.

Maintenance and potential problems

Little maintenance is required. The only potential problem is vigorous self-seeding if there is much bare soil about.

Chinese artichoke
(*Stachys affinis*)

Also known as crosnes

This is a perennial tuber crop, long grown commercially in China and Japan. The name 'crosnes' originates from the French town of Crosne, where they were first grown in Europe.

It forms a low spreading clump, 30-45cm (1'-1'6") high, with each plant producing strings of white tubers at the end of underground stems each autumn. The plants closely resemble the British native hedge woundwort (*Stachys sylvatica*), with square stems and rough leaves (though not fragrant). They bear blue flowers, which are loved by bees.

The tubers are 2.5-5cm (1-2") long to 2cm (3/4") wide, white and cylindrical with distinctive 'rings' (see photo overleaf). Some folk reckon they resemble huge white grubs or chubby maggots.

Several North American related species also have edible tubers, including hyssop-leaved hedgenettle (*S. hyssopifolia*) and marsh woundwort (*S. palustris*).

Hardiness zone: 5

Cultivation

Chinese artichoke grows in any reasonably well-drained soil, though yields are highest in fertile soils. Tubers are harder to harvest from heavy soils. It likes sun or light shade, and plants tolerate high summer temperatures. Tubers will rot in waterlogged soils in winter.

If this crop is grown with a thick organic mulch on the soil surface, the tubers will be very near the soil surface beneath the mulch, making harvest very easy.

Plants do not particularly suffer or deteriorate through overcrowding, though if they do become crowded then tuber size will decrease, so if this is important, make sure you harvest a good proportion of the tubers, leaving enough plants spread out evenly to maintain the required density. Feeding will help keep the tuber size good.

Varieties: There are no named varieties available outside China.

Harvest: Tubers are dug at any age (they don't get woody), after frosts in late autumn and winter as needed – they do not store very well out of the ground. It is unlikely you will ever find every single tuber, and you can expect decent regrowth from a harvested patch the following spring.

Propagation: Plant tubers upright at 10cm (4") spacing in small holes, at a depth of anything between 4cm and 15cm (15/8" to 6"). In my experience the plant is not especially vigorous and needs a little care and attention when young, particularly in regard to weed competition. Growth starts early in spring, so try to plant in late winter at the latest.

Chinese artichoke tubers.

Culinary uses

The tubers need scrubbing clean (best to let them soak in a bowl of water for 10 minutes first), and then can be eaten raw in salads – they have a crisp, crunchy texture and a pleasant, delicate flavour reminiscent of a mixture of apple, globe artichoke, new potatoes and water chestnuts – or lightly cooked by boiling, roasting, etc. They remain crisp after stir-frying, and are sometimes used in place of water chestnuts. In China and Japan they are mainly used for pickling.

The tubers are unusual in that they contain the carbohydrate stachyose. This sweet compound is often found in beans and, like inulin (see page 125), can be only partially digested by most people, but has very beneficial effects on the gut flora and immune system. Like beans, it can cause flatulence.

Maintenance and potential problems

Some weeding is required, especially in spring. Mice and voles can sometimes nibble the tubers. The only other potential problem is that the plant is difficult to get rid of permanently, should you ever want to!

Chinese boxthorn
See Goji berry (*Lycium barbarum*)

Chinese broccoli
(*Brassica oleracea* Alboglabra Group)

Also known as gai lon; kailan

This is an evergreen short-lived perennial (living 3-5 years). It grows to some 45cm (1'6") high and wide; higher if allowed to flower. The leaves are a waxy green-grey, and the main flowering stems are smooth, around 1.5-2cm (5/8-3/4") thick, and chunky. The flowers are usually white, though in China there are yellow- and red-flowered varieties.

Hardiness zone: 8

Cultivation

Like all brassicas, Chinese broccoli likes a fertile well-drained soil and sun or light shade. It is tolerant of very hot weather, and is not particularly sensitive to spacing. Seed can be sown or transplanted at 25-38cm (10-15") apart. With closer spacing, plants are less likely to stay perennial.

After the frosts arrive in autumn, cut plants down to a stump of about 5cm (2"). They will resprout from this in spring.

Varieties: There are few varieties commercially available in the UK or North America, although in China there are early-, mid- and late-season varieties. 'Green Lance' is a productive F1 variety.

Harvest: The upper 20-25cm (8-10") of succulent stem, leaves and flower buds can be repeatedly harvested, from June onwards – the plant recovers well from cutting. Flowering heads can be used even when starting to flower. To overwinter, take a last cut no later than August.

Propagation: It is easy to grow from seed. Sow from early spring through to early autumn, preferably *in situ*; otherwise, pot up seedlings and plant out when large enough. Sowing in midsummer can help to prevent premature bolting. Chinese broccoli is often listed in seed catalogues under the name 'Kailan'.

Chinese broccoli harvested.

Culinary uses

Treat like broccoli. The flavour is an excellent mix of asparagus, kale and broccoli.

Maintenance and potential problems

The exact winter hardiness is still unknown in the UK, so in cold winters it may be worth wrapping plants in fleece for extra protection. Problems are the usual brassica ones – pigeons, caterpillars, etc. – and require the usual responses: net against pigeons, pick off caterpillars or use biological controls. Pigeon pie, anyone?

Chinese cedar
(Toona sinensis)

Also known as Chinese toon; fragrant spring tree

This deciduous tree is not a cedar and not a conifer! Thought to be originally native to eastern, central and south-western China, it now grows wild in many parts of Asia, including Nepal, Korea, Japan and Taiwan.

The tree normally grows up to 8m (26') tall and 30cm (1') in diameter, but occasionally larger. It has brown bark, smooth on young trees, becoming scaly or shaggy on older trees. The leaves are pinnate, usually without a terminal leaflet, with 10-20 leaflets, which are hairy underneath. Flowers are produced in summer in long panicles at the branch tips; each has five white or pale pink petals.

Grown in the UK and North America as an ornamental tree, Chinese cedar is a well known and highly valued perennial vegetable in many parts of southern and South East Asia.

Hardiness zone: 5

Cultivation

Chinese cedar prefers well-drained, fertile soils and tolerates a wide range of pH (5.5-8.0). It is tolerant of humid climates and requires a climate with annual average temperatures of at least 8-10°C (46-50°F). Full sun is required.

Keeping trees shrubby is easy, mostly achieved by harvesting young shoots, and plants can be maintained at a height of 1.5m (5') or so. Chinese cedars kept shrubby can be planted at 1m (3') apart. In parts of Asia, they are often intercropped with lower-growing herbs or vegetables.

Protected cultivation of these trees (in polytunnels or greenhouses) is now widely practised in China to allow for fresh toon to be harvested in the winter, especially during Chinese New Year holidays.

Varieties: An ornamental variety, 'Flamingo', which has pinkish-purple young foliage, is widely grown in Europe and North America. This can also be used as a vegetable.

Harvest: Young leaves and shoots up to 20cm (8") long are repeatedly harvested from trees in spring and summer. The yield from shrubby trees is about 0.5kg (1lb 2oz) per plant per year.

Propagation: Seeds of Chinese cedar are tricky to germinate. They should be cold stratified (see Chapter 3, page 54) for 2-3 months and/or soaked in warm water (25°C/77°F or so) for 24 hours prior to sowing. Keep seeds warm at 25°C after sowing for best germination. Pot on as they start to grow and plant out when large enough.

Propagation is also possible by root cuttings.

Culinary uses

The vegetable is used in four forms:

- Fresh young leaves and shoots from trees kept low and shrubby by harvesting; these have a strong flavour and are usually used lightly cooked.
- Dried leaves and shoots, which are used more as a spice. Fresh leaves and shoots can be dried quite easily, either in warm ambient temperatures or with extra heat. The dried material is usually crumbled to a powder.
- Shoots of young seedlings grown densely in punnets or trays under protection and harvested wholly; these have a more delicate flavour. Only worthwhile where bulk seed is cheap.
- Sprouted seeds, used like other sprouts, such as mung beans. Only worthwhile where bulk seed is cheap.

The young leaves of Chinese cedar are used extensively as a vegetable in China, and are one of the most popular seasonal vegetables. Toon is very aromatic, combining a pungent roasted garlic aroma with a raw onion flavour. The leaves are valued for stir-fries (especially with eggs), salads, frying, pickling and seasoning. Classic dishes include fried egg with toon, and a tofu and blanched toon salad. Toon shoot and walnut salads are also popular.

In China, plants with red young leaves are considered to be of better flavour than those with green young leaves. Both types of plant have green leaves after a few weeks in spring.

The fresh young leaves are very nutritious: they contain 6.3-9.8 per cent protein (high for a vegetable), vitamins B1, B2 and high levels of vitamins C and E. They are relatively high in beta-carotene, and high in calcium and iron. In an evaluation of the antioxidant activity, vitamin C content and total phenolic content of 20 tested vegetables,* Chinese cedar came top in antioxidant activity, top in total phenolics, and high in vitamin C content.

Maintenance and potential problems

Little maintenance is required – harvesting shoots and leaves does most of the work of keeping plants shrubby. If they start getting too large to harvest easily, coppice back to a smaller stump. Established trees can sucker.

There seem to be no significant pests or diseases.

* Sato, T. et al. 'Evaluation of antioxidant activity of indigenous vegetables from south and Southeast Asia'. *JIRCAS Research Highlights, 2002.*

Chinese chives
See Garlic chives (*Allium tuberosum*)

Chinese toon
See Chinese cedar (*Toona sinensis*)

Chinese water chestnut
See Water chestnut (*Eleocharis dulcis*)

Chives
(*Allium schoenoprasum*)

This clumping herbaceous perennial plant, 25cm (10") wide and 30cm (1') high, is widely grown for its tubular-shaped fine leaves, which are usually used for flavouring. It is included here because the leaves and stems can be used in bulk in salads or in stir-fries as a vegetable too.

Chives produces rounded pink or white flowers; like all alliums, it is a good bee plant.

Hardiness zone: 5

Cultivation
It tolerates most soils of reasonable fertility, and requires sun or light shade.

Varieties: Several varieties are available, as well as unnamed seed.

'Black Isle Blush' – flowers are light mauve with a deep pink centre.
'Dwarf' – very compact.
'Extra Fine Leaved' – purple-flowered, often grown for bunching; thin leaves.
'Forsake' – ornamental as well as culinary.
'Grolau' – has thick, dark foliage. Good as a windowsill plant.
'Purly' – has thicker leaves, good in containers.
'Staro' – large, thick-leaved variety, especially good for drying or freezing.

Harvest: Leaves and stems can be harvested throughout the spring, summer and autumn; cut at just above ground level. The leaf flavour declines when plants are flowering. Plants grown under protection or in pots brought inside can extend the season. Flowers can be harvested in summer.

Propagation: Easy to grow from seed or division of existing plants; plant out at 20-30cm (8-12") spacing.

Culinary uses
The leaves and stems have a mild onion flavour and are used in salads, soups, stews and stir-fries. Leaves can also easily be dried or frozen for later use.

The flowers can also be used whole in salads.

Maintenance and potential problems

Plants may need dividing every 3-4 years, otherwise their vigour may decline. The only disease of note is rust. Remove any leaves that are affected.

Chufa
See Tiger nut (*Cyperus esculentus* var. *sativa*)

Cinnamon vine
See Yams (*Dioscorea* spp.)

Collards, tree
See Tree collards (*Brassica oleracea* Acephala Group)

Columbine
(*Aquilegia vulgaris*)

This is a short-lived, tall, branching herbaceous perennial, found in the wild in damp meadows and light woodland. It grows up to 30cm (1') wide and usually up to 70cm (2'4") high, sometimes up to 1m (3') high when flowering. The species has blue flowers.

Columbine is much grown in gardens for the flowers: there are many garden varieties, a lot of which have escaped into the wild.

Hardiness zone: 4

Cultivation

Plant at about 30cm (1') spacing. Columbine grows in most soils except heavy clay, but prefers neutral or alkaline ones. It prefers a little shade in British conditions, tolerating quite shaded conditions. Although short-lived (3 years), it often self-seeds. It readily hybridises with most other *Aquilegia* species, so may not come true from seed.

Varieties: Many garden varieties are available. All *A. vulgaris* varieties can be used as a vegetable.

Harvest: Young leaves can be harvested all through the growing season (but don't pick any that are showing signs of mildew). Flowers are picked from April to July.

Propagation: Easy to grow from seed. Sow in spring after giving a few months' cold stratification (see Chapter 3, page 54).

Culinary uses

The young leaves have a mild flavour and make excellent eating, either raw in salads or lightly cooked (steamed).

The flowers are sweet and good in salads.

Maintenance and potential problems

Replant or allow to re-seed from time to time. Powdery mildew is the most common ailment – improve soil conditions if it becomes a problem.

Crosnes
See Chinese artichoke (*Stachys affinis*)

Daffodil garlic
(*Allium neapolitanum*)

Daffodil garlic is a bulbous perennial that forms a gradually expanding clump, growing to over 20cm (8") wide and 30-50cm (1'-1'8") high. It has white flowers in spring, loved by bees.

This plant is well adapted to dry summer regions, as it goes dormant over summer. It comes into growth in October and grows through the winter (as pictured), flowering in mid-spring and vanishing from sight by July.

Hardiness zone: 7

Cultivation

It likes a position in sun or light shade in any reasonably well-drained soil.

Like many alliums, daffodil garlic is not very weed-suppressing, so either mulch well or grow it through a low ground-covering plant to reduce the weeding.

Varieties: There are no varieties.

Harvest: Harvest the flattish leaves all through the winter; the flowers in spring.

Propagation: Sow seed in spring, or divide existing plants, replanting bulbs in late summer or early autumn.

Culinary uses

The leaves have a mild garlic flavour and are excellent in salads or cooked dishes. The flowers are good in salads.

Although the bulbs are edible, they are small (1-2cm, 3/8-3/4") and really worth harvesting only if you are splitting clumps and have spare.

Maintenance and potential problems

Little required apart from weeding.

Dandelion
(Taraxacum officinale)

Dandelion hardly needs describing, as you'll probably have it as a weed already! It is a herbaceous (sometimes evergreen) perennial with deep taproots, growing some 30-40cm (1'-1'4") high and wide in flower. Its bright yellow flowers are borne mainly in spring but also scattered throughout the growing season. It grows widely in fields, hedgerows and light woodland – and gardens.

Hardiness zone: 4

Cultivation

Dandelion grows in any reasonably moist soil, in sun or partial shade. Plant at 30cm (1') spacing.

Varieties: Some larger-leaved varieties exist (which also have thicker roots).

'Amélioré à Coeur Plein' – bears a large number of leaves, which form a regular tuft or clump, instead of a plain rosette.

It yields a very abundant crop without taking up much ground, and blanches very easily, indeed almost naturally.

'Amélioré Géant' – large-leaved, excellent variety.

'Broad Leaved' – has large, broad, dark green leaves, more deeply lobed along the axis of the leaf than the wild form. The leaves are thick and tender. Plants are semi-erect in habit, and the leaves are easily blanched (see 'harvest' below). In rich soils they can be 60cm (2') wide. Plants do not go to seed so quickly as the wild form.

'Thick Leaved' – large, thick, dark green leaves.

'Vert de Montmagny' – has large, long, dark green leaves, well lobed and finely notched. The leaves are less bitter than in other varieties and are sometimes used unblanched. Vigorous and productive plants.

Harvest: Leaves can be picked at any time in the growing season, though they are less bitter in spring. Plants can also be blanched (just cover to exclude light for a couple of weeks before harvest), which also reduces the bitterness in leaves. Flowers are mainly harvested in spring. Roots can be lifted at any time.

Propagation: Sow seeds in spring, either in containers or *in situ* in the soil – sow on the surface of a seedbed or tray. As they grow, thin out to about 30cm (1') between plants.

Culinary uses

The leaves are often used in salads – wilt them over heat (or dip into boiling water) for few seconds to remove much of the bitterness. They're good with sweet root vegetables or added to rich stews, and are widely eaten in mainland Europe, often with bacon in France. This deep-rooted plant is high in minerals and vitamins.

Flowers can be added to salads, pancakes and omelettes; they are also often used to make wines.

The roots can be dried, roasted and ground to make a coffee-like beverage.

Maintenance and potential problems

You might want to prevent dandelion from self-seeding by picking off flower heads.

Day lilies
(*Hemerocallis* spp.)

Day lilies are clump-forming perennials with grassy-type leaves, growing to at least 45-60cm (1'6"-2') high and 30-45cm (1'-1'6") wide – sometimes forming expanding clumps. Some varieties are semi-evergreen or evergreen but the majority are herbaceous. Garden escapees are found in the wild.

The plants bear masses of large flowers, up to 8cm (3¹/₄") wide, which usually only last a day or two (hence the name) over a period of 3-4 weeks in summer or autumn. The flowers can be yellow, orange or red; there are thousands of named varieties, mostly hybrids, with other colour combinations. Some flower earlier and some later in the season.

Hardiness zone: Usually **4**, but there are hardier varieties that can be grown as far north as zone 2.

Cultivation

Day lilies are easy to cultivate in any soil, even poor soils – they thrive on neglect. They like sun or light shade.

Varieties: *Hemerocallis fulva* 'Flore Pleno' is the main variety grown in China for flower bud production. It appears that many yellow-flowered varieties have sweeter flowers, while some red ones can be slightly bitter. *H.* 'Hyperion' and *H.* 'Stella de Oro' are two excellent yellow varieties. *H.* 'Red Rum' is a nice-tasting, smaller-growing red variety.

Harvest: Flowers and/or flower buds are picked daily once flowering has started. Flower buds should be picked early in the morning before the flower emerges. Fresh flowers are best towards the end of the day. Recently withered flowers can be harvested and dried for seasoning. In China, the flower buds are an important crop, sold fresh and air-dried, and are known as 'golden needles'.

Young leaves and shoots are harvested in spring; rhizomes in winter.

Propagation: Day lilies are mainly propagated by division in spring or autumn. Lift a clump and chop it into quarters, replanting each quarter immediately. All day lily species can be grown from seed but are slow to germinate.

Culinary uses

There are few flower crops that are substantial enough to be called a vegetable, but day lily ranks top of the list. The flowers are not thin-petalled fripperies that one might use as a garnish (as with many other flowers), but are substantial items; sweet with thick, crunchy petals. The flowers can be used raw in salads or are great battered and fried. They can also be stuffed or deep-fried.

The flavour of unopened flower buds resembles that of French beans. The flowers themselves have a sweet, mild flavour, somewhat similar to courgette flowers.

The dried flower buds (golden needles) are widely used in Chinese cooking, reconstituted by soaking in water for half an hour before use. They are used like green beans, with a crisp texture and unique day-lily flavour, often added into soups and in pork dishes. They can also be chopped and added to salads, steamed or fried. They can be used as a seasoning, and have a thickening effect in soups and stews.

Young leaves and shoots can also be eaten (in moderation) in the spring, as can the tuberous rhizomes in winter (also in moderation; these are quite small). The leaves have a mild oniony flavour, and the rhizomes taste a little like a nutty salsify. These parts can occasionally cause digestive upsets in some people when eaten.

Maintenance and potential problems

Young plants need good weed control, but once established, clumps are low-maintenance. Watch out for slug and snail damage on young plants.

Clumps may need lifting and dividing every few years to maintain vigour and promote flowering.

Flower buds that swell unusually and fail to open may be infested with the grubs of the hemerocallis gall midge – pick off these buds and burn them.

Duck potato
See Arrowheads (*Sagittaria* spp.)

Duke of Argyll's tea tree
See Goji berry (*Lycium barbarum*)

Earth chestnut
See Pig nut (*Bunium bulbocastanum*)

Earth nut
See Pig nut (*Bunium bulbocastanum*)

Egyptian onion
(*Allium cepa* Proliferum Group)

Also known as tree onion; walking onion

This is a bulbous perennial, forming an expanding clump of bulbs, and is also called top onion or topset onion. Its origins are lost in the mists of time. It is evergreen in mild climates.

The leaves are tubular, like those of Welsh onion (see page 196); 45cm (1'6") long. Long stems grow to 50-100cm (1'8"-3'3") high, bearing not flowers but a head of bulbils or sets – miniature bulbs, each 0.5-1.5cm (1/8-5/8") across. These bulbils often start growing and producing their own tiny leaves while still in the heads in mid-air (on vigorous plants the bulbils can even form their own bulbils – like a second generation – on their own flower stems).

As the bulbils (or topsets) grow and get heavier, the leaves bend towards the ground. If they touch the soil, some of the bulbils will root, forming a new plant – which is how the plants 'walk' around.

Hardiness zone: 4

Cultivation

Egyptian onion grows in any reasonably well-drained soil, in sun or light shade. It needs regular mulching and/or weeding to prevent too much weed competition. Leaves come up quite early in spring and can remain green late into the year. The young stems can also be used.

Varieties: There are brown-skinned and red-skinned forms of Egyptian onion – the brown is more common.

Harvest: Leaves can be harvested at any time during the growing season; stems in spring.

Bulbils grow in clusters of 3-10 or more at the end of the shoots and are harvested green in July and August, or ripe in late August or early September. Plants sometimes produce similar offsets around their bases, which can be used in the same way at the same time of year.

Bulbs can be dug as needed, mainly in winter and spring. Bulbs and bulbils can be stored over winter in a cool, dry place.

Propagation: Plant bulbils, bulbs or small plants in autumn or spring at about 25-30cm (10-12") apart.

Bulbils of Egyptian onion.

Culinary uses

Leaves and stems are used like spring onions or Welsh onions, raw in salads or in cooked dishes. They have a strong and hot onion flavour.

The bulbils can also be eaten. The ripe ones have papery skins like cloves of garlic, which are a bit fiddly to remove (like garlic, the easiest way is to half-crush the bulbils on a flat surface with the flat edge of a knife, then the papery skin comes cleanly away). It is easier to use the green bulbils, as they don't need peeling and can be put whole into soups and stews.

The bulbs can be used like shallots, and have a mild flavour.

Maintenance and potential problems

Slugs can be a nuisance. The plant can potentially spread itself about by bending over, the bulbil heads touching the ground and rooting there.

If plants become too congested, remove some bulbs in winter and eat them!

Elder, American
See American elder (*Sambucus canadensis*)

Elders
See European elders (*Sambucus nigra* & *S. racemosa*)

Elephant garlic & perennial leek
(*Allium ampeloprasum*)

This species has two distinct forms. Elephant garlic (*Allium ampeloprasum* var. *ampeloprasum*) is grown for the large bulbs, while perennial leek (the botanists haven't quite decided how to separate this from elephant garlic – but note that this perennial leek is not the same as Babington's leek, page 72) is grown for the leaves or thick stems.

Elephant garlic is like a giant version of garlic, producing a bulb that can measure 7-10cm (3-4") across, divided into giant cloves, around 2.5cm/1" across (pictured on previous page with a £1 coin). It grows 60-80cm (2'-2'8") high. It has been cultivated in Europe and Asia since ancient times and there are various different forms. Biennial garden leeks were developed from this species many years ago.

The leaves are broad and flat, like leeks, and it produces a tall, solid flowering stalk in summer, which produces flowers but not bulbils. Unharvested plants gradually spread to form a clump. Plants sometimes sprout small bulbils on the cloves or on the leaf bases, often at least three per head. If these become detached from the parent bulb and left on the ground, they develop into new bulbs.

Perennial leek (also called salad leek or perennial sweet leek) looks like the biennial garden leek but grows from a bulb. It is told apart from Babington's leek by the fact that it does not form bulbils at the top of a flower head. It reaches a height of 45-60cm (1'6"-2'); again forming a spreading clump if bulbs are not harvested.

Both elephant garlic and perennial leek tolerate hot and dry conditions, but are also fine in British conditions, where they are green over winter.

Hardiness zone: 6

Cultivation

Both forms prefer full sun, though tolerate a little light shade. A moist but well-drained soil of reasonable fertility is ideal.

Both are usually grown from bulbs or bulbils. If elephant garlic is grown from the small outer bulbils, it will produce an undivided bulb in the first year; in later years the bulb will divide into cloves.

Varieties: Perennial leeks are still widely grown in the Mediterranean region and include 'Kurrat' from Egypt, 'Tarée Irani' from Iran and 'Poireau Perpétuél' from France.

Harvest: The flavour of perennial leek is milder than that of biennial leek. Tops can be harvested by cutting back to 1-2cm (3/8-3/4") above ground several times per season, and plants will grow back. Elephant garlic bulbs are harvested in summer when top growth yellows.

Propagation: Elephant garlic can be planted at 20x30cm (8x12") as a replant crop, though if left in the ground it will overwinter and all bulbs will regrow, leading to crowded plants. Perennial leeks should be planted at 30cm (1') spacing.

Culinary uses

Elephant garlic cloves can be used in the same way as ordinary garlic, including roasted or baked. The flavour is like mild garlic. Young leaves of elephant garlic can also be used, and have a flavour more like leek than garlic.

Perennial leek leaves and stems are used in the same way as biennial leeks, though they are also often used in salads due to their milder flavour. The bulbs of this form are small but can be used like shallots.

Maintenance and potential problems

Slugs and snails can be a nuisance in wet seasons.

European elders
(*Sambucus nigra* & *S. racemosa*)

These well-known large shrubs or small trees are found in hedgerows and woods all over Europe.

Sambucus nigra (European elder; sometimes called black elder) grows to 4-6m (13-20') high and wide, while *S. racemosa* (red elder) grows to 3m (10') high and wide. They bear white flowers in late spring and mid-spring respectively, followed by the familiar small purple-black fruits.

Hardiness zone: 4-5

Cultivation

Easy to cultivate, these elders prefer a moist soil of good fertility but will grow almost anywhere. They tolerate shade but flower better in sunny conditions.

To cultivate elder as a flower crop, you might want to keep plants bushy so that the flowers are easier to harvest: trim to 1-1.5m (3-5') high every 2 years, or coppice back from time to time.

Varieties: Seedling plants can be used, or named varieties that have been bred for fruit production (most of these have larger flowers, so flower harvesting is quicker). Varieties of European elder include 'Bradet', 'Donau', 'Franzi', 'Godshill', 'Haschberg', 'Ina', 'Sambu', 'Samdal', 'Samidan', 'Samnor', 'Sampo' and 'Samyl'. There are no improved fruiting or flowering varieties of red elder.

Harvest: Harvest flowers by hand in spring. Pick them on sunny days when they are dry and shedding pollen (this is when their flavour is at its peak), picking as little green stalk as possible. Use quickly, or, to dry, shake flowers over a bag to loosen the ripe ones and air-dry.

Propagation: Take hardwood cuttings in late autumn or early winter. Plants can be grown from seed too, which requires stratification of 6-9 months (see Chapter 3, page 54).

Culinary uses

Although this plant has many other uses, elder is listed here for use of the lemony, muscat-scented flowers as a vegetable. A well-known way to cook the flowers is to batter them then deep-fry for just a few seconds. Older recipes use them in stews or sauces served with meat, often using dried flowers. As a flavouring, fresh elder flowers are particularly good with other fruit, e.g. gooseberries and rhubarb.

Maintenance and potential problems

Apart from trimming back, there is little maintenance required. Elders often attract aphids in spring, but these do little damage and allowing them to remain ensures a fast build-up of predators, which will soon clear them away and help elsewhere in the garden. Self-seeding can sometimes be a nuisance – harvesting the flowers will reduce the fruit/seed yield, but if fruit heads are harvested (or removed before ripe) then the problem should not arise.

Everlasting pea
See Perennial sweet peas
(*Lathyrus latifolius* & *L. sylvestris*)

False strawberry
(*Duchesnea indica*)

Also known as mock strawberry

This is an evergreen (or semi-evergreen in cooler climes) creeping perennial, which looks quite similar in leaf to wild strawberry (see page 180) and spreads by similar rooting runners. It has yellow flowers (a sure way to tell it is not a true strawberry) followed by red round fruits. Height 15cm (6"); spread indefinite. Bees like the flowers.

Hardiness zone: 6

Cultivation

False strawberry is easy to grow in any reasonable soil. It prefers some shade and tolerates quite deep shade. Plant young plants at 30cm (1') spacing and they will effectively cover the ground within a season. It makes quite a good ground cover beneath other plants.

Varieties: There are no varieties.

Harvest: Pick young leaves in spring as well as later in the season. Fruits are also available from late spring onwards.

Propagation: By seed in spring, or by detaching runners in summer and potting up or transplanting.

Culinary uses

The leaves are mild in flavour and good in salads. The fruits, incidentally, are tasteless – a bit like eating bags of water – but the seeds on the outside are crunchy, like poppy seeds, and add an interesting texture to salads.

Maintenance and potential problems

Maintenance is really only a matter of stopping it from going where you don't want it to go.

Fennel
(Foeniculum vulgare)

Not to be confused with Florence fennel, which has been derived from this species and which is biennial, fennel is a clump-forming herbaceous perennial. It grows some 40cm (1'4") wide and 1-1.5m (3-5') high when flowering.

It has feathery foliage and pale cream flower heads, like many umbellifers, in summer, and bears heads of seeds in autumn.

Hardiness zone: 5

Cultivation

A well-drained soil is essential, plus sun, though a little light shade is tolerated.

Varieties: Bronze and purple fennel can be used in the same ways.

Harvest: Harvest the fine leaves at any time in the growing season. The flowering stems get tough but smaller stems generally stay tender for the whole season. Harvest seeds in late summer.

Propagation: Fennel is usually propagated by seed in spring (easy); established plants can be divided in spring.

Culinary uses

Fennel is borderline in the herb/vegetable spectrum, but I have included it as a vegetable because the feathery foliage can be used in bulk, in salads especially. In my family we use masses of it added to grain-based salads, e.g. of rice or couscous.

Seeds can of course be used as a flavouring themselves. They also make excellent herb teas.

Maintenance and potential problems

Fennel is not good at suppressing weed competition, so grow it well mulched or interplanted with a low-growing companion.

Fireweed
See Rosebay willowherb
(Epilobium angustifolium)

Fragrant spring tree
See Chinese cedar *(Toona sinensis)*

French scorzonera
(Reichardia picroides)

A rosette-forming, clumping plant from southern Europe, French scorzonera looks like a grey-green-leaved dandelion. It grows about 25cm (10") wide, and when flowering the stems can reach 80cm (2'8") high. Yellow flowers are followed by a head of fluffy seeds, which fly off in the wind once ripe. It is evergreen in very mild winter regions.

Hardiness zone: 8-9

Cultivation

French scorzonera requires a very well-drained soil to overwinter successfully, but will grow from spring to autumn in any reasonable garden soil. It needs sun or light shade.

Varieties: There are no varieties.

Harvest: Leaves can be harvested at any time, even when the plant is flowering.

Propagation: Raise from seed, which is sometimes available commercially. Make sure you save some of your own seed in case plants die in the winter.

Culinary uses

The leaves are tender with a lovely cucumber-type flavour – they are excellent as a major salad ingredient. They can also be added to stews, etc., and need only a few minutes to cook.

Maintenance and potential problems

Plants should be mulched, especially over winter to give the roots extra protection against winter cold. Hardiness is the only real problem – for me plants often die off over winter. Slugs and snails do not seem to touch the plant.

Fuki
See Giant butterbur *(Petasites japonicus)*

Gai lon
See Chinese broccoli *(Brassica oleracea* Alboglabra Group)

Garlic
(*Allium sativum*)

Also known as softneck garlic

Most garlic grown in the UK is 'softneck' garlic (*Allium sativum*), though in many parts of the world a different type is grown called 'hardneck', of which rocambole is one variety – see page 161 for details.

Garlic can be treated as a perennial bulb or as a replant perennial. It grows about 60cm (2') high.

Hardiness zone: 6

Cultivation

It is best planted in autumn between October and early December, in ground that is reasonably well drained. Garlic does not require rich soils and tolerates soils of average fertility. Full sun is required.

Varieties: There are many garlic varieties adapted to different localities, so check out what grows well in your region. Some of the better varieties for British conditions include 'Arno', 'Cristo', 'Germidour', 'Ivory', 'Long Keeper', 'Solent White', 'Spring Wight' and 'Wight Cristo'. 'Mediterranean Wight' is good for 'wet' garlic (see below).

Harvest: If bulbs are not harvested, then in time plants will get overcrowded and bulbs will reduce in size. So try to harvest and replant frequently, if not every year. From time to time it is wise to change location entirely to avoid a build-up of onion diseases.

Bulbs are mature when the leaves turn yellow and start to bend over in July or August. Lifted bulbs should be sun-dried (under cover in dubious weather) before storage. Store in a dry place. 'Wet' garlic is bulbs that are harvested when the plants are still green and fresh, before the skin on the bulb has turned papery.

Leaves can be harvested at any time in the growing season; young stems in spring.

Propagation: This is done either via the harvested bulbs or from bulbs that form at the base of existing plants. Plant from mid-autumn to early spring – the former is preferable, though spring-planted garlic tends to store better. Discard any very small bulbs for planting. Plant at about twice the bulbs' own depth, so larger bulbs/cloves should be planted at about a 4cm (1 5/8") depth and at an average spacing of about 15cm (6") apart. Plant cloves upright, pointed end upwards.

For leaf production from autumn through to spring, you can plant bulbs much closer together – 7-10cm (3-4") apart.

Garlic foliage.

Culinary uses

Garlic in the form of bulbs is a staple culinary ingredient and is used in numerous ways. The trick to peeling the papery skin off garlic is to press down on a clove with the flat side of a knife, half-crushing it – then the whole papery skin will come off really easily.

The young green leaves and stems can be used raw in salads or cooked – in China they are often blanched (as for garlic chives; see page 107). There are usually usable leaves through mild winters.

In spring, the whole plants – green leaves, stems and undivided bulb – can be lifted and used (sometimes called 'baby garlic').

Maintenance and potential problems

White rot, an onion disease, can be a serious problem – make sure you start with healthy bulbs and change the location of the garlic bed every 5 years or so. Rust (appearing as orange blisters) is a common disease – to prevent attacks, improve potash levels in the soil, perhaps by mulching with comfrey leaves.

Garlic chives
(Allium tuberosum)

Also known as Chinese chives; oriental garlic

This widely cultivated perennial forms a slowly expanding clump, living for up to 30 years. It grows 30-50cm (1'-1'8") high and 30cm (1') wide, with long, flattish leaves and mauve flowers loved by bees. The bulbs are small, reaching 1cm (3/8") in diameter. Established plants have thick rhizomes. In warm regions plants may stay evergreen – the leaves die back below about 5°C (41°F) and start back into growth in spring at about 3°C (37°F).

Hardiness zone: 5

Cultivation

Grow in a any reasonably well-drained soil in sun or light shade. It is very tolerant of cold and heat.

Garlic chives is an important vegetable in China, where plants have the green leaves harvested, then are immediately covered to exclude light with clay pots or straw 'tents', so that the new shoots are blanched for 3-4 weeks; the yellowed blanched leaves are then harvested. In cool climates the plants are then allowed to recover, though in warmer climates the process can be repeated the same season. Blanched leaves are softer and milder in flavour.

Varieties: In China there are 'leaf' types and 'flowering' types grown specifically for those parts, but these do not seem to be available elsewhere, so the species is used for both.

Leaf types include 'Broad Leaf'/'Broad Belt', 'Hiro Haba', 'New Belt' and 'Shiva'. Flowering types include 'Flowering Chinese leek', 'Nien Hua' and 'Tender-pole'.

Harvest: Leaves can be harvested at any time through the growing season, cut low (in China the parts blanched white just under the soil are highly valued). Young stems are harvested in spring. Flowers and flower stalks are harvested in summer.

The leaves can be dried and crumbled or frozen to store.

Propagation: Raise from seed or divide existing clumps. Sow seed from spring to early summer, or in autumn. Pot up seedlings in clumps (about ten seedlings per pot) and transplant out when large enough. Plant at about 20cm (8") spacing. Seeds are a little slow to germinate, which makes sowing *in situ* outside a bit more risky. Seed does not retain viability for more than a year or two.

Divide clumps in spring or autumn. Plants generally do not require regular division unless harvested very intensely.

Culinary uses

The leaves, stems and flower stems are tender, with a great mild onion-garlic flavour and can be used in bulk in salads or cooking – great in stir-fries. They are usually chopped into sections and need only a few minutes' cooking to retain the flavour. They're also good in dumplings, pancakes and soups.

The leaves are valued for Korean kimchi (a fermented preserve like sauerkraut). Blanched leaves are served in China with noodles, chicken or pork. Bundles of leaves are sometimes tied together and deep-fried.

Flowers can be added to salads as well as to cooked dishes. They are also dried, ground and salted as a spice in China and Japan.

The young flat leaves of garlic chives.

Although the thick rhizomes are edible, they are small and not really worth it unless you are dividing plants and have spare. There is apparently a large-rooted variety used for pickling in China.

The leaves can be dried for winter use – dry fairly rapidly and crumble into a jar. Leaves and stems (whole or chopped) can be frozen.

Maintenance and potential problems

Little maintenance is required. Like most alliums, garlic chives are poor at suppressing weeds, so mulch well or grow through a low interplant (I currently grow false strawberry beneath mine).

Garlic cress
(*Peltaria alliacea*)

Garlic cress is a clump-forming, southern European herbaceous perennial (evergreen in mild locations), growing to 30cm (1') high and wide, with flower stems sometimes reaching 60cm (2') high. It is a brassica, and bears white flowers in late spring / early summer, liked by bees.

Hardiness zone: 6

Cultivation

Garlic cress is easy to grow in any soil, in full sun or light shade.

Varieties: There are no varieties.

Harvest: Harvest leaves at any time except during hot, dry spells, when they become bitter.

Propagation: Raise from seed in spring, or divide plants in spring or autumn.

Culinary uses

The leaves have a garlic/mustard flavour and can be used in small quantities raw in salads or in larger quantities cooked in soups and stews. The leaves become hotter and more pungent as the growing season progresses, so are best cooked from late spring onwards.

Flowers are best used in salads.

Maintenance and potential problems

Little maintenance is required and there are no real problems. As it is a brassica, it could potentially be attacked by caterpillars, etc., but this does not seem to be common.

Giant butterbur
(Petasites japonicus)

Also known as fuki; sweet coltsfoot; Japanese butterbur

This is a large, robust, creeping herbaceous perennial that bears huge basal leaves (emerging from the base of the plant) and looks a little like rhubarb. It is found in permanently damp sites – by stream sides, in damp meadows and in woodlands, often in shade. It has pale mauve-white flowers in spring before the leaves emerge, which attract bees. Plants can attain a width of 1.5m (5') but can also spread to form larger colonies. They grow over 1m (3') high.

Hardiness zone: 4

Cultivation

Grow in permanently moist, fairly fertile soil in shade, partial shade or sun. Once planted in a spot where it is happy, you'll have it for ever! It is particularly good under trees. Plant at a spacing of 1m (3') or so.

Varieties: The larger variety, *P. japonicus* var. *giganteus*, has huge leaves up to 1m (3') across, held on leaf stalks up to 2m (6'6") long, and makes an impressive stately colony.

Harvest: The flower buds – about the size of artichokes – are harvested as they appear through the ground in early spring.

The leaf stalks (like giant celery stalks) are harvested in spring. They have long been used as a vegetable in Japan, where plants are both cultivated and harvested from the wild.

Leaves and leaf stalks of this plant contain furfuran-type lignan compounds, which are powerful antioxidants thought to be particularly effective in the brain. Note that the flower stalks contain compounds that can cause liver damage.

Propagation: Established plants can be divided in late spring/summer or by planting sections of the underground runners. It can also be grown from seed but this is hard to obtain.

Culinary uses

The flower buds are eaten cooked, in soups and with miso. They have a slightly bitter flavour and are probably best eaten in moderation.

The leaf stalks should be cut into 10-20cm (4-8") segments, boiled for 10 minutes, then dipped in cold water for a minute and the outer fibrous skin peeled off. The sections are then fried (in sesame oil in Japan) or added to soups, stews, etc. The flavour resembles celery.

Maintenance and potential problems

In very dry spells the plants may need irrigation if the soil dries out.

Warning: This plant is rampant and spreading. Once planted you'll not easily get rid of it. You might want to remove flower heads before they have set seed to prevent self-seeding. Intensive harvesting will help to control the plant.

Globe artichoke
(*Cynara cardunculus* Scolymus Group)

This familiar vegetable plant is a large, grey-leaved Mediterranean evergreen perennial thistle, with big leaves and tall flowering stems. The leafy plants reach about 80cm (2'8") high and a similar or slightly larger width, and the flowering stems reach 1.5-2.1m (5-7') high. At the top of the flowering stems, large flower buds form, 8-15cm (3-6") across, which open into intensely blue flowers, much loved by bees.

It is closely related to cardoon (see page 83), and difficult to tell apart except when the flower buds form, which are much larger on globe artichoke.

Hardiness zone: 7

Cultivation

Globe artichoke requires a well-drained soil and sun or light shade, and protection from cold winds. It's not quite as tolerant as cardoon of wet winter soils, which can be fatal to plants.

To maximise productivity, you might want to divide the plants every 3-4 years, detaching the small plants (offsets) that form at the base of main plants – dig them up with their roots and you can use them elsewhere. Also, some feeding will be required if plants are cropped heavily. Established plants can yield 8-10 flower buds each.

Varieties: There are several varieties of globe artichoke. Some are seed-grown and give plants with some variation, while the best varieties are propagated by division (removing offsets).

Mainly seed propagated:
'A-106' – used commercially.
'Concerto' – purple heads.
'Green Globe' – American variety with tight, compact, large green heads. Reputedly hardier than most varieties. (Also propagated by division.)
'Harmony' – green heads.
'Imperial Star' – used commercially, fast-growing and selected for growing

mainly as an annual.
'Lorca' – used commercially.
'Madrigal' – used commercially.
'Northern Star' – an extra-hardy variety.
'Opal' – purple heads.
'Purple Italian Globe' – Italian variety
bearing large, tender purple heads.
'Symphony' – green heads.
'Tempo' – purple heads.
'Violet Globe' – purple heads.
'Violetta di Chiogga' – Italian
early-season variety with purple heads.

Mainly vegetatively propagated:
'Blanca de Tudela' – Spanish variety with
medium-sized green heads.
'Brindisino' – Italian variety with
medium-sized purple heads.
'C3' – Italian variety with large purple
heads.
'Camas de Bretagne' – northern French
variety, large green heads.
'Castel' – French variety, large green
heads.
'Catanese' – Italian variety with
medium-sized purple heads.
'Emerald' – glossy green heads.
'Green Globe' – American variety with
tight, compact, large green heads.
Reputedly hardier than most varieties.
(Also seed-grown.)
'Green Globe Improved' – selection of
Green Globe, shorter and more
productive.
'Gros Vert De Laon' – French variety with
large green heads with large hearts, on
shorter plants than most varieties.
'Niscemese' – Italian variety with
medium-sized purple heads.
'Opera F1' – early-season variety, upright
plant with purple heads.
'Peto' – dark green heads, can be grown
as an annual.

'Purple Romagna' – old Italian variety
with large, round purple heads.
'Purple Sicilian' – heat-tolerant variety for
hot summer areas, produces small purple
heads.
'Romanesco' ('Grosso Romanesco') –
Italian variety with large purple heads.
'Spinoso Sardo' – Italian spiny variety.
'Violet de Provence' – French variety with
medium-sized purple heads.
'Violetto' – Italian purple-headed variety,
hardy.

Harvest: Unopened flower heads (buds)
are usually picked when at their largest,
just before the bracts (large scales) start
to open – but the heads can be picked
even when in flower. Small (immature)
flower buds can also be harvested.

Propagation: Sow seed in spring, pot up
(take slug and snail protective measures)
and plant out when large enough. Cut off
any flower buds that form the first year,
to direct the plant's energy into
developing a strong root system. Also
propagate by division of plants in spring,
transplanting the 'daughters' (offsets that
form at the base of plants) to new
locations.

Culinary uses

Although artichokes are not particularly
nutritious, they are popular for their good
flavour. Flower heads are usually boiled or
steamed whole and are often served in
combination with a sauce (e.g. hollandaise
or mayonnaise) to dip the bracts into. The
sweet, succulent heart of the flower head
is the main part of the crop. Getting at it
requires the piecemeal deconstruction of
the flower bud by tearing off the hard bracts
one by one (eating any nuggets of flesh from

their bases by scraping between your teeth). Then cut away the 'choke' – the hairy inedible immature florets in the centre – leaving the heart, which is eaten whole. Immature flower heads (buds) can be boiled and eaten whole.

The leaf ribs can be eaten like those of cardoon; however, they tend to be smaller and tougher and not particularly worth it.

Globe artichoke seeds yield an oil similar in composition and quality to sunflower oil, and used in the same way.

Maintenance and potential problems

In the UK the main problem is excessively wet winter weather, which can kill plants unless they are in well-drained soils. It is worth winter-mulching plants with a material in a cone shape, to drain rainfall away from the crown. In early spring, when the leaf canopy is smallest, there is potential for weed competition.

Artichoke 'Green Globe' in flower.

Goji berry
(*Lycium barbarum*)

Also known as Chinese boxthorn; Duke of Argyll's tea tree; wolfberry

Best known now for its widely promoted fruits, this is also a vegetable. It is a lax, open shrub, 2-3m (6'6"-10') high and wide, with long, straggly, thorny branches which flop around. Flowers (similar to *Solanum* flowers) in summer are followed by small, oval red fruits in autumn.

Plants can sucker from the base of the plant, so become larger in time.

Note that most authorities regard this and *Lycium chinense* as one and the same species. The fruits have long been used in China for their medicinal and tonic effects.

Cultivation

Grow in any soil or situation – in sun or light shade. (Fruiting is better in sun.) It prefers a well-drained soil and is naturalised in the UK on sandy coastal sites. Established plants are tolerant of drought, cold and heat.

In commercial plantations for leaf production, plants are kept coppiced to a height of 60cm (2') to maximise shoot production. It is certainly easier to harvest shoots from a tight cluster growing from a pruned stem than from larger open shrubs. If you don't want the suckers that may be produced, they can always be dug up and removed.

If plants are getting large or lax, prune or coppice back in winter – they respond with vigorous new growth. Plants can also propagate by tip-layering, so keep an eye on where the long, lax, droopy branches are heading!

Varieties: Several varieties with improved fruit quality are available, some of which have fewer or no spines, but they are all similar in terms of leaf production. They include 'Big Lifeberry', 'Sweet Lifeberry' and 'No.1 Lifeberry'.

Harvest: Harvest leaves mainly in spring – they start to get quite tatty later in the season. Cut fresh shoots some 30cm (1') long. A second harvest may be possible in autumn. If the stems get too tough, the leaves can be stripped in the kitchen and the stems discarded.

Propagation: This can be done either by seed in spring, or by hardwood cuttings or layering. Improved fruiting varieties are propagated by layering or hardwood cuttings – the latter can be planted in their final positions.

Culinary uses

The leaves and young shoots are steamed as a vegetable, with a mild minty or cress flavour. The leaves wilt quickly and should be stripped from older stems, then cooked for 3-4 minutes. In China they are often added to soups or stir-fries or are eaten with rice. They can also be used as a flavouring, particularly in soups.

Maintenance and potential problems

Goji has the potential to become a weed, so you may want to cut it back to stop it from spreading and tip-layering around the garden. Harvesting young shoots to eat will help!

Golden saxifrage
(*Chrysosplenium alternifolium* & *C. oppositifolium*)

Two similar species, *C. alternifolium* (alternate-leaved) and *C. oppositifolium* (opposite-leaved – pictured above) are included here. These are prostrate European evergreen perennials (they may become herbaceous in cold winter regions), growing only 15cm (6") high. They have slightly hairy, square stems and are found in damp shade, often near streams in woods. Those of the opposite-leaved type creep over the ground, rooting as they go, forming dense mats. The alternate-leaved type does not form mats.

They have small flowers in spring, which are yellowish-green and without petals.

Hardiness zone: 5

Cultivation

Give a damp site in shade and acid soil. *C. alternifolium* tolerates alkaline soils too. The plants makes a good ground cover and tolerate some foot traffic.

Varieties: There are no varieties.

Harvest: Harvest leaves and stems all though the year. They will usually need washing because they are so low-growing.

Propagation: This can be done by seed in spring or division in autumn.

Culinary uses

The leaves and stems are crisp and mild; excellent in salads or cooked as greens. There is sometimes a slight bitterness to the leaves before they have flowered.

Maintenance and potential problems

No maintenance and no problems.

Good King Henry
(*Chenopodium bonus-henricus*)

This clumping herbaceous European perennial plant was probably introduced into England by the Romans, who used it widely as a vegetable. It grows to 60cm (2') high and 30cm (1') wide. The stems are often tinted red; leaves are dark green, triangular and wavy-edged, up to 10cm (4") long and 8cm (3¹/₄") wide. If roots are well protected by mulch, it can be grown as far north as zone 3.

The name does not come from one of the English kings, but is an Anglicisation of the German Guter Heinrich – Good Henry – who was apparently a Teutonic elf.

Hardiness zone: 5

Cultivation

It is easy to grow in any reasonably fertile soil, in sun or shade.

Varieties: There are no varieties.

Harvest: The leaves and young shoots can be harvested at any time during the growing season from mid-spring onwards; the seeds in late summer and autumn. Shoots can be blanched to make them sweet by mounding up straw, etc. around plants.

Propagation: Propagate from seed – it doesn't require pre-treatment, though sowing early in spring so it experiences some cold does sometimes aid germination. It's best to start seed in trays and pot up plants, transplanting them later in the season. Good King Henry rarely self-seeds in cultivation. Established plants can be divided when dormant.

Culinary uses

This is a very good spinach plant; just steam the leaves/stems for a few minutes for very tasty greens similar to annual spinach. It's also good layered in lasagne, added to stews and so on. The young flower clusters can also be cooked and eaten like broccoli. The leaves wilt quickly after picking if not kept cool, so try to pick and use on the same day. As with a number of plants, Good King Henry contains oxalic acid, too much of which is not good for the health, but the amounts in this species are very low.

The seeds can also be eaten – treat them like poppy seeds: they're good sprinkled on bread, cakes, biscuits and so on.

Maintenance and potential problems

Just a little weeding is needed in early spring, until the plant has grown enough to suppress weeds.

Grape vines
(*Vitis vinifera* & hybrids)

These well-known vigorous tendril climbers will climb up anything they can cling on to, sometimes reaching heights of 30m (100') in trees. They are best known of course for the fruits, but here grape vines are included for their edible leaves.

Hardiness zone: 5

Cultivation

Very easy to grow for leaves, grape vines will grow in most sites and situations as long as they are in a reasonably well-drained soil. For leaf production, you can grow them in part shade and on north-facing walls – if growing on walls or fences, then normally a network of horizontal wires is provided to allow the plants to cling firmly and/or be trained along.

The vigour of grape vines means that usually they have to be pruned to contain them in any case, so the harvest of leaves can in effect be the size control at the same time – pinch or trim off whole shoots that are getting too long, then pick off the individual leaves to utilise. Grape plants can be maintained in many different forms by this method, so if the plants do not have secondary functions, such as covering a fence or wall, they can be kept as grape bushes, which can be trained on a single 'trunk' at whatever height is convenient, e.g. 1m (3') high. A bush like this will need staking for several years until the main trunk is rigid enough to hold the bushy head of the plant without keeling over.

Varieties: There are numerous varieties of *V. vinifera* (true grape vine) and hybrids of that species with others. They all have edible leaves, and though there are leaf differences there is little to choose between them for quality of leaf. The hybrids tend to be more vigorous, and often more disease-resistant in humid climates, so will be more productive.

Harvest: You can pick leaves from vines that you are cultivating for fruit production too – indeed vines need regular pruning to remove shoots and leaves, to allow sun and air to the fruits. If you are cultivating vines only for leaves, then remove any flowers when you harvest leaves, to maintain vigour and reduce stresses on the plant.

Pick tender leaves all through the growing season – the leaves nearest the growing shoot tips will be the most tender. They wilt quickly, so try to harvest in early morning or just before you are going to use them. Pick leaves whole and do not tear or cut until using them in the kitchen.

Vine leaves can be stored for later use in various ways. To freeze, pack leaves (enough to use for a meal) flat in a plastic bag, exclude as much air as possible, tie and freeze. Once defrosted they should be used immediately. Leaves can also be stored easily in brine, usually rolled into tight cylinders before packing into jars. They can also be easily dried: run a needle and thread through a bunch of leaves and hang them to dry (as per drying herbs); when ready to use, dip the bunch into boiling water for 2-3 minutes.

Propagation: Take hardwood cuttings in winter – very easy.

Culinary uses

Traditional Greek recipes use vine leaves for wrapping parcels of other foods before cooking; the whole parcels are eaten. Vine leaves used for wrapping are usually blanched (placed in boiling water) for a few minutes to make them more supple and easier to use.

However, the leaves can be used in many more ways than as a wrapping. They are rather bland eaten cooked on their own, but are great shredded in salads, layered in pasta dishes like lasagne, or in pies and stews. You don't need to pre-cook or blanch them if they are going in a cooked dish, just lay them in whole or chopped.

Maintenance and potential problems

With regular harvesting of leaves/shoots, there should be little other maintenance required.

Mildews can be a problem on the leaves of certain grape varieties, covering them with patches of white mould. Hybrid varieties tend to be much more resistant to these; also, it is plants under stress (i.e. bearing a large fruit crop) that tend to suffer most, so if you are growing a vine specifically for leaves and do not let it fruit, then problems should be minimal.

Groundnut
(Apios americana)

Also known as potato bean

Groundnut is a twining perennial climbing vine from North America – not to be confused with peanut (*Arachis hypogaea*), which is also sometimes called groundnut. It is a leguminous nitrogen-fixer like beans, and, like climbing beans, it twines up anything it touches to reach the light. It can grow 2.5m (8') high or sometimes a little more, and bears attractive reddish-brown to purple flowers that are loved by bees.

It bears strings of edible tubers some 5-20cm (2-8") beneath the soil surface.

These are 1-6cm (3/8-2¹/2") across – about walnut-sized – round or oval in shape, quite smooth-skinned, and radiate out from the mother plant at intervals along the root 'string'. Thus, if unharvested, the plant gradually spreads to form a patch. The tubers were widely used by Native Americans.

Hardiness zone: 3

Cultivation

Groundnut will grow in most soils, and tolerates heavy and very acid soils. It doesn't like really dry sites. Like most legumes, it is happiest in a sunny site but also where it can climb or clamber up something, so on the southern side of shrubs is ideal.

Shoots are relatively late to emerge in spring (May), but grow very fast once they do so.

Varieties: In recent years some selection and breeding work in the USA has resulted in better-yielding varieties of groundnut, with plants producing larger tubers and tubers less spread out along strings, and some of the plants available commercially (like mine) are sourced from these improved stocks. These plants can yield several kilos of tubers a year. The varieties themselves do not seem to be commercially available in Europe, but may be so in the USA. They include 'Aquarius', 'Corona', 'Draco', 'Gemini', 'Lyra', 'Orion', 'Serpens' and 'Sirius'.

Harvest: The tubers can be harvested all year round, but normally they are dug in autumn and winter. If you allow a patch to develop, then you can dig this over, harvesting most tubers and leaving some (deliberately or otherwise) to regrow. Once you come across a tuber you can easily follow the 'string' that connects it to others (sometimes even pulling a whole string up gently). Tubers are best stored in the ground – they quickly shrivel in dry warmth. They store well in a plastic bag in a fridge.

Propagation: Plant tubers about 30cm (1') apart, at a depth of 7-10cm (3-4"). Groundnut can be grown from seed but this is rarely available. Small plants may take two or three years to establish before they start producing large enough tubers to be worth harvesting.

Culinary uses

Groundnut tubers are starchy and contain 16 per cent protein – very high for a tuber crop (potatoes contain about 5 per cent). When cooked their flavour is like a slightly nutty potato and they have a slightly mealier texture – quite similar to yams. They can be

Harvested groundnut tubers (with a £1 coin).

cooked in any way that potatoes can, i.e. boiled, fried or roasted.

The seeds can also be used like peas – eaten raw or cooked when green, or stored dry then soaked overnight and cooked. However, they are not borne abundantly.

Maintenance and potential problems

Little maintenance required and no problems.

Ground plum
(Astragalus crassicarpus)

Also known as buffalo pea; groundplum milk vetch

This is a bushy, clump-forming, perennial North American prairie plant, growing around 30cm (1') high and wide, making a reasonably ground cover in sun. It is a nitrogen-fixing legume with flowers attractive to bees. Various species of *Astragalus* are used medicinally in many parts of the world, but this one of the few that have good edible parts.

It produces edible young pods, 3cm (1 1/8") long, which look like green plums and have a sweet flavour of peas. The flowers range in colour from white to violet.

Hardiness zone: 3

Cultivation

Groundplum likes sun or light shade and a well-drained soil – it tolerates very dry soils.

Varieties: There are no varieties.

Harvest: Pick the young green pods in summer.

Propagation: Raise from seed in spring – the seed is slow to germinate and, like many legumes, needs scarification treatment (see Chapter 3, page 54).

Culinary uses

The pods, containing green seeds, can be eaten raw or cooked, or pickled. Many *Astragalus* species contain toxins, so are best eaten in small quantities to begin with, in case you are sensitive to the compounds.

Maintenance and potential problems

None of either.

Hardneck garlic
See Rocambole (*Allium sativum* var. *ophioscorodon*)

Harebells
See Bellflowers (*Campanula* spp.)

Herb patience
See Sorrels (*Rumex* spp.)

Honewort
See Mitsuba & honewort (*Cryptotaenia japonica* & *C. canadensis*)

Hops
(*Humulus lupulus*)

Hops are best known for providing the flavouring and preservative used in ales and beers. However, this plant can also be treated as a perennial vegetable.

Hop plants are twining climbers with rough hairy stems, which climb and clamber upwards, to a height of up to 6m (20') with full-size varieties. Normally only female varieties are grown, because the female flowers ('cones') are harvested for use in brewing. The flowers form in late summer and are harvested around September.

Hop shoots are a traditional spring vegetable in hop-growing regions around the world.

Hardiness zone: 5

Cultivation

Hops grow easily in any reasonably moist and well-drained soil. They need something shrubby close by to climb or clamber up, or they can be trained up a stick or cane into a shrub or low tree canopy. If they don't have support they will sprawl across the ground. If you leave the old stems from the previous year, in time the new shoots will usually climb up them.

Once established, plants can sucker and form a larger clump or thicket.

Varieties: There are many brewing varieties and a few ornamentals – all can be used for harvesting shoots. In recent years a few dwarf varieties have been bred, which grow only 2.5m (8') high or so. These include 'First Gold' and 'Golden Tassels'.

Propagation: Either take root cuttings, divide plants in spring, layer stems in summer, or take semi-ripe cuttings in early summer.

Harvest: New hop shoots appear fairly early in spring, and are usually cut at soil level when 15-30cm (6-12") high, but they can be cut off higher shoots. You can cut repeatedly for several weeks, but should finally allow some of the shoots to grow, to sustain the plant as a perennial. The more you cut, the fewer female flowers you will get.

Culinary uses

The young shoots are treated in the same way as asparagus – just cook lightly. It's best to steam them for only a few minutes to preserve the nutty flavour. You can serve them as a vegetable on their own or add sauces of various sorts.

Maintenance and potential problems

Hops can be susceptible to aphids in summer, especially if grown as a monoculture, but the advantage of using the plants as a vegetable is that in spring there are never any pest problems.

Horseradish
(Armoracia rusticana)

This fairly well-known herbaceous perennial is renowned as much for the fact that it is almost indestructible as it is for its spicy roots. In fact it is not included here for the roots (used of course for making hot and spicy sauces and relishes), which I would describe more as a spice than a vegetable, but for the young leaves.

Horseradish is a robust, deep-rooted and clump-forming plant growing 60-100cm (2'-3'3") high and about 40cm (1'4") wide, with long leaves that look like oversized dock leaves.

Hardiness zone: 5

Cultivation

It grows in any moist soil, in sun or partial shade.

Varieties: There is a variegated variety, which is a bit less vigorous.

Harvest: Harvest young leaves in spring, from the moment they start appearing. The leaf quality varies a lot between plants – it is worth trying new leaves from other folk's plants (with their permission of course! They may think you're mad) to find specimens with more tender leaves.

In some parts of the world the new shoots are blanched by covering to exclude light (as for rhubarb), which gives larger, more tender and mild-tasting shoots.

Propagation: This is normally done by root cuttings – easy.

Culinary uses

The young leaves are very nice eaten lightly steamed – they have a mild flavour and pleasant texture. Occasionally the leaves are tender enough to eat raw in salads – depends on the plant.

Maintenance and potential problems

You'll not easily get rid of it!

Hostas
(Hosta spp.)

Various hostas have been used as vegetables in China, Japan and other parts of Asia for a long time, but although they often grown in the UK as ornamentals, few people know that they can also be eaten. Species that can be eaten include *H. crispula*, *H. longipes*, *H. montana*, *H. plantaginae* (pictured above), *H. sieboldii*, *H. sieboldiana*, *H. undulata* and *H. ventricosa*.

All species are woodland plants, growing as clump-forming herbaceous perennials. Growth begins in early or mid-spring, with leaf clusters emerging tightly curled and packed together. These then unfurl and grow rapidly. The height and width of clumps varies with species and variety, from small (30cm/1') up to 1.2m (4').

Hosta flowers come in white, lavender and violet, but of course many of the ornamental varieties have striped and coloured leaves instead.

Hardiness zone: 4

Cultivation

Hostas are happy in any moist soil in a shady situation – they tolerate quite deep shade.

Varieties: There are many ornamental varieties of the species listed on page 121, all of which can be eaten – the larger-growing selections provide more edible material, as the leaf clusters are larger, and they are also easier to cultivate. Large-leaved selections of *H. sieboldiana* include 'Big Daddy', 'Blue Umbrella' and 'Elegans'.

Harvest: The curled leaf clusters – which look a bit like chicory chicons – are harvested in spring by cutting at soil level. Plants need to be a few years old before the first harvest, then the first flush of clusters can be harvested each year. Replacement clusters should be allowed to grow on.

Propagate: This is normally by division of existing clumps in winter. Hostas can be grown from seed in spring, but varieties are unlikely to come true from seed.

A hosta shoot in spring, at the right stage to harvest.

Culinary uses

Hosta leaf clusters are cooked before being eaten, either by steaming, frying or boiling. They are particularly good served with butter or a sauce.

Maintenance and potential problems

The only real problem – and it can be serious – is slugs and snails, which love to eat hosta leaves and stems. Encourage predators like frogs by having a pond nearby, use traps in early spring, and consider using the biological control nematode against molluscs and organic slug pellets (containing iron phosphate).

Ice plant & orpine
(*Sedum spectabile* & *S. telephium*)

These two sedum species are sometimes separated out into the genus *Hylotelephium*, because they are rather different in character, with their large fleshy leaves, whereas most sedums have tiny leaves.

Ice plant (*S. spectabile* – pictured above) and orpine (*S. telephium*) are herbaceous greyish-green perennials that are widely used as ornamentals in gardens. They bear white or pink flowers in heads, which are very attractive to bees. Ice plant grows in clumps about 45cm (1'6") high and wide, while orpine is slightly taller, reaching 60cm (2') high and 30cm (1') wide and spreading slowly.

Hardiness zone: 6

Cultivation

These two species like any well-drained soil and full sun or light shade.

Varieties: Any of the ornamental varieties can be used as a vegetable.

Harvest: Pick the fleshy leaves at any time during the growing season. In very dry spells in summer they can sometimes get a little bitter.

Propagation: Raise from seed (very fine – sow on the surface of a fine compost in spring), divide in spring, or take softwood cuttings in summer.

Culinary uses

Use the leaves in salads, whole or roughly chopped – they are succulent and juicy and really add to a salad on a hot summer day!

Maintenance and potential problems

None of either.

Japanese asparagus
See Udo (*Aralia cordata*)

Japanese butterbur
See Giant butterbur (*Petasites japonicus*)

Japanese parsley
See Mitsuba (*Cryptotaenia japonica*)

Jersey kale
See Tree collards (*Brassica oleracea* Acephala Group)

Jerusulem artichoke
(*Helianthus tuberosus*)

Also known as sunchoke

This is another of the well-known perennial vegetables. Jerusulem artichokes originate from North America and have long been grown for the somewhat knobbly tubers, 5-8cm (2-3¹/₄") long, which are borne in clusters. The plants grow tall, reaching up to 3m (10') high, though often less, and some varieties are lower-growing.

Slowly expanding via tubers to form colonies, Jerusulem artichoke is sometimes utilised as a summer windbreak, though the tall stems can blow over in strong winds. The tips can be pinched out to keep them shorter.

At the top of the stems, small sunflower-like flowers attract bees and hoverflies in the late summer. The dead stems make good kindling in winter.

Hardiness zone: 2

Cultivation

Jerusulem artichoke grows in any moist but well-drained soil in a fairly sunny location. It responds well to manures and other fertility materials incorporated into the soils before planting.

Varieties: There are a number of named varieties including the following:

'Boston red' – tubers large, skins rose-red, knobbly.
'Dave's Shrine' – tubers long, fast-maturing, red-skinned.
'Dwarf Sunray' – smaller-growing than some (2m/6'6"); tubers thin-skinned, knobbly, tightly clustered around the main stem; high yielding. Flowers more regularly each year than most.
'Fuseau' – tubers smooth, large and uniform; very good flavour, heavy cropper.
'Garnet' – tubers long, round, smooth, purple-skinned; very high yielding.
'Gerard' – tubers pink-skinned, good flavour; moderate cropper.
'Golden Nugget' – tubers tapering and carrot-shaped.
'Jack's Copperclad' – tubers a dark coppery-purple, good flavour.
'Mulles Rose' – tubers large, white, with rose-purple-fleshed eyes.
'Red Fuseau' – tubers maroon-red-skinned, smooth, fast-maturing.
'Stampede' – fast-maturing, white tubers.
'Sugarball' – tubers somewhat knobbly, white, sweeter than most; heavy cropper.
'Wilton Rose' – tubers long, smooth, purple-and-cream-mottled skins.

Harvest: The crop should not be harvested until after frost. Tubers are best left stored in the soil – if dug up and left in dry storage, they shrivel. You'll almost certainly not be able to find every tuber, so will get automatic regrowth from what is left each year.

If tubers are not harvested, plants will persist of course, but quickly get crowded and the tuber size decrease rapidly.

Propagation: Plant new tubers in spring, or cut tubers into sections, each with an eye to plant, at 40-60cm (1'4"-2') between plants and 15cm (6") deep. New shoots come up relatively late in spring, but then grow fast.

Jerusulem artichoke tubers.

Culinary uses

The tubers can be eaten raw but are normally cooked, by boiling, frying or roasting. They take about half as long as potatoes to cook. They are good for thickening soups or as the main ingredient in a soup. They have a reputation for being difficult to peel (how knobbly the tubers are varies a lot and is generally less of a problem with named varieties) – to get around this, cook first and peel afterwards: much easier!

Jerusulem artichoke contains starch, but also in autumn about 75-80 per cent of the content is the complex sugar inulin, which is slower and more difficult to digest; hence their reputation for causing flatulence. The ability to digest inulin increases if it is consumed regularly, so the side effects reduce if you do. When consumed, the inulin is converted in the digestive tract to fructose, which can be tolerated by diabetics. Recent research* has shown that inulin can increase the body's ability to absorb calcium, as well as having a beneficial effect on digestion.

The inulin content decreases over winter to a minimum in early spring, because it converts to fructose over time – in spring they can be really sweet. So if you want to avoid gaseous results as much as possible, harvest in spring!

Maintenance and potential problems

No real problems, though if you ever want to get rid of it you will have to keep digging during the spring, as volunteer tubers left behind will sprout. Mice can sometimes nibble on the tubers and spread them around. Rabbits can nibble the new shoots in spring.

Kailan
See Chinese broccoli (*Brassica oleracea* Alboglabra Group)

Kale, perennial
See Perennial kale (*Brassica oleracea* Ramosa Group)

* Abrams, S. et al. (2005). 'A combination of prebiotic short- and long-chain inulin-type fructans enhances calcium absorption and bone mineralization in young adolescents'. *Am J Clin Nutr* 82(2): 471-6.

King's spear

See Yellow asphodel (*Asphodeline lutea*)

Lady's leek

See Nodding onion (*Allium cernuum*)

Leaf beet

See Perpetual spinach & chard (*Beta vulgaris* subsp. *cicla*)

Leek, perennial

See: Babington's leek (*Allium ampeloprasum* var. *babingtonii*); Perennial leek (*Allium ampeloprasum*)

Lemon balm

(*Melissa officinalis*)

Although it is usually regarded as a culinary herb, I am including lemon balm as a vegetable because it is eminently suitable for using in bulk amounts.

It is a clump-forming, aromatic perennial which is herbaceous, though the centre may stay evergreen in mild winter regions. Plants grow 60-80cm (2'-2'8") high and 40cm (1'4") wide.

Hardiness zone: 4

Cultivation

Grow in any fairly well-drained soil, in sun or partial shade – it tolerates a surprising amount of shade.

Varieties: Several varieties, including 'Citronella' and 'Lemonella', have higher levels of essential oils and a stronger, more pungent flavour than the species.

Harvest: Harvest leaves at any time in the growing season, when they are looking fresh. I usually cut stems off about 15cm (6") back from growing tips, and strip the leaves to use in the kitchen.

Propagation: Raise from seed in spring – very easy.

Culinary uses

You can add good quantities of chopped leaves into salads, where they will give a gentle lemon flavour and aroma. Lemon balm is also good for herb teas. The leaves lose a lot of flavour on drying or cooking.

Maintenance and potential problems

It may self-seed if bare ground is nearby.

I prefer to leave the dead stems in place over winter – they aid overwintering insects – but try to cut them down roughly in spring to maximise the light available to young growth.

Lesser stitchwort
(Stellaria graminea)

Lesser stitchwort is a herbaceous perennial that is common in hedges and woodlands in Europe, including the UK. Coming early into growth and flowering in spring with white flowers, it grows or scrambles to 50cm (1'8") high, often over large areas. Bees like the flowers.

Hardiness zone: 4

Cultivation

It is happy in most soils and in light or partial shade. Plant out a large patch of this in a part-shady site in the garden, and it will look after itself.

Varieties: There are no varieties.

Harvest: The shoots and leaves are harvested from spring right through to autumn. Later in the season only the upper half of the shoots is harvested; the lower part becomes too tough.

Propagation: Easily grown from seed – sow in spring.

Culinary uses

Like its close relative annual chickweed (*Stellaria media*), the leaves and shoots are an excellent vegetable. They can be used in bulk in salads, or, lightly cooked – just steam for a few minutes – they are very pleasant, with a mild flavour.

Maintenance and potential problems

No maintenance needed nor problems.

Limes
(Tilia spp.)

Also known as lindens; basswood

Lime or linden trees (known as basswood in North America) are well-known large deciduous trees, often used as street trees in towns and cities. There are species of lime from many parts of the northern hemisphere, and all can be grown for their edible leaves.

Basswood (*T. americana*) and small-leaved lime (*T. cordata*) are hardier (zone 2 or 3) than large-leaved lime (*T. platyphyllos*, pictured on the previous page) and silver lime (*T. tomentosa*) (both zone 5). These four species are the most common in cultivation, along with the hybrid European lime (*T.* x *europaea*).

Bees love the flowers of lime trees, though it seems that they can sometimes overindulge and become incapacitated! Lime trees are excellent mineral accumulators, raising nutrients into their leaves, which, when they fall, rapidly improve soil conditions.

Hardiness zones: 2-5

Cultivation

Lime trees are all moderately fast-growing woodland trees, very shade-tolerant but slow-growing in dense shade. They grow in most soils and situations.

Normally, cultivation as leaf crops means that you'll want to keep trees small rather than have the canopy largely out of reach. The best way to do this is to treat them as a coppice crop, cutting back all growth every few years either to near ground level (true coppice) or higher up (pollarded). In my forest garden I pollard lime trees at a height of 1.2-1.5m (4-5') to keep young shoots out of reach of deer.

The first coppicing is not usually undertaken until trees are 6-8 years old and perhaps 2.5-3m (8-10') high. The frequency of coppicing after that depends on the vigour of the species. I find that large-leaved lime can be cut back every year, as it puts out 2m (6'6")-long shoots over the course of the season, whereas I coppice small-leaved lime only every 4 years or so, as it is less vigorous. Basically,

cut back the tree in winter once too much of the leaf crop is out of easy reach. The branches can be used for firewood, kindling or growing mushrooms on.

Varieties: There are some ornamental varieties, which can be used in the same way.

Harvest: Lime trees, unlike many trees, continue to put out new growth all through the growing season, so there is almost always some fresh growth to harvest. Harvest the younger leaves near the ends of the shoots. Leaves in shade tend to be thinner and more tender too.

Propagation: Lime trees are normally grown from seed. The seed requires long stratification (see Chapter 3, page 54), and is best sown as soon as seed is ripe in summer, allowing it to experience moist, warm conditions through the autumn, then cold, moist winter conditions before it germinates in spring. Sometimes the seed waits a further year before germinating!

Culinary uses

Lime leaves are one of my most-harvested salad crops. Use the leaves as a bulk 'base' ingredient in salads instead of something like lettuce leaves, and liven up the salad with more strongly flavoured leaves and herbs. The leaf quality varies between species – small-leaved lime is the best, with the most tender leaves.

The leaves can also be used in cooked dishes – layer them in lasagne, for example – and also as an ingredient in pesto.

Maintenance and potential problems

Coppicing is the only maintenance required. There are usually no problems, though European lime has a reputation for being badly attacked by aphids – better to grow small-leaved lime.

Lindens
See Limes (*Tilia* spp.)

Lotus
See Water lotus (*Nelumbo nucifera*)

Lucerne
(*Medicago sativa*)

Also known as alfalfa

Lucerne is well known, both as a green manure and as an edible sprouted seed, but the young shoots and leaves also make an excellent vegetable.

It is a very deep-rooted, herbaceous perennial legume – lucerne roots can reach many metres deep. Top growth reaches about 45cm (1'6") high, sometimes more, and often sprawls. The purple flower spikes are loved by bees. It thrives on well-drained soils that are not too acid (not less than pH 6.0), in sun. In temperate climates it often remains green over winter.

Hardiness zone: 5

Cultivation

Lucerne tolerates many climates, from temperate to subtropical, as long as there is adequate rainfall – though it grows in drier conditions than most legumes.

Plants will last for several years but will eventually lose vigour, when the patch should be replaced and a new patch prepared elsewhere – the old patch will be high in nitrogen and well suited for a nutrient-demanding crop to follow.

Varieties: There are some agricultural varieties, which can be used in the same ways.

Harvest: The top 5cm (2") of shoots, including young leaves, is the crop. The leaves become tougher as the shoots grow longer, but the plant responds well to frequent cutting back, so with a patch, aim to cut back a section each week so that you have a constant supply.

Propagation: A lucerne patch is easy to sow – cultivate an area with a good tilth and broadcast the seed thinly before raking in. Alternatively, sow thinly in rows 7-10cm (3-4") apart. The plant is not native to the UK, and the bacteria that it associates with to enable nitrogen fixation is not always present (especially if it has not been grown in that location before) – but the suitable culture can be purchased and mixed with the seed before sowing.

Culinary uses

The young shoots are very nutritious, high in protein and vitamins. They can be used raw in salads or cooked by steaming or adding to stir-fries, soups, etc. The first shoots are usually available quite early in spring, and from plants cut back there can be a supply right through the growing season.

As mentioned, the seeds can of course be sprouted, and there are several easy-to-use seed sprouter containers available. The sprouted seeds are also high in protein and vitamins.

Maintenance and potential problems

Even if you don't require new shoots, lucerne should be cut back after flowering to renew vigour and lengthen the lifespan of the plants.

Mallows
(*Malva* spp.)

Perennial mallows used as vegetables include hollyhock mallow (*M. alcea*), musk mallow (*M. moschata* – pictured above) and wood mallow (*M. sylvestris*). Wood mallow is herbaceous, but the other two are evergreen in mild temperate climates, retaining a rosette of leaves even in several degrees of frost.

These clump-forming mallows can reach 60-100cm (2'-3'3") high and 20-40 cm (8-1'4") wide when in full flower. Wood mallow leaves stay entire, but the leaves of hollyhock and musk mallow change form as the plants flower, becoming more and more finely divided. All these mallows bear flowers about 2-4cm (3/4-15/8") in diameter, pinkish or purple, though there are

ornamental varieties (which are just as good to use as a vegetable) with particularly showy flowers. All flowers are loved by bees.

Hardiness zone: 4

Cultivation

Mallows will grow in any reasonable soil that is not too acid. Do not use fertilisers, because mallows, like lettuces, grown in very rich soils can accumulate a potentially harmful excess of nitrates in their leaves.

Varieties: There are ornamental varieties bred for different flower colours – all can be used in the same ways.

Harvest: Young leaves and shoots can be harvested mainly in winter and spring. The leaves become tougher on flowering plants, though if you want leaves instead of flowers, the plants can be cut back regularly to prevent flowering.

Flowers are harvested in late spring and summer. Pick whole flowers by carefully grasping the petals on opposite sides of the flower and pulling them off (you want to avoid picking the green base to the flower, which is rather tough to eat).

After the flowers, the young fruiting bodies, called 'cheeses', owing to their appearance, make a nice nibble.

Propagation: Grow from seed in spring – easy – or by taking basal cuttings in spring.

Culinary uses

The leaves and shoots make an excellent salad leaf, but are also good for thickening soups or stews, and as a cooked green or deep-fried.

Wood mallow.

The flowers are generally used in salads – I usually sprinkle them on top after the salad is mixed.

Maintenance and potential problems

Mallows are not particularly long-lived perennials, but often self-seed quite happily.

Marsh mallow
(*Althaea officinalis*)

Marsh mallow is a clump-forming, herbaceous perennial found in moist soil. Until they flower, plants are relatively small, but flowering heads can reach 1.5-2m (5'-6'6") high. The flowers are pale pink.

Hardiness zone: 3

Cultivation

It is easy to grow in any moist soil, in sun or part shade, though a friable soil that is not too heavy is easiest for digging the roots. A good bee and butterfly plant, marsh mallow is also used medicinally as an anti-inflammatory.

Varieties: There are a few ornamental varieties, which can all be used in the same ways.

Harvest: Leaves are harvested through the growing season, flowers in late summer.

Dig younger roots (around the edge of the plant, so without disturbing the whole plant) in winter – they look like small parsnips, generally finger-thickness. They can be stored in sand or a similar well-drained medium for several months.

Propagation: Raise from seed in spring.

Marsh mallow roots are starchy and edible.

Culinary uses

The leaves are slightly felty and can be eaten raw, but are nicer lightly cooked or added to stews and soups. The flowers can be used raw in salads.

The roots are starchy and slightly sweet. Younger roots are crunchy. They can be roasted, boiled or steamed, and are best with a sauce or in a stir-fry, for example, as they do not have a strong flavour themselves. The confectionary marshmallow was formerly made from the roots of this plant.

Maintenance and potential problems

None of either.

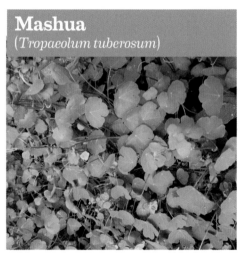

Mashua
(*Tropaeolum tuberosum*)

A perennial scrambling climber, this is one of the many excellent tuber crops that originates from the Andes in South America. It can scramble 2m (6'6") or more up supports or other plants. The leaves are nasturtium-like (though more rounded than ornamental annual nasturtiums) and the attractive flowers, when produced (which is not often in the UK), are orange-red and trumpet-shaped.

A cluster of potato-sized tubers is produced around the base of the plants, from which new shoots will sprout the following spring. Fast-growing, these shoots soon suppress any weed competition.

Hardiness zone: 8

Cultivation

Easy to grow in any reasonably well-drained soil, in sun or light shade.

You do not need to earth up the plants, but if you do you might well increase the tuber crop. Once the plants are well established, however, and the foliage is spreading over the ground, you can't really access the soil to earth them up.

Varieties: Many selections start tuber formation only when the day length is 12 hours or less – i.e. from late September onwards in the UK. However, day-length-neutral varieties, which include 'Ken Aslett', start forming tubers earlier and have the potential to crop more heavily – as good as potatoes. The varieties in cultivation in Europe have white tubers, but yellow and red varieties exist in South America.

Harvest: Harvest leaves through the growing season; flowers in autumn. In long, mild autumns, seeds form, which are similar to annual nasturtium seeds and can be used like capers.

The foliage dies down after the first autumn frosts, after which the tubers can be dug at any time through the winter. The tubers can tolerate frozen soil to a degree – indeed in the winter of 2010/11 mine happily survived aerial temperatures of -10°C (14°F) – but if your winters are significantly colder than this you may need to treat the plant as a replant annual, harvesting all tubers in late autumn, allowing them to air-dry, then storing (in paper sacks) over winter for eating and replanting some the following spring.

Propagation: You can start tubers off in pots or in the soil – they start into growth in low temperatures. Plant tubers around 30cm (1') apart, 3-5cm (1-2") deep, and give the shoots something to clamber up – rough canes, twiggy sticks, or the edge of a shrub or tree nearby (but not single smooth canes, which they will just fall off). Late spring frosts can damage top growth.

Culinary uses

The tubers are not starchy but are high in protein and vitamin C. Young tubers are eaten whole; older and larger tubers should be peeled. Cook by boiling, baking or frying – treat them like other root vegetables such as carrots or parsnips. They have a slight anise/vanilla fragrance and a peppery flavour, quite strong when raw but much milder when cooked. They are especially good in stews.

You can eat the leaves too, as with annual nasturtiums; they are quite peppery – good in salads. The flowers are also very nice in salads.

Mashua tubers.

Maintenance and potential problems

See the advice on the previous page (under 'Harvest') for cold winter areas. There are no pests or diseases.

Mashua flower.

Mint, apple
See Apple mint (*Mentha suaveolens*)

Mint, Bowles's
See Bowles's mint (*Mentha Bowles's mint*)

Mitsuba & honewort
(*Cryptotaenia japonica* & *C. canadensis*)

Mitsuba is also known as Japanese parsley

These plants are clump-forming, herbaceous perennials growing about 30cm (1') high and 20cm (8") wide, with pretty leaflets of three leaves at the end of tender stalks – looking rather like a flat-leaved parsley. Mitsuba (*C. japonica*) has been cultivated as a vegetable for centuries in Japan. Honewort (*C. canadensis*), from North America, can be used in the same way.

Hardiness zone: 6

Cultivation

A woodland edge plant, mitsuba prefers partial shade – the leaves can yellow in full sun. It tolerates any reasonable soil. In ideal conditions it can become a ground-cover plant, spreading by self-seeding.

Varieties: There is a purple-leaved variety available from seed (*C. japonica* f. *atropurpurea*). In Japan there are two main types – kansai (with green stems, grown as a green crop) and kanto (whiter stems, used for blanching) – but these do not appear to be in cultivation outside Japan.

Harvest: Leaves and stems are mainly harvested in spring and autumn. In Japan the stems are sometimes blanched as they grow. The roots may be harvested in autumn or winter; the seeds in autumn.

Propagation: Plants are usually grown from seed, which germinates quickly and can be sown in spring or autumn. Plant out young plants at about 30cm (1') spacing.

Culinary uses

The green leaves and stems are used raw or, more often, cooked – steamed or cooked for a couple of minutes. Their flavour has elements of angelica, celery and parsley. Mitsuba is essential in many traditional Japanese dishes and for seasoning fish soups. It can be used in place of parsley.

The roots and seeds are used for flavouring cooked dishes – roots can be chopped and enclosed in a sachet, which is removed from the dish before serving (they are too tough to eat); the seeds can be used whole or ground.

Young seedlings are sometimes used raw in salads.

Maintenance and potential problems

None of either.

Mock strawberry
See False strawberry
(*Duchesnea indica*)

Monk's rhubarb
See Sorrels (*Rumex* spp.)

Mountain rye
See Perennial rye (*Secale montanum*)

Mountain sorrel
(*Oxyria digyna*)

Mountain sorrel is a small, clump-forming, herbaceous perennial from Alpine Europe, reaching 50cm (1'8") high and 40cm (1'4") wide. It can often self-seed where there is bare soil nearby.

Hardiness zone: 2

Cultivation

It is very easy to cultivate in any reasonably well-drained soil, and in sun or light shade.

Varieties: There are no varieties.

Harvest: Pick leaves and shoots all through the growing season.

Propagation: Grow from seed in spring.

Culinary uses

The leaves are lemony with a melting texture – even better than most sorrels – and are used like sorrel in salads or cooked in soups. As with all sorrels, it should be eaten in moderation owing to the oxalic acid content.

Maintenance and potential problems

You may want to stop it setting seed to prevent self-seeding in nearby cultivated areas.

Mulberries
(*Morus* spp.)

Mulberries are well-known small deciduous trees, 5-10m (16-33') high with rounded canopies. You may wonder what they are

doing in a book on perennial vegetables, but in fact, as well as having delicious fruit, the leaves are used in many parts of the world as a cooked vegetable.

Species include white mulberry (*M. alba*), black mulberry (*M. nigra*) and red mulberry (*M. rubra*). True white mulberry is less hardy than the other two species and can have white or black fruits. There are also hybrids, especially between white and red mulberry, which are hardy and bear fruits that can be white, black or red. Black mulberries bear only black fruits.

Hardiness zones: 5-8

Cultivation

Plant trees in any reasonable soil in sun or light shade. Mulberries need some shelter, as the branches are brittle and liable to breakages on exposed sites.

If leaf production is your aim, then you should aim to grow mulberries as coppiced or pollarded shrubs (see Chapter 3, page 61) and accept that fruiting is definitely a secondary aim. Once established, mulberries can be coppiced every 1-4 years, depending on vigour and how large you allow the plants to get – vigorous plants can grow shoots 1.5m (5') long or more in their first year after coppicing.

Pollarding is my preferred technique – that is, cutting back all growth to around chest height, or 1.2-1.5m (4-5') above ground level – because the new shoots are less susceptible to browsing by rabbits or deer, breakage or frost damage, and because it is easier to underplant these trees as opposed to coppiced trees.

Aim to coppice/pollard/prune back in winter, no later than around March. Mulberries start growth in May – later than most trees – and leaves can be harvested from late May onwards throughout the growing season. Coppiced and pollarded trees of named fruiting selections should fruit the second year after cutting back, until cut back again.

Aim to grow some nitrogen-fixing plants near to the mulberries, to help supply a sustainable source of nitrogen, as they are quite hungry when cropped regularly.

Varieties: There are no varieties selected for leaf production. The leaf quality of white mulberry and its hybrids is better than that of black or red mulberry.

Harvest: Harvest leaves at any time through the growing season. When harvesting leaves, leave the oldest ones and also the shoot tips (to continue growth).

Propagation: Mulberries are quite easy to grow from seed – give 3 months' stratification before sowing in spring. It will be 3-4 years until you can start cropping the tree. Semi-ripe cuttings in summer can also succeed.

Culinary uses

The leaves of white mulberry and its hybrids have a smoother texture than those of black mulberry, which are quite rough. (The texture of red mulberry is in between). In the Mediterranean, black mulberry leaves are sometimes used like vine leaves, wrapped around food prior to cooking. All mulberry leaves can also be used as a cooked vegetable on their own or in dishes – layered in lasagne, for example. They have a mild flavour on their own.

Maintenance and potential problems

Very young trees are susceptible to slug and snail damage to the thin bark – take the usual precautions against these menacing molluscs. Older trees are safe, though you are likely to find grazing snails in the foliage in damp spells.

Multiplier onions
(*Allium cepa* Aggregatum Group)

The multiplier onions, which include shallots (pictured above) and potato onions, form a clump of bulbs, each 2-4cm (3/4-15/8") in diameter – potato onion bulbs are larger than shallots. Plants grow 30-50cm (1'-1'8") high.

Hardiness zone: 5

Cultivation

Grow in any reasonably well-drained soil, in a position in full sun or very light shade. In general, start by planting bulbs (seed is rarely produced) in late winter or early spring.

Varieties:
Shallots:

There are a number of shallot varieties available, including several with red bulbs. The following is just a selection of those available commercially.

'Atlantic' – an early-maturing variety, high yielding.
'Creation' – a seed-grown variety.
'Drittler White Nest' – old variety that produces bulbs of variable sizes.
'Echalote de Poulet' – an old variety valued for its excellent keeping qualities.
'French Delvad' – each bulb yields 8-10 new bulbs.
'French Jermor' – copper-coloured skins, elongated bulbs; each yields 6-8 new bulbs.
'Giant Yellow Improved' – yellow-brown skins.
'Golden Gourmet' – mild, produces good edible green tops.
'Grise de Bagnolet' – a grey shallot highly regarded in France.
'Hative de Niort' – elongated bulbs.
'Jermor' – elongated bulbs with an abundance of green tops.
'Pesandor' – copper-coloured skins, each elongated bulb yields 6-8 new bulbs.
'Picasso' – red-skinned with pink flesh.
'Pikant' – prolific, skins dark reddish-brown.
'Polka' – from Poland, a very good keeper.
'Red Gourmet' – early-maturing, red-fleshed variety.
'Red Sun' – each bulb yields 6 new bulbs.

'Sante' – large, round bulbs.
'Topper' – mild, golden-yellow-skinned bulbs.
'Yellow Moon' – yellow-skinned bulbs.

Potato onion:
Varieties include:
'Jersey' – red-streaked flesh.
'Red potato onion' – red bulbs.

Harvest: Leaves/stems (and young bulbs if desired) can be harvested like spring onions during spring and summer.

Bulbs are usually harvested in late summer and dried like onions for storage over winter. Storage is excellent.

Propagation: Grow from 'sets' (i.e. small individual bulbs), planted in autumn or spring.

Culinary uses

Use the bulbs of shallots and potato onions as you would use onions. The leaves and stems can be used raw or cooked like spring onions (scallions).

Maintenance and potential problems

If replanting, choose a new site to avoid a build-up of onion diseases.

Nettle
See Stinging nettle (*Urtica dioica*)

New Zealand yam
See Oca (*Oxalis tuberosa*)

Nodding onion
(*Allium cernuum*)

Also known as lady's leek

Nodding onion is a perennial bulbous plant originating from North America. It grows to 70cm (2'4") high, with flattish leaves (like garlic chives) and bulbs 1-2cm (3/8-3/4") in diameter. The nodding flowers (hence the name) are usually deep pink.

Hardiness zone: 6

Cultivation

Grow in any reasonably well-drained soil, in sun or light shade.

Varieties: There are no varieties.

Harvest: Use the leaves/stems like spring onions during the spring. Bulbs can be harvested from autumn and over winter, leaving some to regrow.

Propagation: Grow from seed by sowing in spring.

Culinary uses

Use as you would onions.

Maintenance and potential problems

None of either.

Nopale cacti
(*Opuntia* spp.)

Also known as prickly pears

Some readers may wonder at the inclusion of cacti here as perennial vegetables! But, while cacti can be rather a challenge to grow in temperate climes, some are very hardy indeed, although they still require favoured conditions.

There are many *Opuntia* species, originating from Central and North America, including the well-known 'true' prickly pear (*O. ficus-indica*), which is regarded as a weed in many arid regions. This is one of the less hardy edible species, others of which include the beavertail cactus (*O. basilaris*), wheel cactus (*O. robusta*) and *O. streptacantha* (all zone 8).

Some of these less hardy species can reach 3m (10') high. The hardier species, including Eastern prickly pear / Indian fig (*O. compressa*), grizzly bear cactus (*O. erinacea*), spineless / tiger tongue prickly pear (*O. ellisiana*), brittle prickly pear (*O. fragilis*), *O. howeyi*, cane cholla (*O. imbricata*), coastal prickly pear (*O. littoralis*), plains/ twist-spine prickly pear (*O. macrorhiza*), Mojave / tulip prickly pear (*O. phaeacantha* – pictured on the previous page) and *O. polyacantha*, are smaller-growing, usually only 30-50cm (1'-1'8") high.

The pads, or nopales, of most *Opuntia* species are edible, but are covered in intense spines, making them a little more challenging to use than most vegetables.

Hardiness zones: 4-8

Cultivation

To grow nopale cacti, you have to supply a very well-drained soil, a site in full sun, and protection from winter rains. In the UK this means either growing in containers that you bring into a greenhouse or polytunnel over winter, or growing in a well-drained raised bed in a polytunnel or similar structure.

As well as the spineless *O. ellisiana*, spineless varieties of some species, including true prickly pear, are available; while free of the large visible spines, they can still bear glochids at their bases. Non-spineless varieties contain both.

Glochids are tiny hairs which can cause itching and irritation for days. However, there is a simple way to prepare the pads to remove both spines and glochids.

Varieties: See species list (left) – no varieties as such.

Harvest: In summer or autumn, cut pads off with a knife. Obviously you will need to use thick gloves.

Propagation: Raise from seed (quite slow to germinate), or by growing from bought pads, which can be simply planted half-deep into pots.

Culinary uses

Remove spines and glochids by rubbing most spines and glochids off with thick gloves, then singe the pads over a flame and scrape with a knife or use a swivel-type potato peeler. Wash well and double-check!

Nopale pads have a French-bean flavour with hints of asparagus and lemon, and are widely used in Mexican and south-west American cooking, especially served with eggs and salsa.

Maintenance and potential problems

The main problem in a temperate climate is winter wet. Plants really need to be under cover for the whole of the winter, otherwise they are likely to rot.

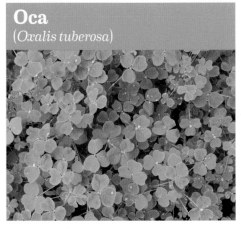

Oca
(Oxalis tuberosa)

Also known as New Zealand yam

This is a bushy perennial from South America – widely grown in Bolivia and Peru, it is the second most important of the Andean tuber crops after potatoes. It grows about 30cm (1') high and 40cm (1'4") wide, with typical oxalis-type leaves with three leaflets. Plants form small-potato-sized tubers, which come in varying colours from white, yellow, orange and pink to dark red and purple, depending on the variety.

Hardiness zone: 7

Cultivation

The tubers are hardy to about -5°C (23°F) soil temperature, so you can grow this as a true perennial only in the milder regions of the UK; otherwise treat it as a replant perennial.

Oca is day-length dependent, so tubers start to form in autumn, when day length is less than 12 hours, and the crop is best after a long, warm autumn. There are apparently some day-length-neutral varieties in Mexico and New Zealand, but these do not appear to be available in Europe or North American yet.

Do not grow in areas where early autumn frosts are a problem.

Propagation: Expose tubers to light in early spring to initiate sprouting (like chitting potatoes). When shoots appear you can pot the tubers up for a while if frosts still threaten, otherwise plant them in a well-drained, fertile soil in full sun. Plant at 30-90cm (1-3') apart, as the foliage sprawls quite widely. They do not require earthing up, but yields can be increased if you do.

Varieties: In South America there are numerous varieties. A few seed companies have started selecting and supplying different varieties in the UK and North America.

'Amarillo' – yellow tubers.
'Grande' – orange to salmon-red tubers.
'Hopin' – light pink tubers.
'Mexican Red' – light red tubers.
'NZ Red' – selected in New Zealand, dark red tubers with black eyes.
'Orange Oca' – orange tubers with red eyes.
'Pure White' – very pale yellow tubers.
'Rebo' (Bolivian Red) – red tubers.
'Scarlet Oca' – deep red tubers with white outlines around eyes.
'Yellow from Orange' – yellow tubers with red lines around eyes.

Harvest: Dig tubers after frosts have killed all the foliage (the first frosts may leave most undamaged), leaving some in the ground for perennial regrowth. Take care not to damage tubers as you dig them. They form in a clump close to the centre of the plants.

The tubers store well in a cool, dark place. Yields of at least 500g (1lb 2oz) per plant should be obtained.

Leaves can be harvested through the growing season.

Culinary uses

The tubers are excellent for eating raw or cooked. When first dug they have sweet-acid flavour (the lemony acidity is from oxalic acid), but if left in the sun for a few days the acidity lessens and they taste sweeter.

They do not need peeling. You can use them in salads (they are crunchy like carrots), or cook them like small potatoes – the cooked flavour is like slightly lemony potatoes and they are superb served with butter or oil. Nutritionally, they are similar to potatoes.

You can also eat the leaves, which taste similar to wood sorrel (see page 200), and can be used in salads, etc. As with other sorrels, they should be eaten in moderation.

Oca tubers.

Maintenance and potential problems

In cold areas, make sure you store some of the tubers over the winter to replant the following spring.

Oriental garlic
See Garlic chives
(*Allium tuberosum*)

Orpine
See Ice plant and orpine
(*Sedum* spp.)

Ostrich fern
(*Matteuccia struthiopteris*)

Also known as shuttlecock fern

This is a very hardy fern from northern temperate regions, well known as a wild edible in North America and Scandinavia.

It spreads via rhizomes to form colonies of plants, each of which can reach 1.5m (5') high and 60cm (2') wide. The ferns are shuttlecock-shaped, hence its alternative name. The curled young shoots uncurl as they grow, giving them the name 'fiddleheads'. This is one of the few ferns now considered safe to eat.

Hardiness zone: 2

Cultivation

Ostrich fern will grow in any moist soil in some shade – it tolerates quite deep shade and acid soil. Plant at a spacing of 60cm (2') or so – plants will spread in time.

Varieties: 'Jumbo' is a vigorous form that grows 2m (6'6") high.

Harvest: Pick the fiddleheads in spring from when they are first seen until they are 5-6cm (2-2 1/2") high, when still tightly curled. After this they rapidly get too tough.

Propagation: Plants can be propagated by division of existing clumps or grown from spores, though these are not always available commercially. They are dust-like and difficult to handle, and need to be sown on the surface of a compost that is kept moist and in shade. Division of existing clumps is easy.

Culinary uses

The young fiddleheads are eaten as a cooked vegetable – boil for 15 minutes (not less, as they can occasionally cause stomach upsets if undercooked). The flavour is like a cross between asparagus and broccoli. They have a crisp texture and are often eaten with eggs.

Maintenance and potential problems

No problems or maintenance needed.

Perennial brassicas

See:
Chinese broccoli (*Brassica oleracea* Alboglabra Group);
Perennial broccoli (*Brassica oleracea* Botrytis Group);
Perennial kale (*Brassica oleracea* Ramosa Group);
Perennial wild cabbage (*Brassica oleracea*);
Tree collards (*Brassica oleracea* Acephala Group)

Perennial broccoli
(*Brassica oleracea* Botrytis Group)

Only one variety of this plant appears to be in cultivation, 'Nine Star' (pictured above. The white flowers are lesser stitchwort – also edible and a good interplant). This looks identical to normal broccoli or cauliflower plants, growing 60-90cm (2-3') high and wide. It is a short-lived perennial, living up to 4 or 5 years. It produces small white cauliflower-like heads in summer.

Hardiness zone: 8

Cultivation

Plant out where brassicas have not been grown recently (to avoid club root problems) in a fairly fertile soil, in sun or very light shade.

Varieties: 'Nine Star' (see previous page).

Harvest: Harvest leaves when small throughout the growing season. Cut flower heads in summer.

Propagation: Plants can be grown from seed, which is relatively easily available, and also from cuttings of side shoots taken in spring.

Culinary uses

Leaves are harvested when fairly small and cooked lightly like spring greens. The flower heads are harvested in summer and used like broccoli.

Maintenance and potential problems

Make sure you stop it from going to seed, as this will reduce the life of the plant. Potential problems are all the usual pests of brassicas – moth caterpillars, pigeons, and so on. If you have lots of trouble from these, you may need to net plants for much of the year, or grow in a fruit cage.

If plants are damaged by pests or weather they can be 'coppiced' – cut right back to a stump 15-30cm (6-12") high, from which they will usually resprout and recover.

Perennial kale
(Brassica oleracea Ramosa Group)

Also known as bush kale

This is one of the earliest domesticated forms of *Brassica oleracea*, described in Roman times. It is evergreen and does not flower readily. Plants are bushy and multi-stemmed, often trailing along the ground, rooting as they go, before ascending vertically.

Only one variety appears to be easily available, 'Dorbenton', also known as 'Daubenton' (pictured above). This looks similar to biennial kale (not curly kale), growing 60-90cm (2-3') high and wide. It is a short-lived perennial, living for 4 or 5 years.

Hardiness zone: 8

Cultivation

Cultivation, harvest and propagation are the same as for perennial broccoli (see left).

Varieties: 'Dorbenton' (or 'Daubenton') is the most easily available.

Culinary uses

As for perennial broccoli (see opposite).

Maintenance and potential problems

As for perennial broccoli (see opposite).

Perennial leek

See:
Babington's leek (*Allium ampeloprasum* var. *babingtonii*); Perennial leek (*Allium ampeloprasum*)

Perennial rye
(*Secale montanum*)

Also known as mountain rye; wild rye

Perennial rye originated as a perennial pasture grass from the Mediterranean region, but has been selected by Peters Seed and Research in the USA over a period of many years to yield a grain similar to true rye (*Secale cereale*). It is a tall plant, growing up to 1.5m (5') high.

Hardiness zone: 3

Cultivation

Perennial rye is much more tolerant of low fertility than are annual cereals. In fact, it lives longer on poor soils (7-8 years) than on rich soils (2-4 years). It should be kept well-weeded.

Varieties: One of Peters' varieties is 'Mountaineer', which bears large seeds that are easily threshed from the shatter-resistant heads. Flowering and grain ripening occurs earlier than for any other perennial rye, and it has moderate rust resistance.

Harvest: Harvest grain in July/August. The grain is good for rolling or milling for cereal use.

Propagation: Sow seed into a weed-free seedbed in autumn or spring, or transplant young seedlings. Perennial grain plants can tiller (branch) to form bushy plants and are best thinned to a spacing of 15-30cm (6-12") – with wider spacing, plants will tiller more.

Culinary uses

Use in the same ways as true rye grain. Cook whole (like oat groats), or crush (like rolled oats) then cook, or grind into a flour and use in breads, etc.

Maintenance and potential problems

The main problem with growing perennial grains is that they cast little shade and are thus prone to weed problems. On a garden scale you can keep plants mulched to prevent weeds appearing, but on a field scale tractor-mounted weeders would probably be required to grow the crop organically.

Perennial sweet peas
(*Lathyrus latifolius* & *L. sylvestris*)

Lathyrus latifolius (everlasting pea) and *L. sylvestris* (wood pea – pictured above) are scrambling tendril climbers from Europe. Perennial (and annual) sweet peas are widely used ornamentally for their flowers, but also in sustainable garden systems for their nitrogen-fixing ability.

They can grow 1-3m (3-10') high with a suitable support, but the higher they grow the less bushy they usually are. The flowers of perennial sweet peas are usually smaller than those of the annuals, and they appear in many different colours. Bees love the flowers.

Hardiness zone: 5

Cultivation

Grow in any well-drained soil that is not too acid, in sun or light shade. Perennial sweet peas interplant well with other vigorous perennials – they will clamber up them to get to the light; a useful source of nitrogen.

Varieties: There are no varieties selected for pod production.

Harvest: Pick young pods from summer through to autumn.

Propagation: Raise from seed. Give hot water treatment (scarify – see Chapter 3, page 54) and sow in spring.

Culinary uses

The young peas inside the developing pods in summer are a delicious snack, tasting very much like fresh garden peas. However, these sweet pea seeds should be eaten only in small quantities, as they contain a toxin that can accumulate in the body, and in large amounts can cause serious illness (this has happened only in famine situations).

Maintenance and potential problems

Mice are attracted to seeds sown in the soil, so it is best to raise young plants and transplant them out.

Seed pods of wood pea.

Perennial wall-rocket
(Diplotaxis tenuifolia)

Also known as wild rocket

This is a small, clump-forming perennial of the mustard family, growing 20-30cm (8-12") wide with flowering stems up to 50-60cm (1'8"-2') high, bearing yellow flowers. It has long leaves, sometimes lobed, which are aromatic when crushed. In warm regions, for example in California, it is considered a weed.

Hardiness zone: 5

Cultivation

As the name implies, wall-rocket likes a very well-drained site – you can place seeds in the nooks and crannies of a wall – and indeed is longer-lived on a poor, very stony soil.

Varieties: At least one variety exists, 'Discovery'.

Harvest: Leaves (and flowers) can be harvested at any time; also the stems when young.

Propagation: Grow from seed, either sowing *in situ* or transplanting young seedlings out.

Culinary uses

The leaves are strongly peppery and are usually used in salads, mixed with milder leaves – common in French and Italian cuisine.

Maintenance and potential problems

Few problems. On a rich soil it is not likely to be long-lived.

Perennial wheat
(Triticum aestivum × Thinopyrum intermedium)

Perennial wheat, like perennial rye, has been selected by Peters Seed Research over a period of many years. It is a tall plant, growing up to 1.5m (5') high.

Hardiness zone: 5

Cultivation

Perennial wheat is much more tolerant of low fertility than are annual cereals. In fact it lives longer on poor soils (7-8 years) than on rich soils (2-4 years). Keep well-weeded.

Varieties: One of Peters' varieties is 'PSR 3628'. This is a perennial winter wheat, 1-1.5m (3-5') tall, which has good disease resistence.

Harvest: Harvest grain in July/August.

Propagation: Grow from seed. Sow in autumn into a weed-free seedbed, or transplant young seedlings. Perennial grain plants can tiller (branch) to form bushy plants and are best thinned to a spacing of 30cm (1') between plants – any wider and plants will tiller more.

Culinary uses

Use in the same ways as annual wheat grain – cook whole, crush like rolled oats or grind to a flour and use in bread, cakes, etc.

Maintenance and potential problems

As with any grains, the main problem is that the plants cast little shade and are thus prone to weed problems. On a garden scale you can keep plants mulched, but on a larger scale you would probably need tractor-mounted weeders to grow the crop organically.

Other perennial grains related to perennial wheat include wild triga wheat or intermediate wheatgrass (*Thinopyrum intermedium*) and x *Agrotriticum* (a hybrid of wheat and

wheatgrass – *Agropyron* spp.). Perennial rice is being developed in parts of Asia.

Perpetual spinach & chard
(*Beta vulgaris* subsp. *cicla*)

Perpetual spinach is also known as spinach beet or leaf beet; chard is also known as Swiss chard

These well-known vegetables are usually treated as biennials, but if they are not allowed to flower (pinch the flowering stems out) then they can remain perennial for several years. They remain evergreen where winter temperatures do not fall below about -6°C (21°F).

Perpetual spinach (*Beta vulgaris* subsp. *cicla*) and chard (*B. vulgaris* subsp. *cicla* var. *flavescens* – pictured above) grow around 60cm (2') high and 40cm (1'4") wide, but if allowed to flower, the flowering stems can reach 1.5m (5') high or more. Both have dark green leaves, and chard has thick mid-ribs, normally white but sometimes other colours.

Hardiness zone: 7

Cultivation

Grow in any well-drained soil.

Varieties: There are varieties of chard selected for different-coloured leaf ribs – bright yellow, orange, pink and red.

Harvest: Leaves and stalks are harvested at any time of year.

Propagation: Grow from seed. Seeds can be sown direct, or young plants raised and planted out. Like all the beetroot family, to which these plants belong, each seed contains several kernels, and usually two or three seedlings will emerge. These are normally thinned to a single seedling while still young.

Culinary uses

The leaves and mid-ribs are usually cooked by steaming or stir-frying, or they can be used in layers in bakes and lasagnes.

Maintenance and potential problems

Few problems. Slugs and snails can nibble leaves, especially in wet weather in spring.

Pig nut
(Bunium bulbocastanum)

Also known as earth chestnut; earth nut

Not to be confused with another plant named pignut (*Conopodium majus*), which is better known by foragers, this species may be the same as black cumin (*Bunium persicum*), though that is not clear. The *Bunium* pig nut is a herbaceous perennial growing some 60cm (2') high and wide, with feathery, finely cut foliage and small umbels of white flowers in summer, which attract beneficial insects. It is an altogether more productive plant than *Conopodium* (which has a single, smallish nutty tuber), because all parts of it are edible.

Hardiness zone: 5

Cultivation

Grow in any soil, in sun or light shade.

Varieties: There are no varieties.

Harvest: Harvest leaves and shoots at any time during the growing season; seeds in late summer and autumn; roots in winter.

Propagation: Sow seed in spring.

Culinary uses

The leaves and stems can be harvested as a herb throughout the growing season, and have a lovely flavour similar to parsley – use in bulk quantities.

The ripe seeds are harvested and used as a spice (similar to cumin). The tuberous roots, up to 4cm (15/8") across, are cooked by roasting or boiling and have a flavour like sweet chestnut.

Maintenance and potential problems

This plant is not hugely long-lived: 4-6 years in my experience. Make sure you save some seeds each year to grow new plants if necessary.

Pink purslane
See Siberian purslane
(*Claytonia sibirica*)

Plantains
(*Plantago* spp.)

Plantains are clump-forming perennials, often found in pastures on reasonably well-drained soils, and bear narrow brown seedheads. Buck's horn plantain (*P. coronopus*), ribwort plantain (*P. lanceolata* – pictured above) and greater plantain (*P. major*) are all good plantains for eating.

Buck's horn plantain has quite narrow divided leaves, a little like rocket (*Eruca* spp.) leaves in shape. All plantains grow about 30cm (1') wide and high.

Hardiness zone: 6

Cultivation

Grow in most soils that are not too slow-draining. Buck's horn plantain is a seashore plant and prefers well-drained soils. Give full sun or partial shade.

Buck's horn plantain is lower-growing than the others, which makes it slightly more prone to weed competition, and also often results in the leaves needing washing well to remove soil. The leaves of ribwort plantain are much more upright and cleaner after harvest.

Varieties: There are some ornamental varieties, but none bred for leaf production.

Harvest: Leaves can be harvested from mid-spring onwards through the growing season. Either cut them with scissors or just tear them off near their bases. They will regrow and can be harvested several times in a season. In very dry spells the leaves may become slightly bitter and tougher. The leaves of flowering plants are still tender.

Propagation: This is usually by seed, which can be sown from spring to autumn. If plants are allowed to set seed they will often self-seed. Plantain seed is small and requires some light to germinate, so is best sown on the surface of a seed compost and the seedlings transplanted before planting out. Space them 15-25cm (6-10") apart. Plants can also be established in pastures by oversowing in early spring and preferably rolling to ensure good contact with the soil. They don't usually need thinning even if they come up thickly, as they tolerate overcrowding.

Culinary uses

The leaves are quite fleshy and succulent, and are excellent in mixed salads as a bulk ingredient, as well as good in soups. They are very gentle on the stomach – they contain allantoin, which is soothing.

Maintenance and potential problems

Bear in mind that it may self-seed if there is bare soil nearby.

Poke root
(*Phytolacca americana*)

Also known as pokeweed; poke

This is a very vigorous herbaceous perennial from North America, growing 2-3m (6'6"-10') high or more, and slowly expanding to form colonies. Large green leaves are borne on thick stems which start green, usually turning reddish as the season progresses (though this change does not always occur in cool-summer climates like that of the UK). Clusters of white flowers are followed by deep-purplish fruits.

Poke root is well known in North America as both a wild edible and traditional medicinal plant. The raw plant contains various toxins and great care should be taken when using it – use only the shoots, as described below. The ripe fruits and raw leaves, shoots or stems will cause sickness if eaten. The fruits were formerly used for ink.

Hardiness zone: 4

Cultivation

Grow in any reasonable soil. It tolerates a range of light conditions, from sun to quite deep shade.

The shoots emerge quite late in spring – not usually until late May in the UK – and poke root can be interplanted with lower-growing, shade-tolerant plants quite easily.

Varieties: There are no varieties bred for shoot production.

Harvest: Harvest new shoots soon after they emerge, at about 20cm (8") height – cut off at ground level like asparagus. The shoots can be up to 2.5cm (1") diameter. Do not harvest if the stems are turning pink.

Propagation: Sow seed in spring. Established plants can also be divided.

Culinary uses

The shoots are toxic when raw and must be prepared properly. Place in a pan of cold water, bring to the boil, then discard the water and replace with new boiling water and boil for 10 minutes, then drain and serve. The cooked shoots have a delicious earthy asparagus flavour.

Maintenance and potential problems

Established plants need little care or attention.

Be sure to let children (and adults) know that the fruits are not edible!

Potato
(Solanum tuberosum)

The potato doesn't need much introduction, as most gardeners growing food will have grown it at one time or another, though as an annual. It is of course a tuberous perennial (as you will probably also know from the regrowing tubers you failed to dig up the previous year!). However, it is very difficult to grow potatoes as true perennials unless you are at high altitude (over about 250m/820' in the UK), because of the rapid infection by viral diseases carried by aphids at lower altitudes.

Another problem is that potatoes cultivated out of South America have very little genetic diversity and so are extremely prone to the damaging potato blight disease. There are in fact numerous *Solanum* species that all go under the name of potatoes in the Andean regions of South America, and traditionally many different selections/species would be grown so that if one did succumb to a disease, most would be fine. Other species are gradually being incorporated by potato breeders into commercial varieties to improve disease resistance. In the meantime, most folk will continue to treat the potato as a replant perennial.

We are worried these days about eating 'poisonous' plants, and it amuses me to think that if potatoes were discovered now they too would probably be described as poisonous, because the green tubers can cause sickness when eaten.

Hardiness zone: 7 as a perennial.

Cultivation

Potatoes are usually grown in rows, which are earthed up to increase tuber formation and to exclude light from the tubers, which turns them green and toxic.

Varieties: There are numerous first early, second early and maincrop varieties. Disease resistance breaks down very quickly, which is why potato breeders are constantly releasing new selections. Contact a good seed potato merchant for up-to-date recommendations.

Harvest: Dig tubers from early summer through to autumn, depending on their maturity.

Propagation: Plant tubers in spring, preferably well chitted (i.e. with 2.5cm/1"

sprouts), as they will crop more quickly and you will be more likely to get a good crop growing organically, even if potato blight does strike. Early varieties are planted closer together (30-40cm/1'-1'4" in the row) than later, maincrop varieties (45-60cm/1'6"-2' in the row).

Culinary uses

Every reader will be familiar with the various ways of cooking potatoes.

Maintenance and potential problems

You can save your own seed tubers for one year, but longer than that is not recommended as they will almost certainly be virus-infected by then.

Potato blight is the main disease. There is no organic remedy: basically you need to cut off and remove infected haulms (aerial parts) soon after you see signs of infection (blackened spots and areas at edges of leaves), then wait three weeks before digging up tubers – this gives time for disease spores on the soil to die, and thus reduces the chance of infection during harvest.

Potato bean
See Groundnut (*Apios americana*)

Potato onion
See Multiplier onions (*Allium cepa* Aggregatum Group)

Prickly pears
See Nopale cacti (*Opuntia* spp.)

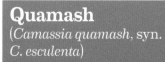

Quamash
(*Camassia quamash*, syn. *C. esculenta*)

Also known as camass

Quamash is a North American bulb with several relatives that are used in the same ways. The bulbs were formerly a crucial staple crop for many native peoples of western North America, who prepared them by steam-baking in huge pits for up to 72 hours! Fortunately there are somewhat faster ways of cooking them, though these still take some time.

Plants grow 80cm (2'8") wide and 20cm (8") high, with long, narrow leaves, and can form large colonies. They are often planted for their blue flowers (though some varieties bear white flowers), which last well as cut flowers. After flowering, plants die down to bulbs for the rest of the year. Most bulbs are about 2.5cm (1") across, though some varieties and species can bear bulbs two or three times this size. The number of bulbs gradually multiplies in time.

Other species include Cusick's camass (*C. cusickii* – large bulbs, hardy to zone 5), large camas (*C. leichtlinii*) and Eastern camass / wild hyacinth (*C. scilloides* – large bulbs, hardy to zone 3).

Hardiness zone: 4

Cultivation

These plants like moist soil that dries out in summer, with good levels of humus, and a position in sun or light shade.

Varieties: Several ornamental varieties exist but none have larger bulbs.

Harvest: You can harvest bulbs sustainably (leaving behind the same amount as originally planted) in the autumn and winter. They store dry for several months.

Propagation: It is easiest to propagate by planting bulbs. Quamash bulbs are best established in grass in the same way as daffodils. (Before harvesting, first cut the surrounding grass low, to make harvest easier.) Buy bulk bulbs from a bulb nursery to establish a reasonable area, and plant at 10cm (4") depth. Alternatively, grow from seed, which requires 3 months of stratification (see Chapter 3, page 54).

Culinary uses

Like Jerusulem artichokes and yacon, the bulbs contain large quantities of inulin, which cannot usually be digested in its raw state. Inulin can increase calcium absorption but also cause flatulence. The long, slow cooking process traditionally used in North America caused the inulin to become digestible.

American experiments have concluded that the best cooking method is by using a pressure cooker and cooking for 9 hours(!), when the bulbs become sweet and soft, with a flavour like winter squash – and do not cause any flatulence. It is possible that (as with Jerusulem artichokes) the inulin levels decrease towards the end of winter, which would mean the cooking time is much reduced.

Maintenance and potential problems

There are few problems. Plants can suffer badly in waterlogged conditions.

Quamash bulbs.

Radicchio
See Chicory (*Cichorium intybus*)

Rakkyo
(*Allium chinense*)

Also known as baker's garlic

This is a perennial bulb growing some 30-40cm (1'-1'4") high, with a clump of vertical leaves arising from bulbs. The leaves are slender and hollow, more sharply angled than those of chives (which it resembles) and bright green.

This species goes dormant from midsummer for a month or two, then starts back into growth and is green over the winter. It flowers in autumn, with striking pinkish-purple or lavender flowers borne on long stalks.

Rakkyo is much grown for its bulbs in China. The bulbs can reach 4-5cm (15/8-2") in diameter and resemble shallots, with reddish-brown skins and pinkish inner flesh.

Hardiness zone: 7

Cultivation

Plant in a well-drained soil in sun or very light shade. It tolerates poor soils.

Varieties: No varieties are available outside China.

Harvest: The bulbs are usually harvested in late summer – the dormant period. The bulbs get larger each year for several years, so it may be worth waiting until clumps are 2-3 years old or more before harvesting some of the bulbs. Flowers are harvested in late summer.

Young bulbs with stems and leaves can be harvested whole.

Propagation: Plant bulbs in spring. Place them singly or in pairs at about 20cm (8") spacing. Rakkyo can also be raised from seed (sown in spring), but this is rarely produced.

Culinary uses

The bulbs have a mild, sweet flavour and are used raw or cooked. The whole plant – bulb, stem and leaves – can be used as a spring onion when young. The bulbs are also widely used for pickling. The flowers are mostly used as a garnish and in salads.

Maintenance and potential problems

As with all alliums, it is wise to rotate plants every now and then to reduce the risk of onion diseases such as white rot becoming established.

Ramps
(Allium tricoccum)

Also known as wild leek

Ramps is the North American version of the European ramsons, or wild garlic (see opposite). It is a shade-tolerant woodland plant which produces broad, smooth, light green leaves in spring, borne on a scallion-like stalk. The leaves, unlike those of ramsons, die down before the flowers emerge on upright stalks – each head holding a cluster of white flowers (similar or slightly smaller in size and number of individual flowers to ramsons). After flowering and producing seed, plants die back completely to a small bulb underground.

Plants grow 15-30cm (6-12") high and wide, often forming vast carpets in their native habitats.

Hardiness zone: 4

Cultivation

Ramps tolerates acid soil.

Varieties: There are no varieties.

Harvest: Harvest leaves and flowers in spring, also with bulbs if required.

Propagation: Sow seed or transplant small bulbs/plants beneath deciduous trees in a moist, humus-rich soil. Plants are likely to self-seed and form colonies over time. Sow seed in autumn or stratify over winter (see Chapter 3, page 54) before sowing in spring.

Culinary uses

Use leaves exactly as with ramsons – the flavour is very similar. If whole plants are lifted to use, then the bulbs too are eaten – used like scallions (spring onions). They go particularly well with eggs.

Maintenance and potential problems

Plants disappear to a bulb by the end of spring, so are best grown in a polyculture with at least one other perennial plant (preferably one that is not early into growth) to maintain a good plant cover over the soil.

Plants are likely to establish colonies over time.

Ramsons
(Allium ursinum)

Also known as wild garlic

Ramsons is a well-known European woodland spring perennial plant, appearing in late winter or early spring, with its broad, mid-green leaves often forming vast carpets of garlic-smelling foliage in native woodlands. White flowers appear on upright stalks in May, and seeds ripen in June. Plants are around 30cm (1') high and wide.

During June the plants die back entirely to an underground bulb and remain dormant right through until the following season.

Hardiness zone: 4

Cultivation

Ramsons likes a humus-rich soil and some shade.

Plants are likely to self-seed and form expanding colonies in time. To limit their expansion you may want to border an area with taller (shade-tolerant) evergreen plants.

Varieties: There are no varieties.

Harvest: Harvest leaves and flowers from late winter through to late spring, with bulbs if desired.

Propagation: Establish your own patch under deciduous trees by either broadcasting seed direct by the autumn, or by transplanting bulbs or young plants – plant at 30cm (1') spacing.

Culinary uses

Leaves, flowers and bulbs all have a strong garlic flavour, though this dissipates quickly during cooking, so add near to the end in a recipe. Ramsons is particularly good with eggs.

Maintenance and potential problems

Plants disappear to a bulb by early summer, so are best grown in a polyculture with at least one other perennial plant (preferably one that is not early into growth) to maintain a good soil cover.

Red valerian
(Centranthus ruber)

Red valerian (not the same as the medicinal valerian) is a deep-rooted European perennial, evergreen in milder regions, which can self-seed in well-drained conditions and in walls. It makes a good ground cover on well-drained sites.

Plants grow 60-100cm (2'-3'3") high by 30cm (1') or more wide, with upright flowering stems bearing deep pinkish-red flowers.

Hardiness zone: 7

Cultivation

This plant does best in well-drained soil but is fine in poor soil. It frequently colonises walls, sometimes causing structural problems. It needs full sun or light shade, and is very drought-tolerant.

Varieties: Several exist, with flowers ranging from pink to red, as well as white.

Harvest: Pick the leaves all season except in long, hot, dry spells. The young shoots can also be picked in spring.

Propagation: Red valerian is easy to grow from seed. Seed can even be sprinkled into small gaps in walls. It's also grown by dividing established plants.

Culinary uses

The leaves and young shoots have a lovely broad bean flavour and can be put in mixed salads or lightly cooked as a vegetable. They can get bitter in long spells of dry weather.

Maintenance and potential problems

The fleshy roots can grow into walls and expand, cracking stones or forcing them apart in time.

Redwood sorrel
(Oxalis oregana)

This low, carpeting perennial from western North America is evergreen in mild areas, spreading via rooting stems. Plants are 20cm (8") high, with instantly recognisable wood-sorrel-type leaves consisting of three heart-shaped leaflets. The flowers are white or pinkish.

The leaves of redwood sorrel are sensitive to light and in full sunlight quickly fold downwards, reopening in shade.

Hardiness zone: 7

Cultivation

Grow in partial or deep shade beneath trees or shrubs, in a moist acid soil.

Varieties: There are a few ornamental varieties.

Harvest: Harvest leaves and shoots at any time during the growing season.

Propagation: Seed is rarely available, so propagate by division.

Culinary uses

Use like the leaves of other sorrels (see page 178): they're especially good either in salads or lightly cooked with mushrooms or fish. As with all sorrels, redwood sorrel contains oxalic acid and so should be eaten only in moderation.

Maintenance and potential problems

It will spread over time.

Rhubarbs
(*Rheum* spp.)

Although in Europe and America rhubarb is known as a 'fruit', it is one of the most common perennial vegetables that people have actually heard of. There are numerous rhubarb species with edible leaf stalks, including those described here. The common garden rhubarb (pictured above, interplanted with lungwort) is designated *Rheum* x *hybridum* or *R.* x *cultorum* and is a hybrid of several species, including Turkish rhubarb.

Rhubarbs are large, sturdy, deep-rooted herbaceous perennials with large leaves. They range from 1m (3') high and wide to over 2.5m (8') high and wide, the height reached by tall, upright, flowering stems. The flowers, often tinged red, are wind-pollinated. Different species have different-flavoured leaf stalks; my favourites are Himalayan rhubarb (*R. australe*; apple-flavoured), and Turkish rhubarb (*R. palmatum*; gooseberry-flavoured). Rhubarb leaves are in fact poisonous, and the stalks are best eaten through spring until only early summer, as the oxalic acid levels in them steadily increase through the growing season.

There is a long history in Asia of rhubarb's use as a vegetable (again, the leaf stalks), particularly in soups and stews.

Hardiness zones: 1-6

Cultivation

Rhubarbs like a humus-rich, fertile soil that is well drained but does not dry out too much, and sun or partial shade. It can be worth incorporating organic matter into the soil before planting.

If plants are harvested heavily, they will need feeding with a nitrogen-rich source to sustain cropping. If you want to maximise leaf stalk production, cut off flowering heads, but this is not essential. Stems can be blanched to make them longer and more tender, by covering to exclude light, e.g. with an upturned pot.

If old plants lose vigour they can be divided (providing material for new plants), which will also reinvigorate them.

Varieties: There are numerous varieties of garden rhubarb. In addition, several of the ornamental types have varieties with different leaf or stem colours.

Harvest: Harvest stalks by pulling rather than cutting: this ensures both the maximum length stalk and also invigorates the roots to produce new shoots (cutting does not have the same effect). Chop off the leaves and compost, or leave on the ground to suppress weeds.

Propagation: Raise from seed or divide established crowns in winter. Rhubarb species hybridise readily and may not come true from seed.

Culinary uses

Rhubarb has many savoury uses, and is particularly good with meat or fish (for example in a sauce with mint), cooked and added to salads, in soups, etc.

In the West it is traditionally used like a fruit, by chopping stalks into short sections and boiling for 5-10 minutes until they soften, then sweetening to taste. The cooked fruit can be added to yoghurts and ice creams, baked in pies, etc. The stalks are also great roasted (add sugar and orange zest, and cover with foil).

The large flower buds can also be eaten cooked, they have a solid consistency and a sour flavour.

Rhubarbs should always be eaten in moderation because of their oxalic acid content.

Maintenance and potential problems
None of either.

Turkish rhubarb.

Rocambole
(*Allium sativum* var. *ophioscorodon*)

Also known as hardneck garlic; serpent garlic

Whereas most garlic grown in the UK is 'softneck' garlic (*Allium sativum*), in many parts of the world a different type is grown, called 'hardneck', of which rocambole is one variety. 'Hardneck' refers to the stiff flowering stems that these types of garlic produce (making them impossible to plait). The flowering stems also often make an amazing complete 360° loop as they grow, and after flowering they do not produce seed but instead produce a head of bulbils – like small cloves – to propagate.

As with softneck garlic, hardneck garlic can be treated as a perennial bulb or as a replant perennial. Note that a second species is sometimes called 'rocambole' – *A. scorodoprasum* – but its more common name is sand leek: it is also edible, with a mild garlic flavour, but is not included here.

Rocambole plants grow about 30cm (1') high until they flower, when the flowering stems can reach 1m (3'3") or more in height.

Hardiness zone: 6

Cultivation

Rocambole is best planted in autumn between October and early December, in ground that is reasonably well drained – it tolerates soils of only average fertility, though needs full sun. It is hardier than softneck garlic. From time to time it is wise to change location entirely, to avoid a build-up of onion diseases.

Varieties: There are many varieties adapted to different regions. In the UK, recommended hardneck garlic varieties include 'Early Wight' and 'Echo'.

Harvest: Allow plants to flower in late spring / early summer – this does not affect bulb formation.

Bulbs are mature when the leaves start to yellow and wilt in July or August. Lifted bulbs should be sun-dried before storage. Rocambole and other hardneck garlics do not generally store as well as softneck garlics. Their stems cannot be plaited like those of softneck garlic, so the tops are best cut off and bulbs stored loose in a net bag.

If bulbs are not harvested, then in time plants will get overcrowded and bulbs will reduce in size. So try to harvest and replant frequently, if not every year.

Harvest leaves from autumn to spring. In spring, the whole plants – green leaves and undivided bulb – can be lifted and used (sometimes called 'baby garlic').

Garlic flower stems of hardneck strains of garlic are a speciality food in China. Bulbs are cultivated in the normal way, the flower stems being cut in early summer when green and the bulbs being left *in situ* to mature.

Propagation: Plant either the daughter bulbs from the base of existing plants, or the small bulbils. Plants from the latter will be quite small in their first year. Plant at about twice the bulbs' own depth, so larger bulbs/cloves should be planted at about a 4cm (15/8") depth and at an average spacing of about 18cm (7") apart. Small bulbils can be initially spaced closer – at about 12cm (5") apart.

For leaf production from autumn through to spring, you can plant bulbs much closer together – 7-10cm (3-4") apart.

Culinary uses

The bulbs are the same as those of softneck garlic and are used in exactly the same ways. The trick to peeling the papery skin off garlic is to press down on a clove with the flat side of a knife, half-crushing it – then the whole papery skin will come off really easily.

The young green leaves are used raw in salads or cooked – in China they are often blanched (placed in boiling water). There are usually usable leaves through mild winters. The flower stems are generally steamed as a side vegetable.

Maintenance and potential problems

White rot of onion can be a serious disease – make sure you start with healthy bulbs and change the location of the garlic bed every 5 years or so.

Rock samphire
(*Crithmum maritimum*)

Rock samphire is a perennial, slightly succulent maritime herb that is found growing on rocks, cliffs, sand and shingle on the upper shoreline around much of the British and European coast.

It grows 15-45cm (6"-1'6") high, often with a woody base. The leaves are greyish-green, fleshy – looking slightly like deer antlers in shape – and very aromatic. It bears yellow flowers in summer. The roots often penetrate deep into cracks in rocks, anchoring plants against strong, turbulent winds and high tides. It is often found naturalised in the dry stone walls of seaside gardens.

This plant was hugely popular in the past, when it was widely harvested, often by people abseiling precariously down cliffs to gather the harder-to-reach specimens. In fact the demand often exceeded supply, leading to supplies being adulterated with both golden samphire (*Inula crithmoides*) and marsh samphire (*Salicornia* spp.)

Whereas marsh samphire will grow only in a salt marsh – and most people don't have one of these – rock samphire can be cultivated on walls, rockeries and flat roofs.

Hardiness zone: 7

Cultivation

Rock samphire needs very good drainage but also a moist substrate and saline conditions. It can be cultivated in walls – preferably dry stone – or in artificial sand/shingle mounds. It prefers a south- or east-facing site, with some shade from the midday sun. Mulch regularly with fresh seaweed or use seaweed meal (dried seaweed) to maintain saline conditions.

Varieties: There are no varieties.

Harvest: Leaves and young shoots are harvested mainly from April to August. In hard winters the tops die back, but in mild winters there may be leaves to use all year.

Propagation: Sow seed in spring or autumn, or divide existing plants. The seeds are quite large and can be poked directly into holes.

Culinary uses

The leaves and young shoots are lemon-flavoured and very aromatic. They can be added to salads or (as traditionally) pickled. The leaves are high in omega-3 oils.

Blanch or lightly steam the leaves for use as an aromatic vegetable with butter or oil, or chop and add to potatoes, sauces, soups or pasta dishes.

Maintenance and potential problems

Rock samphire is quite tricky to grow away from maritime locations.

Rosebay willowherb
(Epilobium angustifolium)

Also known as fireweed

A well-known plant that is usually regarded as a weed, rosebay willowherb (better known in America as fireweed) is a robust herbaceous perennial which spreads via rhizomes to form large clumps. It is widespread on waste ground and, as the name suggests, after fires.

The plant grows 1-2m (3'3"-6'6") high, and has distinctive bright pink flowers.

Many other willowherbs can be used in the same ways, including broad-leaved willowherb (*E. montanum*) – the willowherb most gardeners know as a weed – and hoary willowherb (*E. parviflorum*).

Hardiness zone: 3

Cultivation

Rosebay willowherb – indeed all willowherbs – will succeed in many soils and situations.

Varieties: There are a few ornamental varieties, with different flower colours.

Harvest: Pick leaves and young shoots in spring; the shoots when they are 20-30cm (8-12") long.

Propagation: It is easy to grow from seed, sown in spring.

Culinary uses

The young shoots are cooked like asparagus, which they slightly resemble in flavour, and make a good spring vegetable. The young leaves and the flowers are good salad ingredients. The shoots are excellent pickled. Later in the season the stem pith is cucumber-flavoured and makes a tasty nibble.

There is some evidence that rosebay and hoary willowherbs have anti-prostate-cancer properties.

Maintenance and potential problems

All willowherbs have the potential to spread and become weedy. You may want to stop them setting seed to minimise the spread.

Runner bean
(Phaseolus coccineus)

The runner bean is a well-known vegetable that most folk grow as an annual. In its native habitat it is in fact perennial, though to be grown in the UK (apart from in the very mildest parts) it has to be treated as a replant perennial.

The plants are twining climbers and can reach 3-4m (10-13') high during the course of a growing season (there are also dwarf varieties, but these have little advantage unless you are on a very exposed site). Red or white flowers are followed by the familiar pods. Being legumes, they are nitrogen-fixing.

Hardiness zone: 9

Cultivation

Runner beans do not need particularly fertile soil as they have their own source of nitrogen via their nitrogen-fixing ability. They do like a moist but well-drained soil and sun or slight shade – like most climbers they expect to start life in some shade and climb/clamber up shrubs or trees to get to more light.

To maintain plants as perennials, dig up the underground tuberous roots at the first frosts and store in frost-free, well-drained conditions in sand or a similar medium. Replant out in the spring, a couple of weeks before you expect the latest frosts, and they will soon grow rapidly, flowering and fruiting much more quickly than annual-grown plants.

Varieties: There are numerous varieties, all of which can be grown this way.

Harvest: Harvest pods from summer and through autumn. Dry seed can be harvested in autumn.

Propagation: Initially grow from seed, sowing in mid- or late spring.

Culinary uses

Younger pods can be cooked whole (or sometimes shredded if older), or older pods can be shelled and the seeds extracted to use fresh or to dry for winter use.

Maintenance and potential problems

Slugs and snails can attack young foliage, so take precautions as necessary. Older plants are untroubled by pests.

Salad burnet
(*Sanguisorba minor*, syn. *Poterium sanguisorba*)

Salad burnet is a herbaceous, clump-forming perennial, forming a low rosette of long leaves with many leaflets. It is found in the wild in grassland, and can grow to 50cm (1'8") high when flowering and about 30cm (1') or more wide. It is deep-rooted and a good mineral accumulator.

It was widely grown as an edible garden plant up until the mid-nineteenth century.

Great burnet (*S. officinalis*) is taller and also good to eat.

Hardiness zone: 5

Cultivation

Salad burnet grows in any moist soil; in dry sites the leaf quality declines.

Varieties: There are no varieties.

Harvest: Harvest leaves at any time during the growing season. Do not take more than one-third of the leaves from each plant, otherwise they will be set back too much.

Propagation: Raise from seed or divide plants in spring.

Culinary uses

The tender young leaves are a good salad ingredient. They have a delicate, cucumber-like flavour. Older leaves can be eaten cooked, in soups, stews and so on. Add to dishes at the last minute to avoid losing flavour through overcooking. It is very good with beans.

Maintenance and potential problems

None of either.

Saltbushes
(*Atriplex halimus* & *A. canescens*)

Saltbush (*A. halimus* – pictured above) and four-wing saltbush (*A. canescens*) are evergreen grey-leaved shrubs from open, sunny places – saltbush comes from the Mediterranean and four-wing saltbush from the American prairies. The Mediterranean species is slightly less hardy; both shrubs grow some 1.5-2m (5'-6'6") high and wide in the UK.

Hardiness zones: 7-8

Cultivation

Saltbushes like full sun and a well-drained soil and prefer soils of low to moderate fertility. They are more likely to die in British winters from waterlogged soil than from sheer cold temperatures. If your soil is not well drained, construct a mound, incorporating sand/gravel, etc. to make it really well drained, and plant on the top.

In their early years you may want to protect plants with fleece in very cold winter spells.

Varieties: There are no varieties.

Harvest: Leaves can be harvested all year round, but mainly in the growing season when the bushes are putting on vigorous growth. Cut off new shoots and strip the leaves to use. It is better not to leave stripped branches on the bushes as they can be susceptible to disease.

Propagation: The plants are easy to grow from seed. Cuttings – semi-ripe and hardwood – can also both succeed. Wait until plants are a few years old before planting them out.

Culinary uses

The leaves are slightly salty and make a good addition to salads. They can also be lightly cooked – just steam for a few minutes. Those of saltbush are better quality than those of four-wing saltbush, whose leaves can be bitter at times.

Maintenance and potential problems

It might be wise to take a few cuttings each year in case of a hard winter damaging or killing the mother plant. The cold winters in 2009 and 2010 killed my saltbushes, but I have young ones growing to take their place!

Scallion
See Welsh onion, scallion & bunching onion (*Allium fistulosum*)

Scorzonera
(*Scorzonera hispanica*)

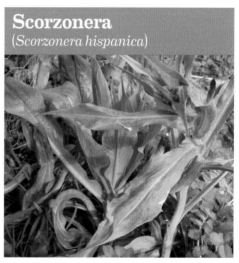

Scorzonera is one of those perennial vegetables that many gardeners have heard of, and seen in seed catalogues, but few have grown. It is always marketed as a root vegetable (though rarely as a perennial), but it is in fact a very good leaf vegetable too.

It is a herbaceous perennial with long, linear leaves and a flowering stalk that can reach 1m (3') high or more. The flowers are bright yellow, looking like oversized dandelions. Plants develop long, black taproots with white flesh inside.

Hardiness zone: 4

Cultivation

Plants prefer a well-drained soil and sun or light shade.

Varieties: There are a number of commercial varieties, all bred for root production.

'Black Giant Russian' – a popular European variety producing long, large roots.
'Duplex' – bears cylindrical roots 20-25cm (8-10") long, blunt-ended, easy to dig.
'Flandria' – uniform cylindrical roots.
'Long John' – uniform, thick, smooth roots.
'Maxima' – heavy cropping with good-sized roots. Slow to flower.

Harvest: If roots are to be harvested, this is done in autumn or winter. The roots get larger in plants of 2 years old or more, and the quality does not decline with age. Harvesting roots does of course kill the plant. The long roots are somewhat prone to snapping, so dig with care!

Leaves are harvested mainly in spring; they can still be harvested later in the growing season, but they won't be as tender. In mild winters, leaves can be available well into winter. Flowers are harvested in late spring / early summer.

Propagation: Establish new plants by sowing seed, which germinates quickly.

Root crops are best sown directly outside and thinned to about 12cm (5") spacing each way. Crops for leaf production can be started inside and small plants transplanted out in spring.

Culinary uses

Use the long roots like other root vegetables – cook by boiling, frying or baking. They have a mild but pleasant flavour and go well with meat or fish, or served on their own as a vegetable with a sauce. The roots, like Jerusulem artichokes, contain inulin, so can cause flatulence if you are not used to them.

Fresh roots bleed easily. It is not always necessary to peel them, but they are easier to peel if you cook them first.

Use the younger leaves and the flowers in salads – they taste like lettuce and have a juicy crunch to them. Older leaves can be lightly cooked as a green vegetables or added to soups and stews.

Maintenance and potential problems

There are no major pests or diseases.

Scorzonera roots.

Sea beet
(Beta vulgaris subsp. *maritima)*

Well known as the parent of beetroot, chard, perpetual spinach, mangel (or mangelwurzel) and sugar beet, sea beet is a perennial (though occasionally annual and biennial forms are found) from the cliffs and seashores of Europe and western Asia. It is a bushy plant, growing around 50cm (1'8") high, but flower heads can be twice that height. It often remains evergreen in winter.

Hardiness zone: 5

Cultivation

Plant out at a spacing of about 30cm (1'). Plants grown in reasonable garden soils are often larger and more productive than the plants seen growing in impoverished conditions by the sea. Good drainage is the most important requirement – sea beet does not like winter waterlogging. Give sun or partial shade.

Varieties: There are no varieties.

Harvest: Harvest leaves from spring through to late autumn or even into winter if mild, and young shoots in spring. If you want to maximise leaf production, plants should not be allowed to flower – pinch out the flower shoots as they form.

Propagation: Sow seed in spring. As with beetroot and chard, each 'seed' actually contains two or three kernels and gives rise to several seedlings, which are best thinned to the strongest one.

Culinary uses

Use as for spinach or chard, lightly steamed or boiled, either as a vegetable on its own or in other dishes.

Like many plants, sea beet contains oxalic acid, but in very low amounts.

Maintenance and potential problems

None of either.

Sea kale
(Crambe maritima)

A fairly well-known plant found wild on the shoreline of shingle beaches around the UK and Europe, sea kale is part of the brassica family and looks like a large silvery-grey cabbage. It forms a clumping herbaceous perennial some 80cm (2'8") high and 60cm (2') wide.

The leaves are similarly shaped to many other brassica leaves, though with a purplish tinge, and as they grow they quickly become quite tough. The flowers, in summer, are white.

Hardiness zone: 4

Cultivation

Sea kale needs a well-drained but fairly fertile soil and full sun. Like most brassicas, it does not like too acid a soil. It is quite long-lived. Traditionally, shoots are blanched in spring by covering them with a deep container or other cover.

Varieties: There are several seed-raised varieties, though only the following two are common. Sea kale plant characteristics are always quite variable from seed.

'Angers' – productive cloned selection, propagated by root cuttings.
'Lily White' – has less purple colouration.

Harvest: Harvest young leaves in spring, blanched shoots in spring, flower heads (unopened to fully opened) in late spring, flowers in midsummer and roots in winter.

To harvest roots you'll need to dig much of the plant up of course – harvest the outer roots and leave the main taproot to regrow. The roots can be stored in moist sand for several months.

Propagation: This can be done by either seed, division or root cuttings.

Sow seed in spring – the seeds appear large but in fact they are fruits containing individual seeds. You can extract the seeds by hand for faster germination (take care not to crush them!). Each fruit is corky, floats and is impervious to seawater – an excellent propagation strategy for the plant. Germination is slow and erratic because of this. Plants take about 3 years to reach full size from seed.

Divide existing plants in spring, separating multi-crowned plants into singles.

Take root cuttings (known as 'thongs') from existing plants in winter. Plants take 2 years to reach full size from thongs.

Culinary uses

Young leaves can be used raw in salads or lightly steamed – they have a mild, cabbage-like flavour.

The blanched shoots are tender with an asparagus/hazel-like flavour.

The delicious unopened flower heads are treated like (and taste like) broccoli, and can be eaten raw or cooked. The opened flower heads have a distinct honey-like smell and flavour and are eaten raw in salads or with fish or meat. Later on, the individual white flowers (about 1cm/3/8" across) can be scattered into salads.

The fleshy roots are rich in starch and are best eaten cooked (roasted or boiled), which makes them much more digestible.

Maintenance and potential problems

Sea kale can suffer from all the usual pests and diseases, but not nearly as badly as most brassicas.

Serpent garlic
See Rocambole (*Allium sativum* var. *ophioscorodon*)

Shallots
See Multiplier onions (*Allium cepa* Aggregatum Group)

Shuttlecock fern
See Ostrich fern (*Matteuccia struthiopteris*)

Siberian pea tree
(*Caragana arborescens*)

Siberian pea tree is a very hardy woody legume originating from north-eastern Asia, which in the UK makes a shrub 2-3m (6'6"-10') high, but in warmer climes it can reach twice that height. It bears yellow flowers in spring – loved by bees – which are followed by green pods up to 5cm (2") long, each containing a number of seeds. It is sometimes grown as a fodder crop for chickens and other poultry.

Hardiness zone: 2

Cultivation

Siberian pea tree, like other *Caragana* species, needs a position in full sun and a reasonably well-drained soil that is not too acid. It prefers a continental climate with hot summers, and is slower-growing in a temperate climate. It is very tolerant of wind exposure.

Varieties: None are specifically bred for pod production.

Harvest: Pick young pods from July onwards when ready. Green seeds can be harvested in summer and ripe seeds for storing in late summer.

Propagation: Sow seed in spring. The seed needs scarification – pour almost-boiling water on it and allow to stand for 12-24 hours before sowing. You'll have to wait 3-5 years until it starts to flower.

Cuttings taken in midsummer, with rooting hormone, can be very successful.

Culinary uses

The young whole pods can be eaten raw or cooked – they taste like young pea pods. When older they become tough.

The seeds are also edible – raw or cooked – when they are still fairly young. The ripe seeds can be stored, then soaked overnight before cooking (boil for 15-20 minutes) like other pea and bean seeds. They can also be sprouted.

Maintenance and potential problems

Young plants are susceptible to slug and snail damage to leaves, so take suitable precautions. Older plants have no problems at all.

Siberian purslane

(*Claytonia sibirica*, syn. *Montia sibirica*)

Also known as pink purslane

This is an Asian perennial from shady, moist sites, which is naturalised in many parts of Europe, including the UK. In mild winters here it remains evergreen; in cooler climes it becomes dormant in winter, surviving as an underground tuber. It also dies back to the tuber in very dry summers.

Plants grow 20-30cm (8-12") high and wide, often self-seeding, especially in shady locations, to form an extensive ground-covering layer. They produce a series of pairs of dark green leaves on long, fleshy

stems. Pale pinkish-white flowers are borne through the spring.

A number of related species, including the American spring beauties *C. caroliniana* and *C. virginiana*, can be used similarly.

Hardiness zone: 7

Cultivation

Grow in any reasonably moist soil, in partial or full shade. In full sun it becomes rather susceptible to weed problems.

Varieties: There are no varieties.

Harvest: Harvest leaves and stems (with flowers if present) at any time of year.

Propagation: Sow seed, or dig up excess self-seeded seedlings, in spring.

Culinary uses

The leaves and long leaf stalks are succulent and are excellent in salads or lightly cooked as a vegetable, with a distinctly beetroot-type flavour. The tubers can also be eaten cooked but are quite small and fiddly.

Maintenance and potential problems

None of either.

Silverbell tree
See Snowbell tree (*Halesia carolina*)

Silverweed
(*Potentilla anserina*)

Silverweed is a low-growing, creeping herbaceous perennial, spreading vigorously via running roots – it is sometimes regarded as a nuisance weed! It was formerly cultivated for its starchy roots in Scotland and served as a staple for many hunter-gatherer peoples.

Plants grow up to 30cm (1') high and spread widely. The leaves are distinctively pale and silvery on the backs, and the flowers are golden-yellow. Each plant produces one to six deep storage roots (pictured overleaf) – as opposed to the thin horizontal running roots near the soil surface – each 15-30cm (6-12") long and 3-7mm (1/8-1/4") across.

Hardiness zone: 5

Cultivation

Grow in any reasonable soil, though light soils are easiest to harvest the roots from. The plants need full sun or light shade. They tolerate some foot traffic.

Varieties: There are one or two ornamantal varieties, which are less productive than the species.

Harvest: Harvest young shoots in spring; harvest storage roots in the dormant season. They grow at a depth of 10-15cm (4-6") and can be lifted and stored in a damp medium over the winter. Plants cultivated in fertile soils yield larger roots.

Propagation: Sow seed in spring or (easiest) divide existing plants at any time – all small pieces of root will grow.

Culinary uses

The young shoots are good in salads or can be added to soups and stews. The leaves are used in herb teas.

The storage roots, though thin, are crisp and starchy, containing more starch per weight than potatoes. Eat raw or cooked by boiling (15-20 minutes), roasting (30-40 minutes), etc. The flavour is like a nutty potato. The roots can be dried and stored quite easily, and were formerly dried and ground into a flour to be used for baking and as a thickener.

Maintenance and potential problems

The only maintenance likely to be needed is stopping it going where you don't want it: if it does, just dig up roots along the border.

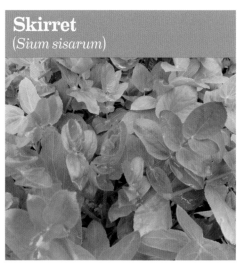

Skirret
(Sium sisarum)

Skirret is a clump-forming, European herbaceous perennial, formerly much grown in vegetable plots for its sweet, edible, bright white roots. It is an umbellifer, found growing in northern Europe and Asia near wild celery, and looks a little like parsnip above ground.

The plants are low and bushy in early spring, some 30cm (1') high and wide, though in late spring they put up flowering stems which can reach 1.2m (4') high.

Hardiness zone: 4

Silverweed roots are starchy.

Cultivation

Skirret prefers a moist, deep, fertile soil but is generally fine in any reasonable soil that does not dry out too much. It needs sun or light shade. Plants appreciate an organic mulch.

Varieties: There are no varieties.

Harvest: From early autumn and through winter, dig the roots of plants that are 2 or more years old – they do not get woody with age. The roots appear like a cluster of finger-thick white parsnips, and get sweeter after frosts. Like other root vegetables, they can be stored in moist sand or similar, or in a root clamp over winter.

Propagation: You can raise plants from seed, which germinates over a period of a few weeks – if you sow *in situ* in the soil, then cover seeds until they germinate, to prevent weed competition causing problems. Sow in drills 15cm (6") apart, thinning plants out to 6cm (2^1/$_2$") within rows. Alternatively, you can sow in a seed tray and pot up seedlings into deep containers such as Rootrainers. The roots do not suffer on transplanting.

Established plants can be easily propagated by division, pulling apart quite readily in spring, once they have started to shoot. Seedlings are quite variable, so any exceptional individuals should be divided and grown on to improve your own stock, especially as there are no improved varieties available to buy.

Skirret roots.

Culinary uses

The finger-sized roots are eaten cooked – boiled or roasted, etc. The flavour resembles a mixture of carrot and liquorice.

In dry sites the core of the roots can become woody; however, the roots can still be cooked and the outer layer stripped off when eaten.

Maintenance and potential problems

Plants may need feeding to remain productive. The roots can become woody after a long dry period if plants are not watered, so irrigation may be necessary at times. The flowers attract beneficial insects.

Snowbell tree
(Halesia carolina)

Also known as silverbell tree

This is a slow-growing, small, bushy deciduous tree from North America, little known in Europe. It grows to 3-4m (10-13') high and wide in time, though is easily kept smaller with some pruning. My 16-year-old trees are about 2m (6'6") high.

The snowbell tree is very ornamental in flower in spring, when it is covered with white bell-shaped flowers. After pollination by bees, these are followed by light green four-winged fruits – these are cropped when they are still young. They grow up to 3cm (1⅛") long.

Hardiness zone: 5

Cultivation

It prefers a fairly sunny situation, but is otherwise tolerant of most soils and situations.

Varieties: 'Wedding Bells' is a smaller, more bushy form, which flowers and fruits prolifically.

Harvest: The young green fruits (seeds), borne profusely, are harvested for 3-4 weeks during June and July, after which they get too tough to eat.

Propagation: Snowbell tree can be raised from seed, which needs 3-4 months of cold stratification (see Chapter 3, page 54) before sowing in spring. Trees will start flowering and fruiting after about 4 years.

Cuttings can also be taken, in early to midsummer, with good success.

Culinary uses

The young green fruits have a cucumber/pea flavour and a great crunchy, juicy texture. They are excellent raw in salads, used to make pickles, cooked briefly in stir-fries and so on.

The flowers can also be used in salads.

Maintenance and potential problems

No maintenance, unless you want to prune the trees to keep them small.

Softneck garlic
See Garlic *(Allium sativum)*

Solomon's seals
(*Polygonatum* spp.)

This is a group of well-known garden plants, usually grown for their pale creamy flowers in spring. They are hardy herbaceous perennials, growing 60cm-2m (2'-6'6") high, gradually spreading via thick creeping rhizomes to form colonies.

All species can be used similarly and include giant Solomon's seal (*P. commutatum*, syn. *P. biflorum* – pictured above), garden Solomon's seal (*P. x hybridum*), common Solomon's seal (*P. multiflorum*), angular Solomon's seal (*P. odoratum*) and whorled Solomon's seal (*P. verticillatum*).

Plants put up new shoots in early spring: the first flush of shoots is the vegetable crop, particularly useful at this time of year.

Hardiness zones: 3-6

Cultivation

Solomon's seals are woodland perennials and like a humus-rich soil in partial or complete shade, though they will tolerate some sun and form a thicker colony in bright conditions. They tolerate acid soils.

Varieties: There are a few ornamental forms with different leaf colours. Variegated forms will be less productive.

Harvest: Cut young shoots in spring when 20-30cm (8-12") high – if the leaves have started to emerge you'll need to cut them off, as they are tough and sometimes bitter. The taller species tend to have thicker shoots and so supply more edible material. Cut only the first flush of shoots, allowing plants to recover and grow normally from the replacement shoots that follow.

Propagation: Solomon's seals are tricky to grow from seed, which is very slow to germinate. It's better to start with plants, which can then be divided easily to produce more plants.

Culinary uses

Treat like asparagus – just cook lightly by steaming, for example, and serve as a vegetable with butter or oil. The flavour is rather like sweet asparagus.

New shoots of common Solomon's seal, ready to harvest.

Maintenance and potential problems

Watch out for slug and snail damage to young plants – established plants are usually fine.

To minimise weed problems, either mulch over the winter with a loose organic mulch or interplant with a low-growing perennial such as wild strawberry or false strawberry.

Sorrels
(*Rumex* spp.)

The *Rumex* genus contains many species, including the docks (usually regarded as weeds) as well as sorrels. Many dock leaves are also edible, usually cooked (for example, layered in lasagne), but their quality never quite equals that of the sorrels.

Sorrel species include garden sorrel (*R. acetosa*), sheep's sorrel (*R. acetosella* – pictured above), monk's rhubarb (*R. alpinus*), herb patience (*R. patientia*), red sorrel / red-veined dock (*R. sanguineus*) and French sorrel (*R. scutatus*).

Sorrels, like docks, are deep-rooted perennials, most forming a robust clump some 40cm (1'4") high – higher when flowering – with long, dock-like leaves, though sheep's sorrel and French sorrel have much smaller leaves and trail low over the soil. Most sorrels are herbaceous, though some varieties of garden sorrel, e.g. 'Schavel', maintain a green rosette of leaves over winter in regions where snow cover is sparse.

Sorrels are all excellent mineral accumulators, especially of potassium and phosphorus.

Hardiness zone: 5

Cultivation

Sorrels are easy to cultivate in any soil. They like a position in sun or light shade. Sheep's sorrel can spread quite fast, with rooting stems as well as seeding plants.

Varieties: There are a few varieties of garden sorrel selected for higher leaf production and sometimes lack of flowering. 'Schavel' does flower but 'Profusion' does not (useful if you don't want any self-seeding). 'Blonde de Lyon' and 'Large de Belleville' (broad-leaved) are commonly grown in France.

Harvest: Leaves can be harvested at any time in the season, though the main time is in spring.

Propagation: Sorrel is usually propagated by seed, sown in spring. The seeds germinate quickly. Plants are also easy to divide.

Culinary uses

The leaves are lemony, due to oxalic acid – they are fine to eat but should be eaten in moderation (i.e. not sorrel soup every day!) as too much oxalic acid is not good for the health. Use raw in salads, cooked in soups and stews, or layered in baked dishes such as lasagne. The leaves are high in minerals.

Maintenance and potential problems

Few problems are encountered. If you are cultivating any soil near sorrel plants, you might want to prevent them from self-seeding.

Spinach beet
See Perpetual spinach
(*Beta vulgaris* subsp. *cicla*)

Stinging nettle
(*Urtica dioica*)

The nettle needs little introduction to most folk! Usually regarded as a weed, it is a potentially tall-growing, spreading perennial, reaching up to 2m (6'6") high and spreading via shallow rhizomes. Nettles are mostly herbaceous but in mild locations can stay green in winter. They are well known for the stinging hairs on the stems and leaves, which can cause nettle rash.

Nettles are high in nitrogen, and large nettle plants indicate soil of high fertility. They support many beneficial insects and should be encouraged – perhaps at an edge or corner of your garden rather than in the middle of other cultivated plants!

Hardiness zone: 4

Cultivation

Nettles grow in most soils and situations, though get less vigorous with increasing shade.

Varieties: There are no varieties.

Harvest: Leaves and young shoots are usually harvested in spring. Use gloves to harvest, or, if you are feeling adventurous, use bare hands: grab the stalks/leaves really firmly and they won't sting.

Propagation: I suppose division would be easiest – just dig some up from an existing nettle patch if you must!

Culinary uses

Well known as a spring wild edible, nettle greens are cooked – steamed, stir-fried, made into soup and so on.

Maintenance and potential problems

Nettles in the garden may well need some controlling. Pulling out stems in late spring is quite a successful way of setting plants back (it may need to be done a few times to get rid of them). You might also want to stop plants seeding by cutting off seedheads before they ripen.

Strawberries
(*Fragaria* spp.)

Strawberries are included here not because of their fruits, but because the leaves of all species can also be eaten. There are many species of strawberry (the cultivated strawberry being a hybrid of several), including:
cultivated strawberry (*F.* x *ananassa*);
Chilean or beach strawberry (*F. chiloensis*);
musk strawberry (*F. moschata*) – hardy to zone 6;
Himalayan strawberry (*F. nubicola*);
wild or woodland strawberry (*F. vesca*) – pictured above;
alpine strawberry (*F. vesca* 'Semperflorens');
green strawberry (*F. viridis*);
American strawberry / scarlet strawberry (*F. virginiana*) – hardy to zone 3.

Cultivated strawberries have been bred as upright plants, to help keep fruit well off the ground, and can reach 40cm (1'4") high,

whereas all the other species listed here are more 'wild' in character and grow close to the ground, around 20cm (8") high, making a better weed-suppressing cover. Some, notably wild strawberry and green strawberry, are evergreen in mild winter locations.

All species apart from alpine strawberries produce overground runners – long, trailing stems that root at intervals where they touch the ground – and spread. I find this habit mostly very useful and have strawberries as an 'under layer' beneath other, larger, perennials, to provide soil cover and keep weeds down.

On all species the white flowers are bee-pollinated and followed by the familiar red fruits; smaller on wild species but often with a more intense flavour.

Hardiness zones: 3-6

Cultivation
Strawberries are fine in most soils, though they don't like really wet soils. They are tolerant of quite a lot of shade, though won't fruit as well in shade.

Varieties: There are fruiting and ornamental varieties, but none selected for leaf production.

Harvest: For leaf production, plants can be cropped at any time of the growing season, though leaves may get tough on plants in sun in summer dry spells.

Propagation: Sow seed in late winter and allow to experience a little cold before warm spring temperatures. It's also easy to separate plants that have propagated naturally on runners.

Culinary uses

Add the leaves to salads or to soups and stews. They have a mild flavour.

Maintenance and potential problems

Strawberries' spreading habit is sometimes regarded as weedy, and there may be places where you have to control their spread by cutting off runners before they can root, or by detaching rooted runners.

Sunchoke
See Jerusulem artichoke
(*Helianthus tuberosus*)

Swamp potato
See Arrowheads (*Sagittaria* spp.)

Sweet cicely
(*Myrrhis odorata*)

One of my favourites of the umbellifer family, sweet cicely is an essential herb/vegetable with a mild flavour and suitable for using in bulk – I would never be without! It is a clump-forming herbaceous perennial, 60cm-1m (2-3') high by 40cm (1'4") wide. Plants are deep-rooted, with white taproots that look like parsnips. Flowering shoots bear heads of white flowers, which are followed by the long, narrow seeds; green when young but maturing deep brown.

There are many umbellifers with similar-looking leaves, some edible and some highly poisonous. However, sweet cicely is the only one with all parts having a strong anise flavour and aroma, so there should be no cause for misidentification of wild plants.

Note: In North America the name 'sweet cicely' is also applied to the species *Osmorhiza longistylis*, which is used in similar ways.

Hardiness zone: 5

Cultivation

Sweet cicely grows in any reasonably well-drained soil in sun or moderate shade.

Varieties: There are no varieties bred for leaf or seed production.

Harvest: Harvest fresh-looking leaves and young shoots throughout the season (new fresh leaves are usually produced in summer after the initial spring leaves get a bit tatty), green seeds in late spring over a period of a few weeks, and roots in winter. The roots can be lifted and stored in sand or in a root clamp like other root crops.

Propagation: It is easy to grow from seed – though it took me years to discover the secret of getting sweet cicely seed to germinate. Basically, the seed needs 5 months of winter cold (stratification) first (see Chapter 3, page 54). Give it less than this (we always have less here in Devon) and it will not sprout. This is why the plant is so much more common further north in the UK. After it has had 5 months of cold, damp conditions, the seed germinates immediately, even in the cold – so if you are stratifying seed in a fridge, make sure you check after 5 months, otherwise you'll have a fridge full of seedlings!

You can also propagate from root cuttings.

Culinary uses

All parts have an excellent anise flavour. Use the leaves and young stems chopped in salads, or added to soups and stews. Use the young green seeds as a spice or just as a snack. Use the roots like other root crops, raw (e.g. grated) or cooked.

Traditionally in the UK, the leaves and stems are cooked with acid fruits (such as redcurrants and rhubarb) – they have a sweetening effect and allow you to halve the amount of sugar used.

Sweet cicely is much esteemed in some culinary cultures as a synergist, i.e. it enhances the flavours of whatever it is cooked with.

Maintenance and potential problems

Rabbits and deer like to eat the young plants, so take protective measures. It hardly ever self-seeds here in the south of England, but further north in the UK and Europe self-seeding can be prolific.

Sweet coltsfoot
See Giant butterbur (*Petasites japonicus*)

Sweet peas, perennial
See Perennial sweet peas (*Lathyrus latifolius & L. sylvestris*)

Sweet potato
(*Ipomoea batatas*)

Sweet potato has a long history in tropical and subtropical regions of the world, notably South America, New Zealand, Polynesia and East Asia. In the last couple of decades, selection work has meant that there are now varieties suitable for cooler climates, where it is grown as a replant perennial. Note that in North America sweet potatoes are sometimes called yams (true yams are *Dioscorea* species).

These vigorous herbaceous vines grow as trailing plants, with stems that reach 1.5m (5') long but do not climb.

Hardiness zone: 9

Cultivation

Even the varieties bred for colder climates need protection for some of the growing season, by using cloches, polythene hoops, coldframes or even by growing in a polytunnel. Sweet potatoes need a reasonably fertile soil and full sun, with a moist but well-drained soil – in dry weather they will need watering to maintain good yields. Too much fertility will encourage leaf production rather than tubers.

Although well known as a tuber crop, in fact sweet potato is grown in many parts of the world either solely or additionally as a leaf crop – the leaves are high in protein. Not all varieties have good leaf flavour.

Varieties: There are a number of varieties suitable for cool regions:

'Beauregard' – orange skin and flesh with long, large tubers, good flavour.
'Georgia Jet' – deep orange flesh, good flavour. Productive and reliable.
'O'Henry' – A compact variety with tubers in a tight cluster beneath the plant. Particularly suitable for container growing.
'T65' – tubers with red-tinted skin and cream-coloured flesh, good flavour. Reliable and vigorous.

Harvest: Harvest tubers as soon as they are large enough – usually leave as late as possible in autumn until cold weather has killed the foliage. Lift the tubers – they will store in the ground only in very mild winter regions. Before storing, the tubers need curing by experiencing about a week at 25°C (77°F) – perhaps in an airing cupboard. Then store at about 14°C (57°F) – in a cool, dry place somewhere in your house. They easily suffer from cold damage and should not be stored in a fridge.

Leaves and young shoots can be harvested at any time during the growing season.

Propagation: Establish by planting tubers, or cuttings of tubers called 'slips'. Plant direct into the soil when the soil is warm (you could pre-warm it with a cloche) or start plants off in pots and transplant them out. Do not use a sheet mulch, because tubers are formed where the trailing stems make contact with the ground.

You can propagate your own slips from tubers by planting tubers in pots in spring in the warmth, and treating the shoots that emerge as cuttings, detaching them at 10-12cm (4-5") in length and potting up in a well-drained compost. These grow to form the slips.

Plant the slips, now with 10-15cm (4-6") shoots, on ridges 30-40cm (1'-1'4") apart, with plants at 25-30cm (10-12") apart along the ridge. The ridges encourage tuber development.

Culinary uses

Use sweet potatoes in the same ways as ordinary potatoes – though they are sweeter (no surprise there then). They are high in dry matter and can be mashed or made into chips, for example.

The top 10cm (4") of the shoot tips and attached leaves should be cooked for 15-20 minutes.

Sweet potato tubers.

Maintenance and potential problems

Some weeding is often necessary. Watering in hot weather is important.

Swiss chard

See Perpetual spinach & chard
(*Beta vulgaris* subsp. *cicla*)

Tiger nut
(*Cyperus esculentus* var. *sativa*)

Also known as chufa

Tiger nut is a rush-like plant from the Mediterranean and Asia, related to papyrus but a rather hardier herbaceous perennial. Usually grown as a waterside plant, but possible to grow in soil too, it grows to about 60cm (2') high with long, narrow leaves. Amongst the fine roots it produces a number of small tubers, banded with stripes, which are the edible 'nuts'.

Cyperus esculentus var. *sativa* is the form cultivated for tubers and does not set seed. Its wild relative *C. esculentus* does set seed; it also spreads via aggressive rhizomes and is known for its potential to become weedy.

The tubers are 1-2cm (3/8-3/4") long, with a single plant capable of producing over 100 tubers.

Hardiness zone: 8

Cultivation

Tiger nuts are quite hardy but yield better where summers are longer and warmer. Although they grow naturally at water margins in wet soil, they can also be grown in normal soil as long as it is kept moist. If you are already growing aquatic perennials then you can easily incorporate tiger nuts with them, for example by growing in a container that is partly sunk into the water.

Varieties: Named varieties exist in Spain but are not generally available.

Harvest: The tubers can be harvested when the foliage has been cut down by the first frosts or is turning yellow. Dig up the plants and work the tubers out from the dense roots, then replant the plants. Dry the tubers for storage. The tubers do not shrivel when dried and can be stored for more than a year.

Tubers are not tolerant of deeply frozen soil, so in cold winter regions you'll need to treat tiger nut as a replant perennial.

Propagation: Plant tubers in spring about 1cm (3/8") deep in pots, keeping them warm, and grow on until the soil has warmed up, when they can be planted out a little deeper than in the pot and about 30cm (1') apart. Or plant tubers straight into soil, at the same spacing, 5cm (2") deep, in late spring.

Culinary uses

Tiger nuts are very like nuts in flavour, with sweet, yellow flesh. They are usually eaten raw, but if lots are produced they can be boiled or steamed and eaten as a cooked vegetable. In Spain they are sometimes eaten roasted and spiced as tapas.

Maintenance and potential problems

Plants in soil will need watering in dry weather. Mice can be a problem, as they like eating the tubers.

Tiger nut tubers.

Tree cabbage
See Tree collards (*Brassica oleracea* Acephala Group)

Tree collards (*Brassica oleracea* Acephala Group)

Also known as Jersey kale, tree cabbage, walking-stick kale, Western Front kale

Tree collards are better known by what are actually variety names – as listed above. None of them form tight heads like a cabbage. Collards are also placed in this brassica group, but they rarely live longer than 2 years. Also included here is 'Ewiger Kohl' (in German meaning 'eternal cabbage'), which is rather longer-lived. Collards are called 'couve' in Portugal, where there are also several perennial forms.

These are short-lived perennials, living 4 or 5 years, sometimes more. The 'tree' types grow with a long stem, which can reach 4m (13') high (or more in mild climates!), appearing rather like a palm tree, with an unbranched trunk topped with a head of leaves. 'Western Front' kale and 'Ewiger Kohl' are smaller plants.

It is also worth mentioning here that wild cabbage (*Brassica oleracea*), which grows wild on the seashore in much of Europe, is also a short-lived perennial (3-4 years typically) that can be cultivated for its edible leaves. Although the leaves are fairly small on established plants, they can still be very productive and tasty.

Hardiness zone: 8

Cultivation

Plant out where brassicas have not been grown recently (to avoid club root problems) in a fairly fertile soil, in sun or very light shade. Stake plants and tie them up to make sure the trunk is vertical, otherwise it is likely to fall over as it grows. It is easier to grow plants very tall if they are by a wall.

If plants are getting too tall and unstable they can be 'coppiced' (see right) or heavily pruned back in autumn – they should send out new shoots the following spring.

Varieties: As noted above – 'Jersey Kale', 'Tree Cabbage', 'Walking Stick' kale, 'Western Front' kale and 'Ewiger Kohl'.

Harvest: Harvest leaves through the growing season.

Propagation: Plants can be grown from seed, but may not be true to type. You can also propagate from cuttings of side shoots taken in spring. It is wise to propagate from existing plants by cuttings every year or two anyway, both to ensure your stock doesn't die in a hard winter and also because you need small green shoots to root as cuttings, and these become rarer in the tree forms on plants older than about 2 years.

Culinary uses

Leaves are harvested when fairly small and are cooked lightly, like spring greens. They can also be blanched and used in salads.

Maintenance and potential problems

Make sure you stop it from going to seed, as this will reduce the life of the plant. Potential problems are all the usual pests of brassicas – moth caterpillars, pigeons, etc. If you have lots of problems from these, then you may need to net plants for much of the year or grow in a fruit cage.

If plants are damaged by pests or weather they can be 'coppiced' – cut right back to a stump 15-30cm (6-12") high, from which they will usually resprout and recover. This is also a method of keeping plants lower and more easily manageable.

Tree onion
See Egyptian onion (*Allium cepa* Proliferum Group)

Turkish rocket
(*Bunias orientalis*)

Turkish rocket is a sturdy, clump-forming perennial, growing to 80cm (2'8") high and 30cm (1') wide, with long, slightly hairy leaves (like an oversized dandelion) and yellow flowers in late spring and early summer. It has deep taproots and is a good mineral accumulator. The flowers are loved by bees. Plants often keep a rosette of leaves over winter in mild regions.

Established plants can form clumps with multiple growing heads.

Hardiness zone: 4

Cultivation

Grow in any reasonable garden soil, in sun or partial shade.

Varieties: There are no varieties.

Harvest: Harvest the unopened flower heads in spring, and continue to harvest flowering heads as they flower all through spring and early summer. Take young leaves in spring and older leaves all through the growing season.

Propagation: Grow from seed in spring, or propagate from root cuttings.

Culinary uses

Treat the flowering heads – opened or unopened – like broccoli or calabrese: either use raw or just cook lightly by steaming or stir-frying briefly. They are like a mustardy version of broccoli.

The young leaves can be used raw or cooked as a green vegetable; the older leaves are best cooked, as they become too hot to eat when raw.

Maintenance and potential problems

Although related to the brassicas, Turkish rocket does not seem to suffer from any of the brassica pests – no caterpillar or pigeon damage – which makes it very useful!

Plants are apt to collapse on to their sides after flowering – not a problem in itself but they can damage other smaller plants alongside. If you dig plants up, every small bit of root will regrow, so be prepared!

Udo
(*Aralia cordata*)

Also known as Japanese asparagus

Udo is a deep-rooted large herbaceous perennial, growing to 1m (3'3") high and wide or more, with large leaves. It looks like an oversized angelica. Almost unknown in the UK, it has long been cultivated as a vegetable in Japan and China, where there are named varieties and it is considered a gourmet vegetable. It is also used medicinally in China to treat pain, particularly from arthritis.

White flowers in summer (which attract beneficial insects) are followed by heads of small black fruits, each fruit about 4mm (1/8") across, containing several seeds. The fruits are not edible.

Hardiness zone: 7

Cultivation

Udo is a woodland perennial and needs some shade to thrive – it tolerates quite deep shade. It will cope with almost any soil type as long as it remains fairly moist in summer.

Plants can be blanched, in the same ways as rhubarb, or earthed up to make them more tender.

Varieties: Named varieties exist in Japan but are not in general cultivation.

Harvest: Harvest the shoots and young leaf stalks in spring, up to a height of about 60cm (2').

Propagation: Raise from seed (requires 3 or more months' stratification (see Chapter 3, page 54), division or root cuttings.

Culinary uses

You can eat the shoots and leaf stalks raw – just peel, soak in water for 10 minutes to remove any bitterness and add to salads. They have a lemony/fennel/asparagus flavour. They can also be chopped thinly and used in soups (added at the last minute). If cooked, they are only ever boiled briefly.

Maintenance and potential problems

Slugs and snails like to nibble on this plant, so take protective measures when small. Established plants shrug off molluscs but still often have a few holes nibbled out of them here and there.

Ulluco
(*Ullucus tuberosus*)

Ulluco is another tuber crop widely grown for centuries in the Andean regions of South America. It is a low, bushy perennial plant, growing to about 30cm (1') high and wide. The tubers themselves are the size of a small potato, and look a bit like oca tubers (pictured on pages 14 and 142).

In regions with cold winters it needs to be grown as a replant perennial, because the tubers are hardy only to soil temperatures of about -5°C (23°F).

Hardiness zone: 7

Cultivation

Ulluco likes a well-drained, fertile soil and full sun.

After planting, some initial weeding may be necessary, but the foliage soon smothers possible weeds. Stems arch over as they grow and tubers can form where they touch the ground. Most tubers form around the bases of plants and these can be encouraged by earthing up around plants.

Ulluco needs a long growing season – tuber formation starts only in early autumn and long, warm, frost-free autumns lead to good crops. Green tubers (which have been exposed to light) are fine to eat, unlike green potatoes. In mild areas tubers can be left in the ground to overwinter, but if not harvested they can become overcrowded within a few years and tuber size will decrease.

Varieties: There are several different-coloured forms, including yellow, red, white, purple, mottled and speckled varieties in South America, though few are in general cultivation. Tuber shape, size and yield do not seem to be related to colour.

Harvest: Harvest tubers carefully in autumn after frosts have cut the foliage down, and store in a cool, dark place. They can store for over 12 months and year-old tubers can be used to regrow the crop.

Harvest leaves through the growing season.

Propagation: Plant tubers in spring – they're usually best started off in pots and planted out after the last frosts. Plant at a spacing of about 20cm (8") between plants, placing pot-grown plants 5cm (2") lower in the ground than they were in the pots.

Culinary uses

The tubers have a crisp texture and nutty flavour and are excellent to eat raw or cooked like potatoes – boiled, fried or baked. The texture is slightly more mucilaginous than that of potato. Do not overcook as they can become tough. They do not need peeling.

The leaves can be eaten cooked as a vegetable too; they taste like New Zealand spinach.

Maintenance and potential problems

Ulluco shares some virus diseases with potatoes, so try to keep this crop separate and some distance from potatoes if possible.

Violets
(*Viola* spp.)

Violets are small, mainly perennial, mostly clump-forming plants. Some species, such as sweet violet (*V. odorata*), spread via rhizomes and self-seed freely. Many are herbaceous, though some are evergreen or semi-evergreen (e.g. sweet violet – one of the best to grow for eating – is evergreen in a favourable climate). They are somewhat slow to get established, and many are short-lived, but most have good shade tolerance. The picture on the left shows the common dog violet (*V. riviniana*), which thrives in shady spots beneath trees and shrubs.

Violets are very low-growing – most grow only 15-20cm (6-8") high and a little wider – so it can be a good idea to grow larger perennials amongst them. They tolerate a little foot traffic.

Hardiness zones: 4-8

Cultivation

Violets like a well-drained but moist soil that is humus-rich. Most prefer partial shade.

Varieties: There are many species and ornamantal varieties, all of which can be used for eating.

Harvest: Pick leaves through the growing season when young and tender; flowers in spring.

Propagation: This can be done by seed, division or layering of runners.

Culinary uses

The flowers, flower buds and leaves can all be used in salads – use flowers in moderation (especially from yellow-flowered species), as they can sometimes cause stomach upsets. The leaves can also be used in cooked dishes – they are mucilaginous and have a thickening effect in soups or stews.

Maintenance and potential problems

Some weeding is likely to be needed, as most species do not form a thick cover over the ground.

Walking onion
See Egyptian onion (*Allium cepa* Proliferum Group)

Walking-stick kale
See Tree collards (*Brassica oleracea* Acephala Group)

Wapato
See Arrowheads (*Sagittaria* spp.)

Water caltrop
(*Trapa bicornis*)

Also known as water chestnut

Rather confusingly, there are two oriental vegetables called water chestnut: this one is also called water caltrop; the other is *Eleocharis dulcis* (see overleaf). Water caltrop is an aquatic, floating plant widely grown in southern Europe for export. The distinctly shaped tubers resemble the caltrop (a spiked ball once used as a weapon), 2.5-6cm (1-2¹/₄") across, with two 'horns'. This species is better for eating than the wild, four-horned type (*Trapa natans*).

Hardiness zone: 4

Cultivation

Grow in a pool or container in 10-30cm (4-12") of water, with a little soil beneath to supply some nutrients (see Chapter 2, page 38). The shiny black tubers are produced at the base of the leaves.

Warm summer temperatures are required for good yields, so in the UK it's best to grow in a polytunnel or greenhouse. This species is hardier than the other water chestnut and does not need such high temperatures.

The tubers are very hardy and can be left to overwinter in a pool, or harvested and stored damp over the winter if you need to drain the growing container.

Varieties: There are no varieties.

Harvest: The tubers are fully ripe when the plants start to die off in autumn. They do not store dry, so should be kept moist in plastic bags or in damp sand.

Propagation: Float tubers in the water in mid- to late spring.

Culinary uses

Water caltrop is much used in oriental cooking. The tubers have to be boiled for at least 1 hour before they are edible (they are

The curious two-horned tubers of water caltrop.

poisonous raw). After cooking they need shelling. Despite this, they are the more popular of the two water chestnuts in China and other parts of Asia.

Maintenance and potential problems

Keep water topped up in hot weather.

Water chestnut
(*Eleocharis dulcis*)
See also Water caltrop (*Trapa bicornis*)

Also known as Chinese water chestnut

This is the other vegetable known as water

chestnut: a sedge with narrow, hollow leaves reaching up to 60-90cm (2-3') high. It has long been grown in China and South East Asia along river margins and at the edges of paddy fields. Edible bulbs form underwater, each mother bulb producing rhizomes, at the end of which more bulbs are formed. Each bulb is about 4cm (1 5/8") in diameter. The bulbs darken with age.

Hardiness zone: 9

Cultivation

Grow in a pool or container with a minimum of 15cm (6") of soil covered by at least 10cm (4") of water (see Chapter 2, page 38).

The nut-like edible bulbs are borne on the end of subterranean runners – a single plant can yield 1kg (2lb 3oz) of bulbs. Warm summer temperatures are required to yield well, so in the UK growing in a polytunnel or greenhouse is recommended.

Varieties: There are no varieties.

Harvest: Bulbs are harvested in autumn soon after the foliage dies down. Water chestnut bulbs are quite tender and should be treated as a replant perennial: store bulbs in moist, frost-free conditions – for example, in moist sand or compost in plastic bags – over winter and until you want to use them.

Propagation: You can start plants off in pots (part-submerged in water) or plant straight in an aquatic situation. Plant bulbs that are starting into growth, in mid- to late spring, 30-40cm (1'-1'4") apart, just under the soil surface.

Bulbs of water chestnut.

Water lotus
(*Nelumbo nucifera*)

Culinary uses

Use the bulbs raw or cooked after peeling. They are very often used in oriental cookery in stir-fries – they need only light cooking. They can also be dried and ground into water chestnut flour, used for thickening soups and stews, and for making a batter for deep-fried vegetables and meats.

Maintenance and potential problems
Keep water topped up in hot weather.

Also known as lotus

Water lotus is well known as an ornamental perennial aquatic plant, with white and pink water-lily flowers. Its habitat is shallow ponds in Asia. It bears large, rounded, waxy leaves, curled at the edges and held clear of the water. Plants can emerge 1m (3') or more above the water surface. Hardiness varies a lot between varieties.

As a vegetable, lotus is mainly grown for the starchy rhizomes, which are buff-coloured and woody-looking, 7.5cm (3") thick by 60-90cm (2-3') long. They are divided into

sausage-like segments, each up to 13cm (5") long and full of air passages. When cut crossways, they look like old-fashioned telephone dials (pictured below right).

The rhizomes will die if frozen, but will usually overwinter without trouble at the bottom of a pond 20cm (8") deep, so if this depth of pond is likely to freeze solid for you, it has to be grown as a replant perennial; otherwise it should be fine treated as a perennial.

The hardier American species *Nelumbo lutea* has yellow flowers and is edible in the same ways.

Hardiness zones: 4-9

Cultivation

Both white- and pink-flowered varieties can be used. Rhizomes with several segments are usually planted in late winter or early spring in mud at a 30° angle with 10-20cm (4-8") of water above them. Ideally, grow in a large shallow container (as a replant perennial if necessary where you are), which will make harvesting the rhizomes much easier. One plant can easily fill 1m (3') in all directions.

When grown commercially the flower buds are removed to focus energy on root production.

Varieties: Ornamental varieties (of which there are many) are fine to use for food production.

Harvest: Harvest rhizomes when the flowers die down, or in any case in autumn if the water is likely to freeze.

Some rhizomes can be stored over winter in fresh water in a frost-free but cool place, e.g. in a bucket of water in a garage. They can also be stored in moist sand.

Leaves are harvested during the growing season; seeds in autumn.

Propagation: Divide plants in spring, or sow wet scarified seeds (see Chapter 3, page 54) in spring at 25°C (77°F) or so.

Culinary uses

The leaves, flowers, seeds, young fruits and rhizomes are all edible.

The young rhizomes are starchy with a crisp texture and a mild flavour – boil first, as they are too hard to eat raw, and then use in salads or, as in Chinese cookery, in stir-fries and soups, or deep-fried in batter. They are often cut in slices to reveal the intricate air passages inside.

The seeds are harvested after the seedhead turns brown. The tough outer skin is removed, as is the bitter green embryonic shoot; then they can be eaten raw, roasted or used in soups. They have a chestnut flavour.

Rhizomes of water lotus.

The young leaves are eaten cooked (they are toxic raw) and are also used to wrap and steam meat, rice, etc. in the same way as vine leaves. The flowers can be used as a garnish.

Maintenance and potential problems

Harvesting in a deep pond can be a wet experience!

Watercress
(Rorippa nasturtium-aquaticum, syn. R. nasturtium)

Watercress is a perennial brassica that has been used for food since at least Roman times. Plants are straggling, up to 1m (3') long and found in the wild on stream sides, notably where the water is neutral to alkaline in pH. It spreads by rooting along the stems.

A number of closely related species were formerly lumped together as *Nasturtium officinale*, and can all be eaten and cultivated in the same way. This one is the main commercial species.

Watercress contains isothiocyanates, which have antibiotic activity, perhaps explaining its long use as a tonic and health-giving plant. It also contains high levels of vitamin C and minerals.

Hardiness zone: 3

Cultivation

It is easy to grow from seed, or you can root bought watercress by keeping it in a jar of water. Taking cuttings of wild plants can also succeed, but you run the risk of introducing viral diseases into cultivation.

Watercress does not require aquatic conditions – a permanently moist-to-wet soil will suffice. It does not like stagnant water. It can be grown in containers with other aquatics, but you'll have to change the water every day or two and make sure it does not overheat. Or you could make an island in the middle of a container and plant the watercress on the top.

See the note in Chapter 2 (page 39) about liver fluke – be careful if you have grazing animals anywhere nearby that can access the water in which plants are growing.

Varieties: There are no varieties in general cultivation.

Harvest: Watercress can often be harvested all year round, especially in commercial beds where constant fresh running water ensures that beds do not freeze in cold weather; it also protects the plants from frost damage. The more the plants are cut, the bushier they become.

Propagation: This is done by division: stems in water readily start producing roots and can be transplanted.

Culinary uses

Watercress is often eaten now as it used to be in years gone by – raw in salads and in sandwiches, or in a hot or cold soup. When cooking with watercress, do not cook it for too long, so that the flavour and colour is retained. However, if sourced near grazing animals it must be washed and well cooked to avoid the risk of liver fluke infection.

Maintenance and potential problems

Flea beetles (as on brassicas) can be a serious problem – submerge plants under water for a few days to treat an infestation.

Welsh onion, scallion & bunching onion
(*Allium fistulosum*)

Welsh onion (pictured) is a fairly common herbaceous perennial allium in British gardens, though it is also one of the most important of the onions grown in China and Japan. There is no connection to Wales! It forms a clump 30-50cm (1'-1'8") high, comprising a clump of small bulbs, each bearing long, thin leaves that are circular in cross-section and about 1-2cm (3/8-3/4") in diameter. It usually stays green over winter. Purple flowers are borne in summer.

The scallion/bunching types have thicker, white stems and do not form bulbs.

Hardiness zone: 5

Cultivation

Welsh onion as a perennial is usually planted as a bulb and the leaves are the crop: cut a few times a year, allowing the plant to recover after each harvest. Plants can also easily be grown from seed – scallion and bunching varieties are usually grown from seed. Welsh onion and clumps of scallions can also be divided.

Plant in sun or light shade in any reasonably well-drained, fertile soil. They prefer near-neutral pH. Welsh onions need no special treatment. Scallion and bunching varieties grown in China and Japan are often earthed up as they grow, to blanch the growing stems, making them whiter and more tender.

Scallion and bunching varieties in China and Japan are divided into multi-stemmed and single-stemmed types. The multi-stemmed types are closer to Welsh onion, 'tillering' (branching) to produce clumps with up to 20 leaves. The single-stemmed types develop a leek-like stem up to 25cm (10") tall and 2.5cm (1") in diameter, topped by about six green leaves. Both types are often intercropped with other vegetables.

Varieties
Welsh onion:
'Red Welsh Onion' – has red bulbs.

Scallion/bunching varieties (multi-stemmed) for leafy shoots and thin stems (some with red stalks):
'Asagi' – grown for its thin, tender leaves.
'Deep Purple' – deep reddish-purple stems.
'Edo'– thin, tender leaves.
'Four Seasons' – good flavour.
'Hikari' – thin, tender leaves.
'Katana F1' – tall, thick stems.
'Kujo' – light green leaves, tender white stalks.
'Kyoto Market' – thin, tender leaves.
'Menegi' – grown for the delicate young leaves.
'Red Beard' – red stalks, green leaves.
'Redhead' – has only a few stems, which are reddish.
'Rouge' – small-diameter stems.
'Spring Slim' – has a moderate number of medium-diameter stems.
'White Lisbon' – neat foliage.
'White Nebuka' – long, slender, white stalks in tight clusters.
'Winterhecke' – has many stems and short, small leaves.

Scallion/bunching varieties (single-stemmed) for leaves and thick stems:
Summer/autumn use:
'Feast' – wide leaves and long stems.
'Gallop' – vigorous, upright with deep green leaves.
'Guardsman' – dark blue-green leaves, very hardy.
'Heshiko' – tender leaves on long stalks.

'Hybrid Gallop' – good-quality leaves and stems.
'Kalgaro' – has large-diameter stems.
'Laser' – long, white stems, upright plants, mild flavour.
'Nabechan F1' – thick stems with a sweet flavour.
'Natsuguro' – long, tender stems.
'Oasis F1' – Long, slender stems, very fast-growing.
'Photon' – mild-flavoured, dark green leaves.
'Sentry' – upright, stems harvested over a long period.
'Shimonita' – produces fat white stalks.
'Summer Isle' – sweet mild flavour, dark green leaves.
'Tokyo Long White' – long stems.
'Tycoon' – tall stems, dark green leaves.
'White Spear F1' – thick stems, blue-green leaves.

Winter use:
'Evergreen' – deep green leaves.
'Fuyuyo' – tender stalks and leaves, good flavour.
'Ishikura Improved' – medium height, productive.
'White Evergreen' – slim stalks, tender and mild flavour.

Harvest: Harvest leaves and stems all year round from plants at any stage of growth, from seedlings to mature plants.

Harvest bulbs of Welsh onion in late summer or autumn.

In very cold winter climates, mature bunching onions are partially dried to store over winter. In northern China they are sun-dried in the wind, so the outer layers become papery dry – this preserves the inner layers of stem and leaves. The plants are then piled in heaps and covered with mats, and checked frequently through winter.

Propagation: Grow from seed sown in spring. These onions are sometimes grown as annuals – seed can be sown thickly and small shoots or leafy scallions harvested a few months later.

As a perennial, space (or thin) plants at about 20cm (8") apart.

Single-stemmed scallion/bunching onions.

Culinary uses

Use the leaves as for spring onions in salads or cooked dishes (they need only a little cooking). The thick stems are used more like leeks or as a substitute for bulb onions – excellent in soups and stews. They're especially useful in winter.

The bulbs are used exactly like shallots or small onions.

Maintenance and potential problems

Once in a while you should probably replant bulbs in a new location to reduce the risk of build-up of onion root diseases, e.g. white rot.

Young plants can be susceptible to slug and snail damage.

Western Front kale
See Tree collards (*Brassica oleracea* Acephala Group)

White deadnettle
(*Lamium album*)

White deadnettle is a sprawling perennial, growing 20-60cm (8"-2') high, often forming dense patches in the wild, in hedge banks and on roadsides. It has nettle-shaped leaves, but paler than those of stinging nettle and without stings. It bears white flowers, loved by bees.

Hardiness zone: 4

Cultivation

It is easily grown in any soil in a situation with some sun, though is tolerant of partial shade. It is sometimes used deliberately as a ground-cover plant.

Varieties: There are some ornamental varieties.

Harvest: Harvest leaves at any time in the growing season; shoots just in spring.

Propagation: Raise from seed or detach rooted runners.

Culinary uses

The leaves and young stems (before flowering) are juicy and tender – great in salads, or steam lightly and use as a vegetable with butter or oil. They can also be incorporated into other dishes, e.g. with a grain like rice or with couscous. The leaves on older plants are also good.

Maintenance and potential problems

It is likely to try to spread!

Wild arugula
See Wild rocket (*Eruca selvatica*)

Wild garlic See Ramsons
(*Allium ursinum*)

Wild leek
See Ramps (*Allium tricoccum*)

Wild rocket
(*Eruca selvatica*)
See also Perennial wall-rocket
(*Diplotaxis tenuifolia*)

Also known as wild arugula

The common name 'rocket' or 'roquette' is used for a number of different species, and 'wild rocket' is even used for both this species and *Diplotaxis tenuifolia*! Salad rocket or arugula (*Eruca vesicaria* subsp. *sativa*) is the annual relative of this plant.

Eruca selvatica is a herbaceous perennial brassica with finely cut leaves and yellowish flowers, loved by bees. It originates from southern Europe and grows some 30-50cm (1'-1'8") high and 20cm (8") wide.

Hardiness zone: 7

Cultivation

Grow in any reasonably well-drained soil, in sun or light shade.

Varieties: There are no varieties.

Propagation: Raise from seed. Either sow in containers and transplant out, or sow direct in the soil in drills 20cm (8") apart and 5mm (1/8") deep. Thin to 15-20cm (6-8") between plants.

Harvest: Harvest leaves, shoots and flowers at any time during the growing season, usually well into early winter. Rather than cut whole plants, take a few leaves from each plant in a patch: this will help to keep them productive.

Culinary uses

The leaves are hotter and more pungent than those of annual rocket and are great for adding to salads, mixing with blander leaves such as those from lime trees.

Maintenance and potential problems

There are few problems – the usual brassica pests seem to leave it alone. A severe winter can set plants back, so it is wise to save a few seeds each year for possible propagation. It can self-seed easily.

Wild rye
See Perennial rye (*Secale montanum*)

Wolfberry
See Goji berry (*Lycium barbarum*)

Wood pea
See Perennial sweet peas (*Lathyrus latifolius* & *L. sylvestris*)

Wood sorrel
(*Oxalis acetosella*)

This is a herbaceous perennial of European woodlands, where it is happy to form carpets. It spreads by seed and grows only 20cm (8") high, with individual plants about the same width. Heart-shaped, clover-like leaves fold up at night and in rain, as do the small white flowers borne in spring.

The plant forms a network of small taproots, 15-20cm (6-8") deep, 5-6cm (2-2 1/2") long by just under 1cm (1/4") wide.

Hardiness zone: 3

Cultivation

Wood sorrel likes a humus-rich soil that is moist but well drained. It requires some shade, and tolerates quite deep shade.

Varieties: There are no varieties selected for leaf production.

Harvest: Leaves can be picked throughout the growing season, and flowers in spring. Taproots can be harvested at any time.

Propagation: You can raise it from seed, which requires winter stratification (see Chapter 3, page 54). Alternatively, divide existing patches.

Culinary uses

Wood sorrel has long been eaten for food – the leaves have a wonderful lemony flavour and are used raw in salads or cooked in soups. Like the true sorrels, the leaves contain oxalic acid (hence the flavour) so should be used only in moderation. The flowers are nice in salads, while the taproots are sweet and delicious raw in salads.

Maintenance and potential problems

None of either.

Yacon
(Smallianthus sonchifolia, syn. *Polymnia edulis & P. sonchifolia)*

Yacon is a large, vigorous herbaceous perennial originating from high in the Andes in South America, where it is greatly valued as a tuber crop. The tubers are hardy to soil temperatures of about -5°C (23°F), so in most parts of the UK it must be grown as a replant perennial.

It grows large and sturdy, 1-2m (3'3"-6'6") high and 60-90cm (2-3') wide, with distinctive large felty leaves and thick stems. It sometimes forms small yellow flowers at the top of each stalk in late summer.

Below ground it has a small clump of knobbly growing tips, with large storage tubers, which look like potatoes, radiating out in a circle. In South American varieties these can be white, yellow, orange, pink, red or purple. Unlike oca and ulluco, yacon is not sensitive to day length for tuber formation.

Hardiness zone: 7

Cultivation

Easy to grow in most soils and climates, yacon likes a well-drained but moist, fertile soil and sun or light shade. It prefers a hot, humid climate but seems to like UK conditions, and crops well here.

Named varieties are not yet commercially available in the UK or USA, where unnamed varieties with light brown skin are grown and are very productive. There are reports of the variety 'Morado', which has reddish tubers and leaves, not being as productive as others.

Yacon is quite a hungry feeder, so, if possible, mulch plants with something that will also feed them, and/or have some nitrogen-fixing and accumulator plants nearby to aid fertility.

On a windy site you might have to stake the stems to stop them from being blown over – they can snap at ground level if they do. In long periods of dry weather, plants will appreciate irrigation.

Varieties: There seem to be no named varieties of yacon outside South America.

Harvest: Unless you are in a region with very mild winters and can leave them in the ground to store, harvest tubers carefully (they are brittle and damage easily). They can reach the size of a large potato, and store well in a cool, dark place. If you are in an area with cold winters, you can also lift the crowns (cutting off stems at the tops), which include the knobbly propagation roots, and store these in a slightly moist compost or similar material over the winter.

Lifted tubers should be left in the sun for a few days to cure if you are intending to eat them, and will become sweeter during the process, and during storage over winter.

Propagation: You can grow yacon either from the growing tips or from tubers. An existing plant makes a lumpy mass of growing tips at the bottom of the stem. These can be cut apart in spring: each section should be a lump of root around 1.2cm (1/2") square with a growing tip on it. These should be potted up immediately in moist compost and grown on, to be planted out well after the last frosts. Plant at about 1m (3'3") apart, as they become big plants, though they take some time to fill the space, so in the meantime there is the opportunity to intercrop with a fast-growing annual.

Alternatively, you can leave existing masses of growing tips in the ground when you harvest tubers, though in time plants will get crowded if all growing tips are allowed to grow.

If growing from tubers, plant in spring, a few weeks before the last frosts are due. Alternatively, if your winters are mild, you can deliberately leave some in the ground over winter.

Culinary uses

The tubers are excellent for eating raw or cooked (like potatoes), being juicy, sweet, crisp and crunchy, with a flavour which includes elements of pear, apple, watermelon and celery. As with Jerusulem artichokes, their starch is in the form of inulin – and for folk unused to eating them they are relatively indigestible and can cause flatulence, though (as with Jerusulem artichokes) the more you eat them, the more digestible they

Yacon tubers can be as big as baking potatoes.

become. This also means that although they are good source of minerals and vitamins, little of the starch is digested, making them a low-calorific vegetable. It is possible that (as with Jerusulem artichokes) the inulin levels decrease over winter.

Peel the tubers before use, and then use raw in salads (sliced or diced), or cooked – for example, in stir-fries (when they resemble water chestnut in texture). Alternatively, steam or boil for 30 minutes. Individual tubers can weigh over 500g (1lb 2oz), so often need cutting into smaller pieces before cooking.

Yacon is also apparently beneficial to the gut flora that boost the immune system and aid digestion.

If the tubers are crushed and then pressed, using the same techniques as for pressing apples, a sweet juice is obtained. In fact the name 'yacon' means 'water root' in the Inca language, and the tubers were valued as a wild source of liquid refreshment. The juice can then be concentrated by boiling down to get a sweet syrup, which is delicious and also low-calorific.

Maintenance and potential problems

The foliage of young plants can sometimes be nibbled by slugs and snails, but older plants are robust. Heavy-cropping plants take a lot out of the soil, so feed and mulch well. Yacon has no problems with virus diseases.

There are reports in the UK of plants failing to produce tubers after cultivation for several years, as if they lose this ability for some reason. So you may need to restock with new tubers from time to time.

Yams
(*Dioscorea* spp.)

Also known as air potatoes

Most people think of yams as tropical plants that we can't even consider here in the UK, but this is not true. There are several species that grow as perennial climbers in cooler climates, dying back in winter to an underground tuber, which is edible. Species for temperate regions include cinnamon vine / Chinese yam (*D. batatas*) and Japanese yam (*D. japonica* – pictured above).

Some yams are also called air potatoes, because they form round aerial 'tubers', one from each leaf axil, which can easily be harvested. These mini-tubers can be cooked and eaten in exactly the same way as the underground tuber, though they don't get as large. With Japanese yam and cinnamon vine, the aerial tubers grow to about 1cm (3/8") in diameter, but the plants produce lots of them. The plant known as air potato (*D. bulbifera*) forms larger aerial tubers, though it really needs warmer summers than we currently get in the UK – it is considered a weed in parts of the southern United States.

Yams are twining vines, best planted on the southern side of large shrubs so they can scramble up into better light conditions. They can grow over 4m (13') high and 30cm (1') wide. The glossy, heart-shaped leaves are very similar to those of bindweeds and the related wild black bryony (*Dioscorea communis*), which is not edible. The flowers are tiny but very fragrant – cinnamon-like.

Plants usually produce two or three pale cream-coloured tubers, which get larger every year and can reach over 1m (3') long. They are broadly cylindrical, though in time they tend to swell at the lower ends up to a thickness of 7-10cm (3-4"). The flesh can be reddish in some selections.

Hardiness zone: 5

Aerial tubers of Chinese yam.

Tubers from young plants of Chinese yam (Dioscorea batatas).

Cultivation

These yams prefer a fertile, well-drained but moist soil with plenty of humus. Yams need as much sun as possible to do well. The new shoots come up quite late in spring, so keep weeds down beforehand.

If unsupported, plants will sprawl over the ground, but if they can climb by twining they will. I usually give them a cane to grow up, at least to start with, and then perhaps train them into the sunny side of a large shrub.

Varieties: 'Dr Yao' is a variety of cinnamon vine selected for its productivity.

Harvest: Harvest aerial tubers in late summer and autumn.

The underground tubers are hardy enough to be left in the soil over winter in many parts of the UK, though tubers older than 4-5 years can start to get woody. Harvest them in winter. If you don't get the whole tuber out, just dig out what you can, as plants will usually regrow from the tiny buds that are numerous on them. Tubers will store in a barely moist medium, such as sand, in cool temperatures through the winter. They will also store well loose in a fridge.

Propagation: Plants can be grown from the aerial tubers as well as from the underground ones. Either plant directly once the soil has warmed up in spring, or start off in pots and plant out after danger of frosts has passed (the shoots are frost-tender). They're also good for growing in containers – the deeper the better. Space plants about 30cm (1') apart.

The shoots that emerge in spring can also be detached, with a piece of tuber attached, and potted up.

Culinary uses

Both sorts of tubers can be boiled, fried or baked – they have a floury texture and a mild but very nice flavour. Use in any way like potatoes. Baked yams taste like baked potatoes and crisps – great for kids!

Maintenance and potential problems

Yams are late to emerge in spring, so can easily become weedy if neglected.

Yellow asphodel
(*Asphodeline lutea*)

Also known as king's spear

This is a clump-forming herbaceous perennial from southern Europe, often grown as an ornamental. It grows 60cm (2') high (with flower heads up to 1.5m/5') and 30cm (1') wide, and forms a cluster of finger-sized roots.

Hardiness zone: 6

Cultivation

Yellow asphodel likes a well-drained soil and sun or light shade.

Varieties: There are a few ornamental varieties but none bred for shoot production.

Harvest: Young shoots are harvested in late summer, autumn, winter in very mild locations (where it can be evergreen) and spring.

Propagation: It is easy to raise from seed, but it can take a long time to germinate. You can also divide established clumps – best in late summer or early autumn.

Culinary uses

The young shoots are excellent cooked – just steam for a few minutes like asparagus. They are excellent. The flowers are sweet and used in salads.

The roots are not huge, but are abundant and easily harvested, usually in late autumn and winter. The are eaten cooked and have a good nutty flavour.

Maintenance and potential problems

Snails and slugs like to munch on the new shoots, so take precautionary measures in spring! Rabbits will browse the plant too.

Appendix: Common and Latin names

This table gives the Latin names of all the plants cited by common name in Part 1, as well as of all those that have their own entry in Part 2. For those species that are listed in Part 2 as part of a species group (e.g. strawberries), it includes the more well known of those species (e.g. alpine strawberry) as well as those whose common names do not contain the main species name (e.g. duck potato, a species of arrowhead).

A few species mentioned in Part 1 (*Elaeagnus* spp.; *Indigofera* spp.) have no common name, so are not included in this listing.

Latin names of species		
Common name	**Latin name**	**Also known as**
air potato	*Dioscorea bulbifera*	
alexanders	*Smyrnium olusatrum*	
alpine strawberry	*Fragaria vesca* 'Semperflorens'	
alum root	*Heuchera americana*	
American elder	*Sambucus canadensis*	
amur maackia	*Maackia amurensis*	
angelicas	*Angelica* spp.	
anise hyssops	*Agastache* spp.	
apple mint	*Mentha suaveolens*	
arrowheads	*Sagittaria* spp.	
artemesias	*Artemesia* spp.	
asarabacca	*Asarum europaeum*	
asparagus	*Asparagus officinalis*	
asters	*Aster* spp.	
autumn olive	*Elaeagnus umbellata*	
Babington's leek	*Allium ampeloprasum* var. *babingtonii*	perennial leek
bamboos	*Arundinaria gigantea* (cane reed) *Phyllostachys* spp. *Pleioblastus* spp. *Pseudosasa japonica* (arrow bamboo) *Semiarundinaria* spp. *Yushania* spp.	

(Cont.)

Common name	Latin name	Also known as
barren strawberry (2 similar species)	*Waldsteinia fragarioides* *Waldsteinia ternata*	
basswood	*Tilia americana*	
beans	*Phaseolus* spp.	
bee balms	*Monarda* spp.	
beech	*Fagus sylvatica*	
bellflowers	*Campanula* spp.	harebells
betony	*Stachys officinalis*	
bindweeds	*Convolvulus* spp.	
bird's foot trefoil	*Lotus corniculatus*	
black locust	*Robinia pseudoacacia*	false acacia
black mulberry	*Morus nigra*	
bladder campion	*Silene vulgaris*	
bladder senna	*Colutea arborescens*	
bloodroot	*Sanguinaria canadensis*	
bog myrtle	*Myrica gale*	
borage	*Borago officinalis*	
Bowles's mint	*Mentha* Bowles's mint	
bracken	*Pteridium aquilinum*	
breadroot	*Psoralea esculenta*	
brooms	*Cytisus* spp.	
bugle	*Ajuga reptans*	
burdocks	*Arctium* spp.	
burnet saxifrage	*Pimpinella saxifraga*	
burnets	*Sanguisorba* spp.	
bush clover	*Lespedeza bicolor*	
butterburs	*Petasites* spp.	
cabbages	*Brassica* spp.	
Californian bayberry	*Myrica californica*	
cane reed	*Arundinaria gigantea*	
cardoon	*Cynara cardunculus*	
catsfoot	*Antennaria dioica*	

(Cont.)

Common name	Latin name	Also known as
Caucasian spinach	*Hablitzia tamnoides*	
ceanothus	*Ceanothus* spp.	
chamomile	*Chamaemelum nobile*	
chard	*Beta vulgaris* subsp. *cicla* var. *flavescens*	Swiss chard
chickweed	*Stellaria media*	
chicory	*Cichorium intybus*	radicchio
Chilean rhubarb	*Gunnera tinctoria*	
Chinese artichoke	*Stachys affinis*	crosnes
Chinese bramble	*Rubus tricolor*	groundcover raspberry
Chinese broccoli	*Brassica oleracea* Alboglabra Group	kailan, gai lon
Chinese cedar	*Toona sinensis*	Chinese toon, fragrant spring tree
chives	*Allium schoenoprasum*	
cinnamon vine	*Dioscorea batatas*	Chinese yam
cleavers	*Galium aparine*	goosegrass
clovers	*Trifolium* spp.	
coltsfoot	*Tussilago farfara*	
columbine	*Aquilegia vulgaris*	
comfrey	*Symphytum officinale*	
comfreys	*Symphytum* spp.	
common alder	*Alnus glutinosa*	
coneflowers	*Echinacea* spp.	
copper beech	*Fagus sylvatica* Atropurpurea Group	purple beech
cow parsnips	*Heracleum* spp.	
creeping dogwood	*Cornus canadensis*	
creeping jenny	*Lysimachia nummularia*	
crown vetch	*Coronilla varia* (syn. *Securigera varia*)	
daffodil garlic	*allium neapolitanum*	
daisy	*Bellis perennis*	
dandelion	*Taraxacum officinale*	
day lilies	*Hemerocallis* spp.	
docks	*Rumex* spp.	

(Cont.)

Common name	Latin name	Also known as
duck potato	*Sagittaria latifolia*	American arrowhead; wapato
dwarf comfrey	*Symphytum ibericum*	
dyer's greenweed	*Genista tinctoria*	
earthnut pea	*Lathyrus tuberosus*	
Egyptian onion	*Allium cepa* Proliferum Group	tree onion, walking onion
elephant garlic	*Allium ampeloprasum* var. *ampeloprasum*	
European elder	*Sambucus nigra*	black elder
everlasting pea (a perennial sweet pea)	*Lathyrus latifolius*	
false lupins	*Thermopsis* spp.	
false strawberry	*Duchesnea indica*	mock strawberry
fennel	*Foeniculum vulgare*	
feverfew	*Tanacetum parthenium*	
foam flower	*Tiarella cordifolia*	
four-wing saltbush	*Atriplex canescens*	
French scorzonera	*Reichardia picroides*	
French sorrel	*Rumex scutatus*	
garlic	*Allium sativum*	softneck garlic
garlic chives	*Allium tuberosum*	Chinese chives, oriental garlic
garlic cress	*Peltaria alliacea*	
giant butterbur	*Petasites japonicus*	fuki, sweet coltsfoot, Japanese butterbur
giant fennels	*Ferula* spp.	
globe artichoke	*Cynara cardunculus* Scolymus Group	
goji berry	*Lycium barbarum*	Chinese boxthorn, wolfberry, Duke of Argyll's tea tree
golden marguerite	*Anthemis tinctoria*	
golden saxifrage	*Chrysosplenium alternifolium* and *Chrysosplenium oppositifolium*	
goldenrods	*Solidago* spp.	
Good King Henry	*Chenopodium bonus-henricus*	
gorse	*Ulex europaeus*	
goumi	*Elaeagnus multiflora*	

(Cont.)

Common name	Latin name	Also known as
grape vines	*Vitis* spp.	
greater bird's foot trefoil	*Lotus uliginosus*	
green alder	*Alnus viridis*	
ground elder	*Aegopodium podagraria*	
ground ivy	*Glechoma hederacea*	aleroot
ground plum	*Astragalus crassicarpus*	buffalo pea, groundplum milk vetch
groundcover raspberry (2 similar species)	*Rubus* 'Betty Ashburner' *Rubus pentalobus*	
groundnut	*Apios americana*	potato bean
gunnera	*Gunnera magellanica*	
hemp agrimony	*Eupatorium cannabinum*	
herb patience	*Rumex patientia*	
Himalayan sea buckthorn	*Hippophae salicifolia*	willow-leaved sea buckthorn
hog peanut	*Amphicarpaea bracteata*	
hollyhock	*Alcea rosea*	
honewort	*Cryptotaenia canadensis*	
hop	*Humulus lupulus*	
horse mint	*Mentha longifolia*	
horseradish	*Armoracia rusticana*	
horsetail	*Equisetum* spp.	
hostas	*Hosta* spp.	
ice plant	*Sedum spectabile*	
Italian alder	*Alnus cordata*	
Japanese pagoda tree	*Sophora japonica*	
Japanese yam	*Dioscorea japonica*	
Jerusalem artichoke	*Helianthus tuberosus*	sunchoke
kidney vetch	*Anthyllis vulneraria*	
knapweeds	*Centaurea* spp.	
laburnums	*Laburnum* spp.	
lady's mantle	*Alchemilla mollis*	

(Cont.)

Common name	Latin name	Also known as
large-leaved lime	*Tilia platyphyllos*	
lemon balm	*Melissa officinalis*	
lesser periwinkle	*Vinca minor*	
lesser stitchwort	*Stellaria graminea*	
limes	*Tilia* spp.	lindens; basswood in the US
liquorice	*Glycyrrhiza glabra*	
liquorices	*Glycyrrhiza* spp.	
lovage	*Levisticum officinale*	
lucerne	*Medicago sativa*	alfalfa
lungwort	*Pulmonaria officinalis*	
lungworts	*Pulmonaria* spp.	
lupins	*Lupinus* spp.	
mallows	*Malva* spp.	
marsh mallow	*Althaea officinalis*	
mashua	*Tropaeolum tuberosum*	
meadow parsnips	*Thaspium* spp.	
milk vetch	*Astragalus glycyphyllos*	
milk vetches	*Astragalus* spp.	
mints	*Mentha* spp.	
mitsuba	*Cryptotaenia japonica*	Japanese parsley
monk's rhubarb	*Rumex alpinus*	
mountain mint	*Pycnanthemum* spp.	
mountain sorrel	*Oxyria digyna*	
mulberries	*Morus* spp.	
mulleins	*Verbascum* spp.	
multiplier onions (includes shallot and potato onion)	*Allium cepa* Aggregatum Group	
musk mallow	*Malva moschata*	
Nepalese raspberry	*Rubus nepalensis*	groundcover raspberry
nodding onion	*Allium cernuum*	lady's leek
nopale cacti	*Opuntia* spp.	prickly pears

(Cont.)

Common name	Latin name	Also known as
northern bayberry	*Myrica pensylvanica*	
oca	*Oxalis tuberosa*	New Zealand yam
oleaster	*Elaeagnus angustifolia*	
oregano	*Origanum vulgare*	pot marjoram
orpine	*Sedum telephium*	
ostrich fern	*Matteuccia struthiopteris*	shuttlecock fern
partridge berry	*Mitchella repens*	
perennial broccoli	*Brassica oleracea* Botrytis Group	
perennial kale	*Brassica oleracea* Ramosa Group	bush kale
perennial leek (note that Babington's leek is also known as perennial leek)	*Allium ampeloprasum*	salad leek, perennial sweet leek
perennial rye	*Secale montanum*	mountain rye, wild rye
perennial wall-rocket	*Diplotaxis tenuifolia*	wild rocket
perennial wheat	*Triticum aestivum* x *Thinopyrum intermedium*	
perennial wild cabbage	*Brassica oleracea*	
periwinkles	*Vinca* spp.	
perpetual spinach	*Beta vulgaris* subsp. *cicla*	spinach beet, leaf beet
pig nut	*Bunium bulbocastanum*	earth chestnut, earth nut
pignut	*Conopodium majus*	
pilotweed	*Silphium lanciniatum*	
plantains	*Plantago* spp.	
poke root	*Phytolacca americana*	pokeweed, poke
potato	*Solanum tuberosum*	
quamash	*Camassia quamash* (syn. *Camassia esculenta*)	camass
rakkyo	*Allium chinense*	baker's garlic
ramps	*Allium tricoccum*	wild leek
ramsons	*Allium ursinum*	wild garlic
red alder	*Alnus rubra*	
red elder (a European elder)	*Sambucus racemosa*	

(Cont.)

Common name	Latin name	Also known as
red valerian	*Centranthus ruber*	
redbuds	*Cercis* spp.	
redwood sorrel	*Oxalis oregana*	
restharrow	*Ononis spinosa*	
rhubarbs	*Rheum* spp.	
ribwort plantain	*Plantago lanceolata*	
rocambole	*Allium sativum* var. *ophioscorodon*	hardneck garlic, serpent garlic
Rock cranesbill	*Geranium macrorrhizum*	
rock samphire	*Crithmum maritimum*	
rosebay willowherb	*Epilobium angustifolium*	fireweed
rosemary	*Rosmarinus officinalis*	
runner bean	*Phaseolus coccineus*	
Russian comfrey	*Symphytum* x *uplandicum*	
Russian liquorice	*Glycyrrhiza echinata*	
sages	*Salvia* spp.	
salad burnet	*Sanguisorba minor* (syn. *Poterium sanguisorba*)	
saltbush	*Atriplex halimus*	
sanicle	*Sanicula europaea*	
savorys	*Satureja* spp.	
scorzonera	*Scorzonera hispanica*	
sea beet	*Beta vulgaris* subsp. *maritima*	
sea buckthorn	*Hippophae rhamnoides*	
sea hollies	*Eryngium* spp.	
sea kale	*Crambe maritima*	
sheep's sorrel	*Rumex acetosella*	
Siberian pea tree	*Caragana arborescens*	
Siberian purslane	*Claytonia sibirica* (syn. *Montia sibirica*)	pink purslane
silverberry	*Elaeagnus commutata*	
silverweed	*Potentilla anserina*	
Sitka alder	*Alnus sinuata*	
skirret	*Sium sisarum*	

(Cont.)

Common name	Latin name	Also known as
small-leaved lime	*Tilia cordata*	
snowbell tree	*Halesia carolina*	silverbell tree
soapwort	*Saponaria officinalis*	
Solomon's seals	*Polygonatum* spp.	
sorrels	*Rumex* spp.	docks
spurges	*Euphorbia* spp.	
stinging nettle	*Urtica dioica*	
strawberries	*Fragaria* spp.	
sunflowers	*Helianthus* spp.	
swamp potato	*Sagittaria sagittifolia*	
sweet cicely	*Myrrhis odorata*	
sweet fern	*Comptonia peregrina*	
sweet peas	*Lathyrus* spp.	
sweet potato	*Ipomoea batatas*	
sweet roots	*Osmorhiza* spp.	
sweet vetches	*Hedysarum* spp.	
sweet violet	*Viola odorata*	
sweet woodruff	*Galium odoratum* (syn. *Asperula odorata*)	
tansy	*Tanacetum vulgare*	
thymes	*Thymus* spp.	
tickseeds	*Coreopsis* spp.	
tiger nut	*Cyperus esculentus* var. *sativa*	chufa
toadflax	*Linaria vulgaris*	
tree collards	*Brassica oleracea* Acephala Group	Jersey kale, tree cabbage, walking-stick kale, Western Front kale
tree lupin	*Lupinus arboreus*	
Turkish rocket	*Bunias orientalis*	
udo	*Aralia cordata*	Japanese asparagus
ulluco	*Ullucus tuberosus*	
valerian	*Valeriana officinalis*	
vetches	*Vicia* spp.	

(Cont.)

Common name	Latin name	Also known as
violets	*Viola* spp.	
wand flower	*Galax urceolata*	
water caltrop	*Trapa bicornis*	water chestnut
water chestnut	*Eleocharis dulcis*	Chinese water chestnut
water lotus	*Nelumbo nucifera*	lotus
watercress	*Rorippa nasturtium-aquaticum* (syn. *Rorippa nasturtium*)	
wax myrtle	*Myrica cerifera*	bayberry
Welsh onion, scallion & bunching onion	*Allium fistulosum*	
white clover	*Trifolium repens*	
white deadnettle	*Lamium album*	
white mulberry	*Morus alba*	
wild ginger	*Asarum canadense*	
wild indigos	*Baptisia* spp.	
wild rocket	*Eruca selvatica*	wild arugula
wild strawberry	*Fragaria vesca*	woodland strawberry
wintergreen	*Gaultheria procumbens*	
wisterias	*Wisteria* spp.	
wood pea (a perennial sweet pea)	*Lathyrus sylvestris*	
wood sorrel	*Oxalis acetosella*	
wood vetch	*Vicia sylvatica*	
yacon	*Smallianthus sonchifolia* (syn. *Polymnia edulis*; *P. sonchifolia*)	
yams	*Dioscorea* spp.	air potatoes
yarrow	*Achillea millefolium*	
yarrows	*Achillea* spp.	
yellow asphodel	*Asphodeline lutea*	king's spear

Resources

Seed suppliers

Agroforestry Research Trust (UK)
46 Hunters Moon, Dartington, Totnes, TQ9 6JT
www.agroforestry.co.uk
mail@agroforestry.co.uk

Bountiful Gardens (USA)
18001 Shafer Ranch Rd, Willits, CA 95490, USA
Tel: (+1) 707 459 6410
www.bountifulgardens.org
bountiful@sonic.net

B & T World Seeds (France)
Paguignan, 34210 Aigues-Vives, France
Tel: (+33) 468 91 29 63
www.b-and-t-world-seeds.com
matthew@b-and-t-world-seeds.com

Chiltern Seeds (UK)
Bortree Stile, Ulverston, Cumbria, LA12 7PB
Tel: 01229 581137
www.chilternseeds.co.uk
info@chilternseeds.co.uk

Evergreen Seeds (USA)
Evergreen Y. H. Enterprises, PO Box 17538,
Anaheim, CA 92817, USA
www.evergreenseeds.com
eeseedsyh@aol.com

Fedco Seeds (USA)
P.O. Box 520, Waterville, ME 04903, USA
Tel: (+1) 207 873 7333 / 207 430 1106
www.fedcoseeds.com

J. L. Hudson, Seedsman (USA)
Box 337, La Honda, CA 94020-0337, USA
www.jlhudsonseeds.net

Jekka's Herb Farm (UK)
Rose Cottage, Shellards Lane, Alveston,
Bristol, BS35 3SY
Tel: 01454 418878
www.jekkasherbfarm.com
sales@jekkasherbfarm.com

Johnny's Selected Seeds (USA)
955 Benton Avenue, Winslow,
ME 0490, USA
Tel: (+1) 877 564 6697
www.johnnyseeds.com
communications@johnnyseeds.com

Kitazawa Seed Co. (USA)
P.O. Box 13220, Oakland, CA 94661-3220,
USA
Tel: (+1) 510 595 1188
www.kitazawaseed.com
customerservice@kitazawaseed.com

The Real Seed Catalogue (UK)
P.O. Box 18, Newport near Fishguard,
Pembrokeshire, SA65 0AA
Tel: 01239 821107
www.realseeds.co.uk
info@realseeds.co.uk

Richters Herbs (Canada)
357 Highway 47, Goodwood, ON L0C 1A0,
Canada
Tel: (+1) 905 640 6677
www.richters.com

Rühlemann's (Germany)
Auf dem Berg 2, 27367 Horstedt / ROW,
Germany
Tel: (+49) 0 42 88 92 85 58
www.ruehlemanns.de

Seeds of Diversity (Canada)
P.O. Box 36, Stn Q, Toronto, ON M4T 2L7,
Canada
Tel: (+1) 866 509 7333
www.seeds.ca
mail@seeds.ca

Suffolk Herbs (UK)
Monks Farm, Coggeshall Road, Kelvedon,
Essex, CO5 9PG
Tel: 01376 572456
www.suffolkherbs.com
sales@suffolkherbs.com

Territorial Seed Co. (USA)
P.O. Box 158, Cottage Grove, OR 97424, USA
Tel: (+1) 800 626 0866
info@territorialseed.com
www.territorialseed.com

Thomas Etty Esq. (UK)
Seedsman's Cottage, Horton, Ilminster,
Somerset, TA19 9RL
Tel: 01460 298249
www.thomasetty.co.uk
sales@thomasetty.co.uk

Plant suppliers

Agroforestry Research Trust (UK)
See under seed suppliers

Cool Temperate (UK)
45 Stamford Street, Awsworth, Nottingham,
NG16 2QL
Tel/Fax: 0115 916 2673
www.cooltemperate.co.uk
phil.corbett@cooltemperate.co.uk

Edulis (UK)
Flowers Piece, Ashampstead, Reading,
Berks, RG8 8SG
Tel/fax: 01635 578113
www.edulis.co.uk
edulis.nursery@virgin.net

Heronswood Nursery (USA)
300 Park Avenue, Warminster, PA
18974-4818, USA
Tel: (+1) 877 674 4714
www.heronswood.com
info@heronswood.com

Jekka's Herb Farm (UK)
See under seed suppliers

Poyntzfield Herbs (UK)
Black Isle, By Dingwall IV7 8LX, Ross &
Cromarty, Scotland
Tel/Fax: 01381 610352
www.poyntzfieldherbs.co.uk
info@poyntzfieldherbs.co.uk

Richters Herbs (Canada)
See under seed suppliers

Rühlemann's (Germany)
See under seed suppliers

Tripple Brook Farm (USA)
37 Middle Road, Southampton, MA 01073, USA
Tel: (+1) 413 527 4626
www.tripplebrookfarm.com
info@tripplebrookfarm.com

Further reading

Crawford, M. (2010) *Creating a Forest
Garden: Working with nature to grow
edible crops*. Green Books

Diacono, M. (2010) *A Taste of the
Unexpected*. Quadrille Publishing

Fern, K. (1997) *Plants for a Future: Edible and
useful plants for a healthier world*.
Permanent Publications

Hickmott, S. (2004) *Growing Unusual
Vegetables: Weird and wonderful vegetables
and how to grow them*. Eco-logic Books

Irving, M. (2009) *The Forager Handbook: A guide to the edible plants of Britain*. Ebury Press

Jacke, D. & Toensmeier, E. (2005) *Edible Forest Gardens: Ecological vision and theory for temperate climate permaculture*. Chelsea Green Publishing

Larkcom, J. (2007) *Oriental Vegetables*. Frances Lincoln

Logsdon, G. (2009) *Small-scale Grain Raising: An organic guide to growing, processing and using nutritious whole grains, for home gardeners and local farmers*. Chelsea Green Publishing

Toensmeier, E. (2007) *Perennial Vegetables*. Chelsea Green Publishing

Weise, V. (2004) *Cooking Weeds: Vegetarian recipes*. Prospect Books

Picture credits

The photographs in this book were taken by Martin Crawford, apart from the following.

In public domain: Garlic foliage (page 106), Udo (page 188), Water caltrop tubers (page 192), Water chestnut bulbs (page 193), Milky bellflower (page 79), Mojave/tulip prickly pear (page 139), Perennial rye (page 145).

Asparagus (page 70): Rasbak. http://commons. wikimedia.org/wiki/File:Asperges_Asparagus_ officinalis.jpg

Chicory 'Rossa di Treviso' (page 86): Goldlocki. http://commons.wikimedia.org/wiki/ File:RadicchioTrevisoprecoce.jpg

Chinese broccoli (page 89, top): Forest & Kim Starr. http://commons.wikimedia.org/wiki/ File:Starr_081031-0424_Brassica_oleracea.jpg

Chinese broccoli (page 89, bottom): Kowloonese. http://commons.wikimedia.org/wiki/File:Gailan.jpg

Chives (page 92): H. Zell. http://commons.wikimedia. org/wiki/File:Allium_schoenoprasum_001.JPG

Dandelion (page 95): iStock

Egyptian onion (page 98): H. Zell. http://commons. wikimedia.org/wiki/File:Allium_cepa_viviparum_ 001.JPG

European elder (page 101): Petr Vilgus. http:// commons.wikimedia.org/wiki/File:Bez_cerny.jpg

Garlic (page 105): Francesco Perito. http:// commons.wikimedia.org/wiki/File:Aglio_pulito_ particolare.JPG

Garlic chives (page 107): Sakura. http://commons. wikimedia.org/wiki/File:Garlic_chives.jpg

Globe artichoke (page 110): Stok. http://commons. wikimedia.org/wiki/File:Cynara5.jpg

Globe artichoke 'Green Globe' (page 112): Mike Peel. http://commons.wikimedia.org/wiki/ File:Artichoke_%27Green_Globe%27.jpg

Greater burnet saxifrage (page 82): H. Zell. http:// commons.wikimedia.org/wiki/File:Pimpinella_ major_001.JPG

Hosta plantaginae (page 121): Nova. http:// commons.wikimedia.org/wiki/File:Funkia_ babkowata_Hosta_plantaginea_01.jpg

Large-leaved lime (page 127): Karduelis. http:// commons.wikimedia.org/wiki/File:B%C3%BCy% C3%BCk_yaprakl%C4%B1_%C4%B1hlamur-2.jpg

Lucerne (page 129): H. Zell. http://commons. wikimedia.org/wiki/File:Medicago_sativa_001.JPG

Mitsuba (page 134): Mbc. http://commons. wikimedia.org/wiki/File:Mitsuba.jpg

Nodding onion (page 139): PlantStockPhotos

Oca tubers (page 14): Eric Hunt. http://commons. wikimedia.org/wiki/File:Oxallis_tuberosa.jpg

Perennial wall-rocket (page 147): Leo Michels. http://commons.wikimedia.org/wiki/ File:Diplotaxis_tenuifolia_IP0209094.jpg

Perennial wheat (page 147): Scott Bontz, The Land Institute

Poke root (page 9): iStock

Potato (page 152): Amanda Cuthbert

Rakkyo (page 155): Kenpai. http://commons. wikimedia.org/wiki/File:Allium_chinense1.jpg

Rocambole (page 161): Tauno Erik. http:// commons.wikimedia.org/wiki/File:Allium_ sativum_harilik_kyyslauk_estonia.JPG

Runner beans (page 165): H. Zell. http://commons. wikimedia.org/wiki/File:Phaseolus_ coccineus_001.JPG

Scallion/bunching onion (page 198): iStock

Scorzonera (page 168): Goldlocki. http:// commons.wikimedia.org/wiki/File:Schwarzwurzel WurzelnBundware.jpg

Shallots (page 137): Goldlocki. http://commons. wikimedia.org/wiki/File:EschalotteBestand.jpg

Sweet potato (page 182): H. Zell. http://commons. wikimedia.org/wiki/File:Ipomoea_batatas_001. JPG

Sweet potato tubers (page 184): Llez. http:// commons.wikimedia.org/wiki/File:Ipomoea_ batatas_006.JPG

Swiss chard (page 148): Mike Peel. http://commons. wikimedia.org/wiki/File:Swiss_Chard_1.jpg

Tiger nut (page 184): Blahedo. http://commons. wikimedia.org/wiki/File:Cyperus_esculentus.jpg

Tiger nut tubers (page 185): Tamorian. http:// commons.wikimedia.org/wiki/File:Cyperus_ esculentus_012_.jpg

Trailing bellflower (page 78): H. Zell. http:// commons.wikimedia.org/wiki/File:Campanula_ poscharskyana_001.JPG

Tree collards (page 185): From the tree collards blog at http://treecollards.blogspot.com/

Ulluco (page 189): Fotolia

Ulluco tubers (page 14); iStock

Water caltrop (page 191): Shizhao. http:// commons.wikimedia.org/wiki/File:Water_caltrop_ on_lake.JPG

Water chestnut (page 192): Tau'olunga. http:// commons.wikimedia.org/wiki/File:Eleocharis_ dulcis.jpg

Water lotus (page 193): Shizhao. http://commons. wikimedia.org/wiki/File:Nelumbo_nucifera-beijing.JPG

Water lotus rhizomes (page 194): FotoosRobin. http://commons.wikimedia.org/wiki/File:Lotus_ root.jpg

Watercress (page 195): Olivier Pichard. http:// commons.wikimedia.org/wiki/File:Nasturtium_ officinale_marais-blangy-tronville_80_ 25052007_1.jpg

Welsh onion (page 196): Dalgial. http://commons. wikimedia.org/wiki/File:Allium_fistulosum_2.JPG

White deadnettle (page 198): H. Zell. http:// commons.wikimedia.org/wiki/File:Lamium_ album_001.JPG

Wood pea (Page 146, top): Olbertz. http:// commons.wikimedia.org/wiki/File:Unbekanntes_ Bahndammgew%C3%A4chs2_(2).JPG

Wood pea (Page 146, bottom): Annelis. http:// commons.wikimedia.org/wiki/File:Mets%C3%A4n %C3%A4tkelm%C3%A4n_palkoja_Lathyrus_ sylvestris_HP7867_C.jpg

Yacon tubers (page 202): Farmcore. http:// commons.wikimedia.org/wiki/File:Yacon_tubers. JPG

Yellow asphodel (page 205): CFGPhoto

Index